# BIRDS OF NEW ZEALAND

and Outlying Islands

M.F. Soper

# BIRDS OF NEW ZEALAND

## and Outlying Islands

Whitcoulls Publishers
Christchurch London

First published 1984


Whitcoulls Publishers
Christchurch, New Zealand



ISBN 0 7233 0724 5

Typesetting by Quickset Platemakers Ltd,
Christchurch
Printed in Singapore through Hedges and Bell
Printing (S. E. Asia)

# CONTENTS

# CONTENTS

# CONTENTS



## PHOTOGRAPHS

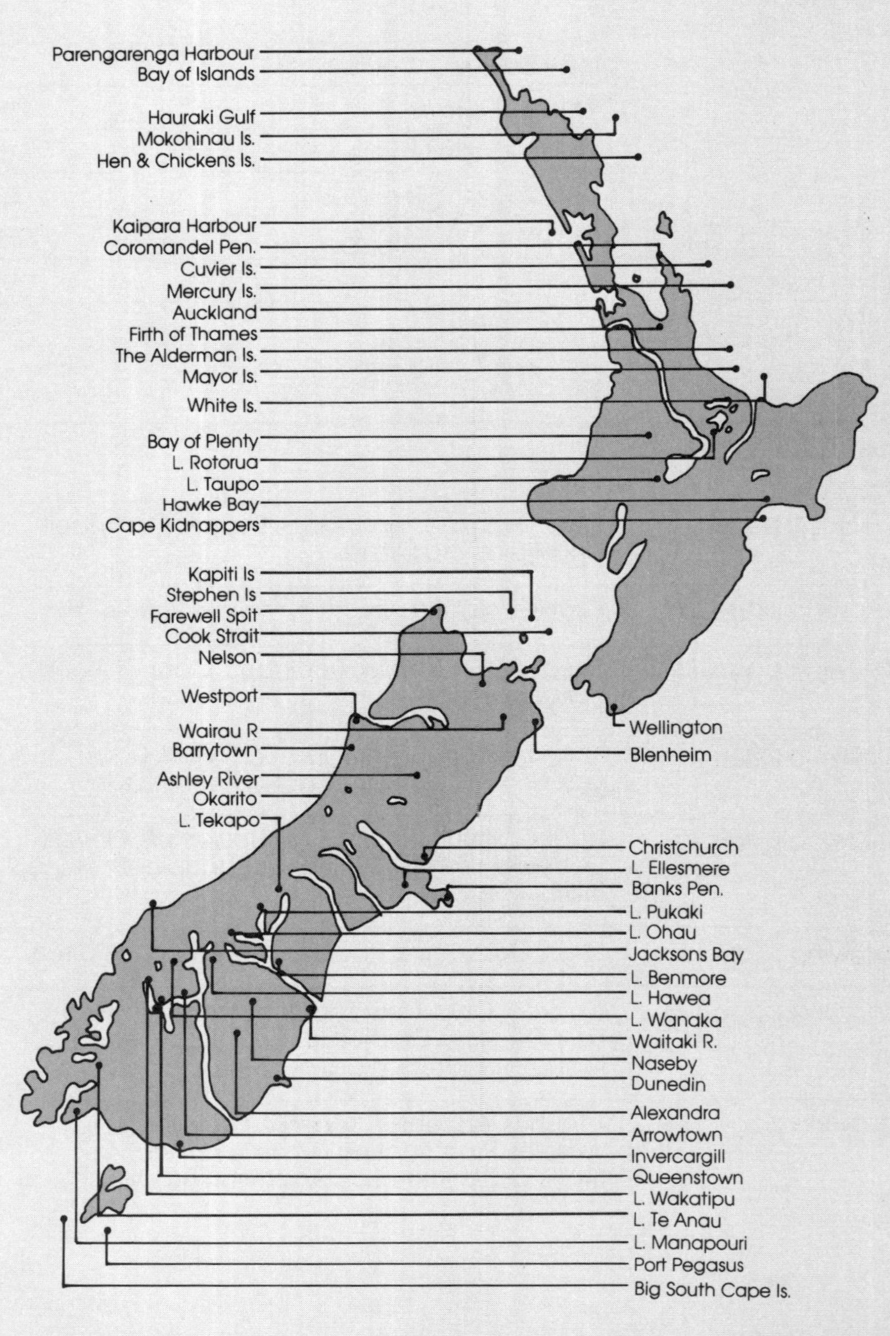
Parengarenga Harbour
Bay of Islands
Hauraki Gulf
Mokohinau Is.
Hen & Chickens Is.
Kaipara Harbour
Coromandel Pen.
Cuvier Is.
Mercury Is.
Auckland
Firth of Thames
The Alderman Is.
Mayor Is.
White Is.
Bay of Plenty
L. Rotorua
L. Taupo
Hawke Bay
Cape Kidnappers
Kapiti Is
Stephen Is
Farewell Spit
Cook Strait
Nelson
Westport
Wairau R
Barrytown
Ashley River
Okarito
L. Tekapo
Wellington
Blenheim
Christchurch
L. Ellesmere
Banks Pen.
L. Pukaki
L. Ohau
Jacksons Bay
L. Benmore
L. Hawea
L. Wanaka
Waitaki R.
Naseby
Dunedin
Alexandra
Arrowtown
Invercargill
Queenstown
L. Wakatipu
L. Te Anau
L. Manapouri
Port Pegasus
Big South Cape Is.

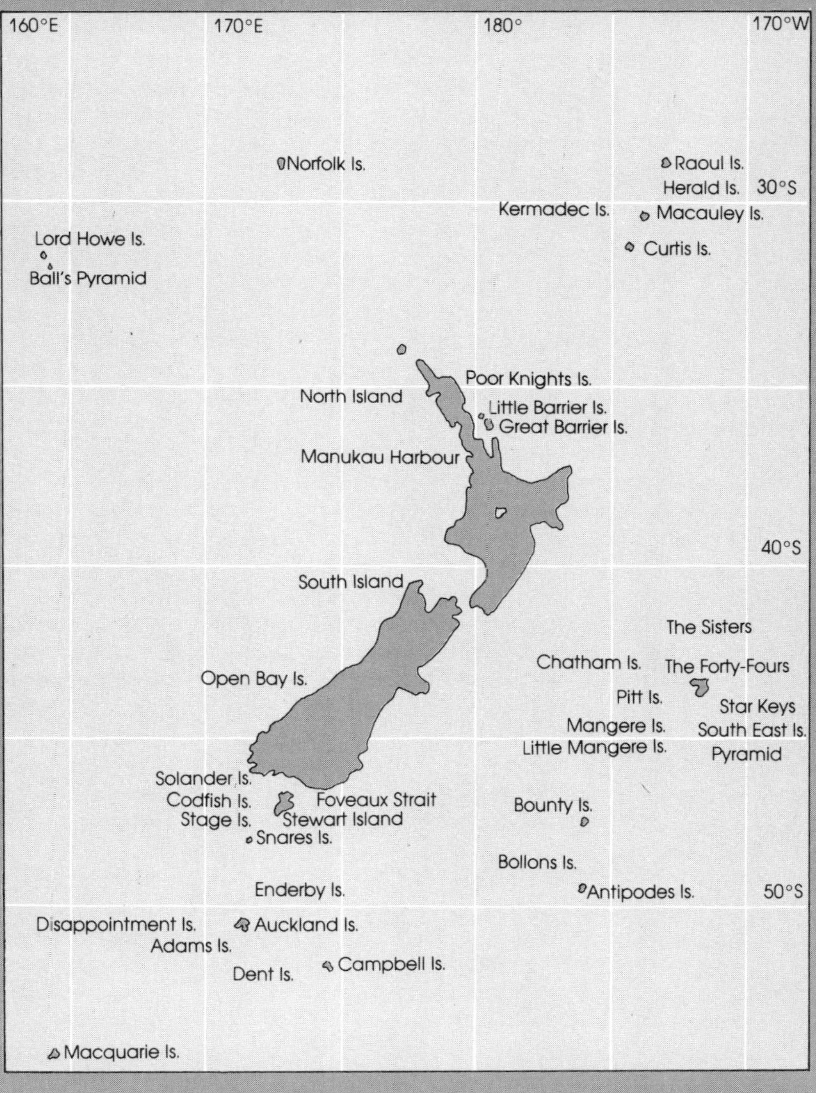

160°E
170°E
180°
170°W
Norfolk Is.
Raoul Is.
Herald Is.
30°S
Kermadec Is.
Macauley Is.
Curtis Is.
Lord Howe Is.
Ball's Pyramid
Poor Knights Is.
North Island
Little Barrier Is.
Great Barrier Is.
Manukau Harbour
40°S
South Island
The Sisters
Chatham Is.
The Forty-Fours
Open Bay Is.
Pitt Is.
Star Keys
Mangere Is.
South East Is.
Little Mangere Is.
Pyramid
Solander Is.
Codfish Is.
Foveaux Strait
Bounty Is.
Stage Is.
Stewart Island
Snares Is.
Bollons Is.
Enderby Is.
Antipodes Is.
50°S
Disappointment Is.
Auckland Is.
Adams Is.
Dent Is.
Campbell Is.
Macquarie Is.

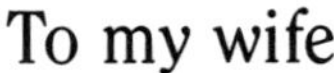

To my wife

# INTRODUCTION

The number of living and recently extinct birds listed in the *Annotated Checklist of the Birds of New Zealand* 1970 and the *Amendments & Additions* 1979 (see bibliography) is 305. Of this total, 10 native species are recently extinct as breeding birds (since A.D. 1800) or so presumed, 104 are non-breeding migrants, visitors, and stragglers, 90 are breeding sea and shore birds, 64 are native land and freshwater birds (36 being endemic) and 36 are introduced. All are mentioned in the following pages.

The New Zealand region, as encompassed by the *Checklist*, includes the main and offshore islands; the outlying island groups of Kermadec, Chatham, Bounty, Antipodes, Snares, Auckland, Campbell and Macquarie; the islands of the Ross Sea; and the Antarctic Ross Dependency. Norfolk and Lord Howe Islands, though they contain New Zealand elements in their flora and fauna are essentially Australian in their affinities and are excluded.

Of the 295 extant species, 55 are vagrants that have been recorded less than 20 times and mostly less than 10. A further 55 (approximately) are unlikely to be seen without visits to the outlying island groups — though this number will be reduced if one is able to spend time at sea.

Two endemic land birds are confined to the North Island of New Zealand and its offshore islands — the Whitehead and the Stitchbird. To these may be added the New Zealand Dabchick (which seems to have abandoned the South Island), the Little Spotted Kiwi (apparently now surviving only on Kapiti Island) and the Kokako (the South Island subspecies of which is now apparently extinct).

Endemic land birds confined to the South Island are Great Spotted Kiwi, New Zealand Little Bittern (if still extant), Takahe, Kea, Kakapo, Orange-fronted Parakeet, Rock Wren, Brown Creeper and Yellowhead. Kakapo and Brown Creeper also occur at Stewart Island.

The Kermadec Islands have 24 breeding species, none endemic. The dominant land birds are Tui, Red-crowned Parakeet and Starling. Seabirds are in large numbers, especially Kermadec Petrel, Black-winged Petrel, White-naped Petrel, Wedge-tailed Shearwater, Red-tailed Tropicbird, Masked Booby, White-capped Noddy, Grey Ternlet and Sooty Tern.

The Chatham group has 60 breeding species of which 6 are endemic: Taiko, Chatham Island Petrel, Chatham Island Oystercatcher, Shore Plover, Black Robin and Chatham Island Warbler. In addition, the Chatham Island Mollymawk is a most distinctive subspecies. The islands are the stronghold of the Northern Royal Albatross and have huge colonies of Buller's Mollymawk, Giant Petrel, Broad-billed Prion, Fairy Prion, Sooty Shearwater and White-faced Storm Petrel — to mention only the most conspicuous.

The Bounty Islands are a major breeding ground for Erect-crested Penguins, Salvin's Mollymawks and Fulmar Prions. The only other species breeding here are the Bounty Island Shag and a few Cape Pigeons, Southern Black-backed (Dominican) Gulls and Antarctic Terns.

The Antipodes Islands have a single endemic: the Antipodes Island Green Parakeet. The islands are notable for the colonies of Soft-plumaged Petrel and Little Shearwater, the very large numbers of Erect-crested and Rockhopper Penguins, the rather small-sized, dark-plumaged Wandering Albatrosses, the colony of the nominate race of the Black-browed Mollymawk and the good population of the Subantarctic Snipe. The remaining species breeding are: Light-mantled Sooty Albatross, Giant Petrel, Cape Pigeon, Fairy Prion, Sooty Shearwater, Grey Petrel,

White-chinned Petrel, White-headed Petrel, Black-bellied and Grey-backed Storm Petrels, Common Diving Petrel, Southern Skua, Dominican Gull, Antarctic Tern, New Zealand Pipit, Red-crowned Parakeet, Hedge-sparrow and Lesser Redpoll. In addition, Silvereyes and Starlings probably breed, or have bred, in small numbers.

The Snares are among the very few subantarctic islands to have so far escaped the introduction of cats, rats and other predators. There is one endemic: the Snares Crested Penguin. The islands are notable for the vast numbers of Sooty Shearwaters and for the breeding colonies of Buller's and Salvin's Mollymawks. The other sea birds breeding are Cape Pigeon, Broad-billed, Fairy and Fulmar Prion, Mottled Petrel, Common Diving Petrel, Southern Skua, Red-billed Gull and Antarctic Tern. There are 8 regularly breeding land and freshwater birds: Grey Duck, Snares Snipe, Black Tit (a very distinct subspecies), Snares Fernbird, Song Thrush, Blackbird, Silvereye and Redpoll.

The Auckland Islands have 45 breeding species, including 20 land and freshwater. None are endemic. The islands contain the world's largest known breeding colonies of Wandering Albatross and Shy Mollymawk; huge numbers of Antarctic Prions, a distinct, flightless subspecies of the Brown Duck, one of the world's most southerly breeding populations of a Falcon, a race of the Subantarctic Snipe, a Banded Dotterel, and a unique though probably now extinct species of Merganser. Conspicuous among the land birds are Tui, Bellbird, Red-crowned and Yellow-crowned Parakeets, Pipit, Tomtit and Redpoll.

Campbell Island is the stronghold of the Southern Royal Albatross and is the only known breeding site of the New Zealand race of the Black-browed Mollymawk. It is the major breeding ground of the region for the Grey-headed Mollymawk and has small numbers of Wandering and Light-mantled Sooty Albatrosses. In all, 32 species breed at Campbell: 5 albatrosses, 3 penguins, 6 petrels, 2 shags, the flightless duck (on Dent Island), Grey Duck, Southern Skua, Dominican and Red-billed Gulls, Antarctic Tern, Skylark, Song Thrush, Blackbird, Hedge-sparrow, New Zealand Pipit (very rare), Silvereye, Redpoll, Chaffinch, Starling and House Sparrow.

Macquarie Island has one endemic: the Royal Penguin, present in huge numbers. The main island is plagued with introduced cats, rats and Wekas and as a result the breeding status of some species is uncertain. The following are known to breed regularly: King, Gentoo, Royal and Rockhopper Penguin, Wandering, Black-browed, Grey-headed and Light-mantled Sooty Albatross, Cape Pigeon, both species of Giant Petrel, Antarctic Prion, Sooty Shearwater, Blue Petrel, White-headed Petrel, Grey Petrel, Macquarie Island Shag, Grey Duck, Weka, Southern Skua, Dominican Gull, Antarctic Tern, Starling and Redpoll. The Macquarie Island Rail and the Macquarie Island Red-crowned Parakeet were exterminated by cats in the 1890s.

Finally, the islands of the Ross Sea, along with the New Zealand segment of the Antarctic, have breeding colonies of Emperor, Adele, Chinstrap and Gentoo Penguin, Antarctic Fulmar, Antarctic Petrel, Cape Pigeon, Snow Petrel, Antarctic Prion (probably), Wilson's Storm Petrel and Antarctic Skua.

In the compilation of a book such as this, dependence on the reported knowledge of others is substantial. In particular, I wish to acknowledge my debts to the *Checklist* and to that mine of information and essential companion *The New Guide to the Birds of New Zealand* by R. A. Falla, R. B. Sibson and E. G. Turbott. This work is a 'must' for all. These and other works consulted are listed in the bibliography. As to myself: I have now been watching and photographing New Zealand's birds for over 30 years. During this time, through the generosity and help, which I most gratefully acknowledge, of the Directors and Officers of the Wildlife Service of the Department of Internal Affairs, I have been able to visit most of the outlying island groups. I have not been to Antarctica, Snares or Macquarie. My wife and I have been to many of the Muttonbird Islands — especially during the early days of Saddleback transfers — and we have both been to Norfolk and Lord Howe Islands which, though not strictly in the region, provided valuable 'rounding off' experiences.

Nevertheless, as an amateur there is a limit to the time one can spend and the species one can photograph, and so not every species is illustrated. To my wife I offer most grateful thanks, not just for the typing of this and previous manuscripts but for her unstinting help with all the problems that are associated with the photography of elusive subjects.

# APTERYGIFORMES

## **Kiwis** Apterygidae

Nocturnal, flightless, ratite birds confined to New Zealand. Feathers hair-like, wings rudimentary, tail absent. Females larger than males and with longer bills. Nostrils at the tip of the bill, not at the base as in all other living birds. Three species.

### The Brown Kiwi

*Photo 1*

*Apteryx australis* 50 cm.

Plumage dark grey, strongly streaked with black and brown. North, South and Stewart Islands.

### The Little Spotted Kiwi

*Apteryx oweni* 40 cm.

Plumage pale grey, spotted dark brown. Now apparently extinct over its former South Island range but surviving in good numbers on Kapiti Island where introduced early this century. A small, endangered population on D'Urville Island has recently been transferred to Maud Island. Only 1 North Island record in historical times: Tararuas 1875.

### The Great Spotted Kiwi or Roa

*Apteryx haastii* 50 cm.

Plumage as for the Little Spotted Kiwi and easily mistaken for that species but has a distinct chestnut tinge on the back. South Island only, principally western Nelson.

Of all the birds peculiar to New Zealand, kiwis are the most famous. Yet outside of zoos little is known of their life history, for their nocturnal ways make them extremely difficult to observe in the dense rain forests of the remote ranges they inhabit.

With their shaggy plumage, muscular hindquarters and pear-shaped outline, kiwis are most unbirdlike creatures. The legs and feet are heavy and powerful and they are well able to defend themselves with lightning-swift, slashing, downward kicks. They can move fast, with long, loping strides. They are credited with a good sense of smell and may be heard snorting and sniffing as they explore the leaf litter of the forest floor. They have large ear orifices and undoubtedly hear well. Their sense of touch is also good, aided by the many catlike whiskers at the base of the bill. Their eyesight, however, appears poor, and for nocturnal birds, their eyes are remarkably small.

Kiwis nest mostly in burrows, but hollow logs and similar cavities are also used. The normal clutch is 1 (2 in captivity) and the eggs are large for the size of the bird. The egg of the Brown Kiwi is about 125×80 millimetres and weighs about 430 grams — roughly one-seventh of the female's body weight. That of the Little Spotted Kiwi measures 110×70 millimetres and weighs 300 grams, or one-quarter of the female's body weight. Incubation is by the male only and in the Brown Kiwi takes 75-80 days. After hatching, the chick remains in the burrow, guarded, but not fed, by the female for 5 days. Thereafter it fossicks for itself, guarded and assisted by the parents.

Kiwis feed largely on worms and insect larvae for which they probe to the full length of their long bills. Kiwi probes in the soft earth are a characteristic and easily identified sign of the birds' presence, for they are triangular in outline when the bill has been buried to the hilt. They manoeuvre the bill like a person enlarging a hole with a crowbar and, with a good worm at the end, become really excited! They also eat land slugs and snails, and at Mason Bay I have seen them taking sandhoppers from the tide wrack thrown up on the beach.

The voice of the male kiwi is a shrill *ki-wi* repeated 5 or 6 times on a rising scale; that of the female is similar but lower in pitch and hoarser. They call mostly at dusk and the male usually calls first. They also grunt and snort, and they hiss when alarmed. Chicks make a cheeping noise.

During the day, kiwis may camp in clumps of fern or under a log. They do not necessarily return to a burrow or go underground. They can swim and appear indifferent to heavy rain.

The displays of kiwis are little recorded. I have seen them preening each other's head and neck, standing face to face rather than side by side, and I have seen them rubbing bills together. They also chase round and round in tight circles.

My personal experience of kiwis is limited to the Stewart Island form of the Brown Kiwi. Kiwis are reasonably numerous at Stewart Island and may sometimes be seen out and about on dull and overcast days. In this they differ from kiwis elsewhere. Their responses to one's attempts to photograph them vary. I recall 5 days my wife and I spent in a pup tent and a hide near and at the burrow of a kiwi at Port Pegasus. Those kiwis would not co-operate at all. Perhaps it was the weather — a series of snow flurries and hail showers with the temperature seldom much above freezing — but we saw them outside the burrow only once. At the other extreme is a pair watched at Mason Bay. Those birds would emerge at dusk and stay at the entrance of the burrow for half an hour or so, stretching and preening, taking no notice of me in full view 3 metres away. Perhaps more typical is the pair with a small chick I photographed with a friend some years ago. This pair had a well-used burrow in open forest near the top of a steep slope. As is common at Stewart Island, the slope was interlaced with the roots of trees and in places honeycombed with cavities and hollows, many of which were occupied by Little Blue Penguins which purred and grumbled under our feet as we walked over the springy surface.

To sit quietly in the forest on a calm, warm evening and wait as the world around you goes slowly to sleep, can be a most pleasant experience. Although it is over 25 years ago, I still recall those evenings vividly. From across the water of the bay came the weird, retching noises of a colony of shags whose chicks were being fed in the last remaining minutes of daylight. In the forest the strange, moaning howls of the Little Blue Penguin added eerie overtones to the stillness. Gradually, as the darkness closed in, the noises died away and the outlines of the forest grew more and more dim. I remember wondering if we would be able to see the kiwis should they appear. Already our eyes were playing tricks and we were imagining grey shapes looming silently out of the burrow.

Then we felt footsteps and a kiwi came running up from behind us. It was as well we detected its approach, for when it stopped a few paces away, it suddenly gave vent to an ear-splitting series of calls. Kiwis can be heard from well over a kilometre; at 2 metres they are deafening! The female came out of the burrow and answered with a series of hoarser cries equally unnerving when heard at such close range. Both birds then vanished into the forest and we could hear them rustling about in the fern and leaves on the slope below. It was three-quarters of an hour before one of them returned and disappeared down the burrow, where it remained for a further three-quarters of an hour before reappearing. As by this time it was pitch dark and impossible to see what was happening, we packed our cameras and returned to camp.

The next night we tied a torch with a red bulb over the entrance of the burrow, hoping that kiwis would be like owls, unable to perceive red light. The male duly arrived at dark and called. The female emerged and answered and both then went off into the forest. About half an hour later, we noticed something just within the entrance of the burrow. This, we realised, was the chick, but it would not come forward into the circle of light thrown by the torch. After a while, however, the torch began to flicker and grow dim and, by peering intently, we could just make out the diminutive form prodding about the cleared ground in front of the burrow. It did not stay long before retreating back underground.

Our last night provided an unexpected drama. We set up our cameras and flashlights and, as usual, the male came running along the track, making the ground tremble with his heavy tread. He called and then, just as the female was about to emerge, a third kiwi appeared and made to go down the burrow. What followed was dramatic in its violence. Both kiwis exploded out of the burrow, to the accompaniment of violent, spitting, hissing noises, crashed into our tripods, shot between our legs and vanished into the forest, swearing profusely. No doubt we had seen last year's offspring being evicted in no uncertain terms now that the parents had a new youngster. After that, it was quite some time before either of the adults reappeared. We were entertained, however, by the chick, which moved quietly about the entrance of the burrow, mostly just out of full view and seldom within the circle of light thrown by the torch. So our few nights with the kiwis ended, some of the most enjoyable I have had with my camera.

1 The Stewart Island Brown Kiwi; (inset) a kiwi chick.

**2** A King Penguin in the final stages of moult, Campbell Island.

**3** Yellow-eyed Penguins displaying.

**4** A Gentoo Penguin photographed at Antipodes Island.

**5** The Yellow-eyed Penguin.

**6** A Chinstrap Penguin photographed at Antipodes Island.

**7** The Little Blue Penguin.

**8** Erect-crested Penguins, Antipodes Island.

**9** The Bounty Islands are a group of granitic outcrops barren of vegetation and without permanent water. During the southern summer they are inhabited by untold thousands of Erect-crested Penguins Bounty Island Mollymawks and Fulmar Prions.

**10** A pair of Rockhopper Penguins, Antipodes Island.

**11** Campbell Island. A view looking south along the west coast with Mt Paris in the distance. Five species of albatross breed at Campbell: Royal, Wandering, Black-browed, Grey-headed, and Light-mantled Sooty.

**12** The Fiordland Crested Penguins.

**13** Carnley Harbour, Auckland Islands. Adams Island, which holds the world's largest colony of Wandering Albatrosses, is to the right of the picture.

**14** An Erect-crested Penguin colony, Antipodes Island. Anchorage Bay and the cliffs of North Cape can be seen beyond.

**15** Campbell Island; the south coast and Monument Harbour. Elephant seals haul up here and Giant Petrels nest in the nearby tussock.

# SPHENISCIFORMES

## **Penguins** Spheniscidae

Flightless, marine birds adapted to the colder waters of the Southern Hemisphere. Wings modified into rigid flippers that do not fold and with which they swim. The feet are used for steering. In the water they have the streamlined shape of dolphins and the dolphins' habit of porpoising. Plumage dense and compact with the feathers reduced to scale-like structures. All species are in shades of blue-black above and white below with ornamentation, if any, confined to the head. Feet webbed. Legs set far back. Stand upright on land. Bill covered with horny plates. Voices powerful — mostly a cacophony of unmusical brays, yells, trills and trumpetings, distinctive for each species, but musical and attractive in the Emperor and King Penguin. Long lived. Slow to mature. Sexes alike though males larger and with more robust bills. Normally mate for life, returning each year to the same meeting place. Breed in colonies which are often enormous, though the species that breed on the New Zealand mainland do so in loose aggregations among vegetation with most pairs out of sight of their neighbours. Most species are found in subantarctic, not antarctic waters. Food fish, squid and krill captured in varying proportion and at varying depths, depending on the species. All species are able to withstand long periods of starvation and habitually do so when moulting (which takes about a month), when incubating (which the majority do for 2 weeks or so at a time) and when guarding the chick. Seventeen species; 14 on the New Zealand list, 5 of which breed only in the region.

### The Emperor Penguin

*Aptenodytes forsteri* 115 cm.

A truly antarctic species seldom seen north of the winter pack, the Emperor Penguin resembles a King Penguin in plumage pattern, but is twice as heavy and distinctly taller. There is only one New Zealand record — Oreti Beach 1967 — but Coulman Island in the Ross Sea has a colony of 100,000, which is about a third of the world population. This penguin breeds during the long antarctic winter, with the male incubating the single egg on his feet (they make no nest) without relief for 60-65 days. The female returns at or near the hatch and takes over while the male feeds at sea (which is still some distance away). Thereafter, they change over with increasing frequency as the ice breaks up. The chicks creche at about 50 days and become independent at 150-170 days.

### The King Penguin

*Photo 2*

*Aptenodytes patagonicus* 90 cm.

The King Penguin is slimmer and more elegant than the Emperor Penguin and, like it, has a conspicuous bright orange tear-drop patch on the side of the head that extends down as a thin orange line to join an orange flush on the upper breast. It has an orange patch on the sides of the mandible where the Emperor has a lilac one. In the New Zealand region it breeds only at Macquarie Island. Elsewhere it breeds at the Falklands, South Georgia, Marion, Prince Edward, Crozet, Kerguelen and Heard. It straggles to Antipodes, Campbell and Auckland Islands, but rarely to New Zealand. This species has an unusual breeding cycle that lasts 13 or 14 months, after which it immediately breeds again and so becomes out of step with the seasons. In the third year, it breeds so late that the chick, if it hatches at all, does not survive the winter. King Penguins at best rear 2 chicks in 3 years, a cycle unique for penguins.

## The Yellow-eyed Penguin

*Photos 3, 5*

*Megadyptes antipodes* 76 cm.

This distinctive, robust penguin is found only in the New Zealand region. It has a yellow eye, yellowish cheeks and crown and a band of yellow encircling the back of the head. It breeds along the east coast of the South Island north to Banks Peninsula, at Stewart Island, at the Auckland Islands and at Campbell Island. It is a sedentary species and may be found ashore in the vicinity of its breeding grounds all the year round. Breeding occurs from September to February. The colonies are not large and the birds are often widely scattered. The nests, which are well formed, are typically placed in dense vegetation and often quite some distance inland in thick forest or heavy scrub. On some of the islands round Stewart Island this urge to move well inland sometimes finds the birds trekking right across a small islet to nest almost on the shoreline on the other side. They never seem to learn, however, to take the resultant short cut to the sea, but continue to come and go the long way round each time!

The normal clutch is 2 and the incubation period is about 42 days. Both parents incubate, taking turns of 2 or 3 days at a time. When the chicks hatch, one parent remains at the nest on guard, while the other goes to sea. The pattern is for one parent to go to sea in the morning and return in the late afternoon or evening. It then feeds the chicks and both parents stay at the nest overnight. In the morning the other parent goes to sea, and so on. The young are fed on regurgitated fish and squid and leave for the sea when about 16 weeks old. As a rule, both chicks are reared.

## The Gentoo Penguin

*Photo 4*

*Pygoscelis papua* 76 cm.

An antarctic species, it has an orange bill with a black ridge and triangular patches of white above and behind the eyes which meet across the crown. It breeds on the antarctic continent, on the islands of the Scotia Arc and South Indian Ocean and in the New Zealand region at Macquarie. It has straggled to Campbell and Antipodes Islands and to the Otago coast. It is a rather timid species that prefers easy landing places and gentle slopes on which to breed. Like all 3 *pygoscelis* penguins, it walks with short, careful steps, head thrust forward. It is present at its breeding islands all year. It lays 2 eggs and often raises both chicks. Incubation takes about 40 days. The chicks creche at 6 weeks and are independent at 12-14 weeks.

## The Adelie Penguin

*Pygoscelis adeliae* 70 cm.

An antarctic species seldom seen north of the winter pack. This bird is, to many people, the stereotype of the penguin clan, made familiar by documentary films. It is identified by its jet-black head with white eye-rings, and its short, stubby, black-tipped, brick-red bill. It breeds in Antarctica, including the Ross Sea area and on antarctic islands, and has straggled to Macquarie Island. It lays 2 eggs on a nest of stones. The incubation period, mostly by the male, is 33-37 days. The chicks are independent at about 50 days.

## The Chinstrap Penguin

*Photo 6*

*Pygoscelis antarctica* 66 cm.

The black 'chinstrap' on the white face and throat is distinctive. An antarctic species, its principal colonies — which are immense — are on the islands of the Scotia Arc. It is increasing its range and has recently been discovered breeding on the Balleny Islands in the Ross Sea. It has straggled to Macquarie, Campbell and Antipodes Islands. The Chinstrap is the most belligerent of the *pygoscelis* penguins. It lays 2 eggs which are incubated for 35-39 days. It may rear 2 chicks — though usually 1 — which are independent at about 10 weeks.

## The Little Blue Penguin

*Photo 7*

*Eudyptula minor* 40 cm.

The Little Blue Penguin is the common penguin of New Zealand coastal waters and the only penguin to breed in the North Island. It is also the only penguin to breed in Australia, where it is known as the Fairy Penguin. It is common at the Chatham Islands but does not extend south to the Snares (except as a straggler) or beyond. Six subspecies are described and include the Banks Peninsula-Motunau Island form, *albosignata*, with conspicuous white markings on its flippers that is known as the White-flippered Penguin. All races are blue-grey above and white below and are without head ornaments.

Little Blue Penguins are the smallest of the penguins. They are timid birds, nocturnal on land, and breed in burrows and caves. Another site — under buildings — is known only too well to the owners of seaside cottages. In such cases action usually has to be taken, for the nocturnal noises of the Blue Penguin are something to be reckoned with. The call of the Blue Penguin is a long, expiratory, moaning wail followed without pause by a long, inspiratory wail of slightly higher pitch — and so the birds go on, and on, and on.

During May and June, Blue Penguins are mostly out at sea, but they are back again in July when eggs are laid. They lay 2 eggs and usually rear 2 chicks. The incubation period is 35-40 days and both sexes incubate. The chicks are fed each night and are ready to depart for the sea in November when they are 8 weeks old. The adults leave at the same time but in January come ashore again to moult. Following the moult, they have another period at sea before returning in April to form pair bonds and start the cycle again.

While the above is the usual, many variations occur. Birds that have lost their clutch may lay again and birds in the southern part of their range breed later than those in the north. Consequently, depending on location, eggs may be found from June through to December, and birds may be seen in residence almost any month of the year.

## The Rockhopper Penguin

*Photo 10*

*Eudyptes chrysocome* 63 cm.

With their golden-yellow crests, geranium-red eyes and volatile temperaments, Rockhopper Penguins have a personality all their own. They are the most widely distributed of all penguins and breed on almost every subantarctic island group. In the New Zealand region they breed at Antipodes, Auckland, Campbell (where they are the dominant penguin) and Macquarie Islands. They visit Snares, have been recorded at Chatham and straggle to the South Island coast. Their status at the Bounty Islands is uncertain.

When subadult, and between breeding seasons, Rockhopper Penguins are entirely pelagic — to the extent that they have been seen with barnacles on their feet.

On land they hop, both feet together, and they prefer rocky terrain. Indeed, Rockhopper Penguins choose the most difficult landing grounds, places where the sea tumbles them about unmercifully. Their colonies are nearly always on rocky ground at some distance above the sea and they tend to place their nests under the overhang of rocks and in caves. They associate freely with other crested penguins — with Erect-crested Penguins at Antipodes and Royal Penguins at Macquarie — and in each case occupy the higher and more broken ground.

Rockhopper Penguins arrive back at their breeding grounds in October and lay in November. They lay 2 eggs, the first being small and usually discarded but, should it hatch, only 1 chick is reared. Incubation takes 32-34 days and is by both sexes in shifts of about 2 weeks. The female does the first shift, then the male, then the female again and then when the chick hatches the male guards for 3 weeks while the female feeds it. The chicks become independent at about 70 days.

## The Fiordland Crested Penguin

*Photo 12*

*Eudyptes pachyrhynchus* 71 cm.

This penguin differs from the other crested penguins in having no visible bare skin round the gape. It differs from the very similar but slightly larger Snares Crested Penguin in showing 4 or 5 whitish streaks on each cheek. It is an endemic species, breeding throughout Fiordland, in parts of South Westland (especially on Open Bay Island and the nearby headland of Jackson's Bay), at the Solander Islands (which have large colonies) and along the west coast of Stewart Island, including some offshore islands such as Codfish.

Fiordland Penguins are attractive birds and the sight of a group, fresh and clean from the sea, their golden crests blowing in the wind as they stand on a rock at the edge of the surf, is not quickly forgotten. They are winter breeders, returning to their breeding grounds in June. Between breeding seasons they are pelagic, their exact movements not known, but they straggle to Snares, Auckland, Campbell and Macquarie Islands, are recorded with some frequency from Tasmania and occasionally even Cape Leeuwin. They nest in the coastal forest and wherever possible go underground — into rockfalls and caves and the cavities between and under the roots of trees. The eggs are laid in July and are hatched in August after an incubation period of 35 days. Two eggs are laid, the first smaller than the second, and though both usually hatch, only 1 chick is reared. Incubation is in shifts, with the female doing the first, and when the chicks hatch the male guards them for 2-3 weeks while the female brings food. Thereafter both parents feed the chick which becomes independent at about 10 weeks. By December all colonies are deserted.

## The Snares Crested Penguin

*Eudyptes robustus* 73 cm.

This is an endemic species breeding only at the Snares Islands where it is the only breeding penguin. It is very similar in appearance to the Fiordland Penguin but is slightly larger, has a more robust bill, shows visible pale pink bare skin round the gape and has uniformly black cheeks showing no white streaks. This species is seldom seen away from the Snares Islands, though it is pelagic between breeding seasons. It straggles to New Zealand and has been recorded at Antipodes, Campbell and Macquarie Islands.

Snares Crested Penguins return to the Snares in September and lay their eggs in October. Two eggs are laid, the first being small and usually abandoned, and the incubation period is 34 days. Should both eggs hatch, only 1 chick is reared. The chicks become independent at 10 weeks and leave for the sea in January.

The population of this penguin at Snares is between 30,000 and 50,000 in more than 100 colonies scattered through the olearia scrub, and reached by following streams that drain to the eastern side of the island. They also breed on the Western Chain (a string of 5 small rocky islands lying to the south west), which they share with Salvin's Mollymawks, Fulmar Prions and Cape Pigeons.

## The Erect-crested Penguin

*Photos 8, 14*

*Eudyptes sclateri* 71 cm.

The Erect Crested Penguin is distinguished by its erect and rather bristly-looking crest. It is an endemic, breeding only in the New Zealand region, and has its headquarters at the Bounty Islands and the Antipodes. At the Bounty Islands its numbers are almost beyond counting, covering some islands to their highest points. At Antipodes the numbers are thought to be nearly as great, if less dramatic in their impact. They also breed in small numbers associated with the Rockhopper colonies of the Auckland Islands and Campbell. They straggle to Macquarie, Snares, Chathams and New Zealand and have attempted to breed on Otago Peninsula.

Erect Crested Penguins are rather stodgy birds compared with the volatile Rockhoppers so often associated with them. They prefer relatively easy landing places and at the Antipodes Islands (where, incidentally, one has the unexpected sight of parakeets foraging round the nests) they site their colonies mostly on gently sloping ground that is easy of access. They are pelagic between breeding seasons, returning in September and laying in October. Two eggs are laid, the first small and usually discarded, and the incubation period is about 35 days. The chicks depart for the sea in January.

## The Royal Penguin

*Eudyptes schlegeli* 76 cm.

The crest of this species is orange-yellow and droops in a floppy, untidy manner over the back of the head and behind the eyes. It has a conspicuously long and massive bill that seems out of proportion to the head. It is an endemic, breeding only at Macquarie Island. It straggles with some regularity to Campbell Island, but rarely to New Zealand. The Royal Penguin is very similar to the Macaroni Penguin except that it has white cheeks and a white throat. Occasional individuals, however, have dark cheeks and a dark throat and these can be difficult indeed to identify. The amount of bare skin showing at the gape — greater than in the Royal Penguin — is said to be a useful pointer.

Royal Penguins occur in vast numbers at Macquarie Island, with colonies ranging from 1000 to more than 100,000 birds and a total population of over 2 million. They prefer open flat ground, which they reach by following streams, and often have Rockhopper Penguins associated with them in the more broken ground beyond. Eggs are laid in October and, as is the pattern for all crested penguins, the first is small and usually abandoned. Incubation takes 35 days and is by the female for the first 14 days, then by the male for 14 days, then by the female again and then, when the chick hatches, the male guards for about 3 weeks while the female brings food. Thereafter the chicks collect in creches and they become independent by late January.

## The Macaroni Penguin

*Eudyptes chrysalophus* 76 cm.

A very rare straggler to Campbell and Macquarie Islands, this penguin is very similar to the Royal Penguin except that the cheeks and throat are dark. It has the same oversized bill. It breeds on the Falkland Islands, the islands of the Scotia Arc, Bouvet, Marion, Prince Edward, Crozet, Kerguelen and Heard. A noisy aggressive species, its breeding cycle is about 1 month later than that of the Royal Penguin, but is otherwise similar.

## The Magellanic Penguin

*Spheniscus magellanicus* 71 cm.

There is a single New Zealand record for this South American species — an exhausted individual found in the surf at Waimarama Beach, near Napier, in March 1972. New Zealand is so far beyond the species' normal dispersal that the likelihood of it having been carried here on a ship cannot be discounted.

# PODICIPEDIFORMES

## **Grebes** Podicipedidae

Small to medium-sized, aquatic, diving birds with broadly lobed toes and legs set so far back as to make progress on land difficult and seldom attempted. Essentially birds of shallow freshwater lakes with emergent and fringing vegetation. Fly with reluctance and seldom seen to do so, though some can fly well as the recent colonisation of this country by 2 species from Australia testifies. Temporarily flightless during the moult. Sexes alike. Plumage dense and with a satin sheen. Ornamentation confined to the head. Habitually eat feathers and feed feathers to the young. Nest on the water, building a floating nest anchored to emergent or overhanging vegetation. Carry young on their backs. Young boldly patterned with black and white stripes. Form flocks in winter. Nineteen (20) species; 4 on the New Zealand list, all breeding, 1 endemic.

### The Great Crested Grebe

*Photo 16*

*Podiceps cristatus australis* 50 cm.

The Great Crested Grebe is widespread over temperate parts of Europe, Asia, Africa and Australia. In New Zealand it is an uncommon bird confined to the South Island where it is sedentary on certain lakes of Canterbury, Westland and Fiordland. The total population is estimated to be about 250 birds, most of them in Canterbury.

The Crested Grebe is about the size of a small Grey Duck. It has black crests on the head, a chestnut ruff round the neck, a dark back and a pure silky-white undersurface. Unlike its relatives in Europe and Asia, the New Zealand Crested Grebe does not lose its crests and ruff during winter, nor does it show any winter dispersal. Australian birds — to which the New Zealand birds are identical, indicating a relatively recent immigration to this country — behave in the same way.

Crested Grebes build floating nests of weed and debris dredged from the bottom and anchored to emergent or overhanging vegetation. The clutch is usually 3 to 5 and the eggs are laid at 2-day intervals. Both sexes incubate, changing over frequently in the early stages, thereafter less often, and the eggs are covered with nest material when left unattended. The incubation period is 28 days. The chicks hatch over a period of days and leave the nest soon after they are dry, to be carried about on the parents' backs. They are fed by the parents on small fish, water snails, aquatic insects and the like and are offered feathers from the start. The feathers apparently form a plug in the stomach to prevent fish bones from passing through to the intestine and presumably assist the process of entangling them into pellets which are subsequently regurgitated. The behaviour is said to be unique to grebes, but New Zealand Rock Wrens also eat feathers.

### The New Zealand Dabchick

*Podiceps rufopectus* 28 cm.

Unlike the Crested Grebe, the New Zealand Dabchick is an endemic species that has been in New Zealand a very long time. It is related to the Australian Hoary-headed Grebe and these 2 species have features that set them apart from all other grebes. The Dabchick's throat and breast are rusty red, its upperparts blackish and the underparts silvery. The head is black, glossed with green, and is overlaid with a number of fine, hair-like, whitish feathers akin to those of the Hoary-headed Grebe but of finer texture and difficult to see in the field. The Dabchick has a conspicuous, pale, yellowish-white eye and a stout, tapered bill. An alert and wary bird, it is difficult to get close to.

For practical purposes, the New Zealand Dabchick is today confined to the North Island where it is widespread and in places plentiful. Dabchick-like birds seen in the South Island are now more likely to be Australian Little Grebes or Hoary-headed Grebes.

Dabchicks are apparently reluctant to fly during daylight hours. At night, however, and especially in winter, it is evident that they move about quite extensively, for they soon occupy newly formed sewerage ponds and farm dams. Their food consists more of fresh water snails, insects, crustaceans and other animal life than of fish and this is borne out by the shorter, stubbier, less dagger-like bill. They display by twisting the head rapidly from side to side, by diving and by brief, splashing runs along the water.

Dabchicks have an extended breeding season with nests being found from August to March. Possibly 2 broods are reared. Chick survival is low and the main predator appears to be the eel. The usual clutch is 2, sometimes 3, and the incubation period is about 21 days. Like other grebes, Dabchicks feed feathers to their young and carry them about on their backs.

## The Hoary-headed Grebe

*Podiceps poliocephalus* 28 cm.

First recorded in New Zealand in 1975 swimming on the sea of the boat harbour of, of all places, Snares Island, the Hoary-headed Grebe has since bred successfully in Southland and has been recorded from a number of locations in both the North and South Islands. At a distance, this grebe bears some resemblance to the New Zealand Dabchick but the fine, white, hair-like feathers on the head are much more profuse and usually easily visible. The front of the neck is white, not rusty red. In winter, the conspicuous head pattern is lost and it then becomes difficult to distinguish from the winter and immature plumages of the Dabchick and the Little Grebe. This species flies more readily than the other grebes and in Australia disperses in winter in flocks, often to salt water. In those parts of Australia where numbers are large, it breeds in colonies. Colonies of up to 400 have been reported, with the nests only a metre or so apart.

## The Australian Little Grebe

*Photo 17*

*Tachybaptus novaehollandiae* 25 cm.

The Australian Little Grebe was first recorded on a small pond near Arrowtown in 1968. The illustration shows the particular bird. A lone individual, it spent much time calling and skittering over the water. It staked out a territory, which it defended against the pond's resident coots, and even built a nest in a rather desultory way. It was all rather sad. It stayed 2 years and then disappeared. Since then, Little Grebes have been reported widely and have bred successfully in a number of both North and South Island localities.

In breeding plumage, the Little Grebe is unmistakable. It has a bright yellow line of bare skin running diagonally from the eye to the bill. The throat is black. In winter it becomes rather nondescript, as do the other small grebes. It has a most attractive, trilling call note and in spring is distinctly vocal. It is a wary bird and at the first hint of danger sinks silently beneath the surface, leaving not a ripple. Careful search is then needed to relocate it — usually some distance away and with only its head breaking water. All grebes have a nice adjustment of buoyancy: with air trapped in the feathers they float, and with the air expelled by compressing the plumage, they sink. Small grebes, especially, have the trick of silently submerging until only the periscope of the head remains.

Besides Australia, this species also occurs in New Guinea, Rennel Island, the New Hebrides (now Vanuatu) and New Caledonia.

# PROCELLARIIFORMES

Oceanic birds with the nostrils in tubes. Four families: Albatrosses and Mollymawks; Petrels, Prions and Shearwaters; Storm Petrels; Diving Petrels.

## **Albatrosses and Mollymawks** Diomedeidae

Very large pelagic birds adapted to life at sea. Come to land only to breed. Wings long and narrow. Bill covered with horny plates and hooked at the tip. Nostrils in lateral tubes. Feet webbed. Walk on land. Sexes alike, though males slightly larger. Swim and dive. Feed on fish, squid and krill. Drink sea water, excreting the excess salt through nasal glands. Long lived. Mate for life. Breed in colonies. Lay 1 egg, not replaced if lost. Subantarctic except for 3 species in the North Pacific and one at the Galapagos. In all 14 (15) species; 10 on the New Zealand list, of which 7 breed in the region, 2 of them nowhere else.

### The Wandering Albatross

*Photos 18, 19*

*Diomedea exulans* 80–135 cm.

Wandering Albatrosses have a circumpolar distribution and a wide latitudinal range — south to the edge of the pack, north to about 25°S. In the New Zealand region they breed at Antipodes, Auckland, Campbell and Macquarie Islands, and Adams Island, of the Auckland group, has the world's largest colony — an estimated 13,500 pairs. Elsewhere, Wandering Albatrosses breed at South Georgia, Tristan da Cunha, Gough, Marion, Prince Edward, Crozet and Kerguelen Islands. The total world population is about 36,000 pairs.

Wandering and Royal Albatrosses are much the same size and can sometimes be difficult to tell apart. Each is a predominantly white bird with a white back and each has a wingspan of up to 3.25 metres. Juvenile Wandering Albatrosses pose no identification problem since they are predominantly dark brown, except for the underwing and face. As they get older, however, the dark markings are progressively lost; fairly rapidly during the first 3 years, thereafter more slowly. Eventually, birds of the larger, southern race, especially the males, become entirely white, except for black wing tips and some black vermiculation on the body feathers. It is these old birds that are so difficult to distinguish from Southern Royals. Others — such as the smaller birds that breed at the Antipodes Islands — apparently retain some dark mottling of the body feathers all their lives, making them easily identifiable at any time. Both races have horn-coloured bills that are evidently well supplied with blood vessels, as they flush pink with excitement and turn blue with the cold.

Wandering Albatrosses do not breed till they are 8-10 years old. They spend their first 5 or 6 years at sea and then commence visiting their future breeding grounds, which are usually the ones at which they were reared, and over the next 2 or 3 years become acquainted with the sites and form pair bonds. Once mated, they normally mate for life, as do all albatrosses. During those early visits to the colony they collect together in groups known as 'gams'. Of the various courtship rituals they undertake — such as bill-clappering and bowing — the most exciting is the 'ecstatic', in which they stretch themselves upwards to their fullest extent, point the bill vertically to the sky, extend the wings to their maximum stretch — and scream!

Only 1 egg is laid and, should it be lost, the birds abandon the attempt for that year and try again the next. Incubation takes 78 days, by each parent in turn, in shifts of about a week. The chick is guarded for the first 4 or 5 weeks, thereafter it is left on its own while both parents hunt for food. As a rule, the chick is fed every second or third day and it leaves the nest when 277 days old, on average. The whole cycle occupies all of 12 months and so successful breeders have a year at sea before breeding again.

There are 2 described subspecies of Wandering Albatross and both occur in the New Zealand region. At Macquarie Island is the large, southern race (*chionoptera*) that with age turns almost entirely white. At Campbell and the Auckland Islands is a slightly smaller bird (*exulans*) that seems always to retain some brown markings, especially on the crown of the head. At the Antipodes Islands is a substantial population (estimated at 6000 birds, including non-breeding juveniles) of birds that are yet smaller again and that seem to retain considerable brown mottling of the plumage throughout their lives. These may yet prove to be a third (undescribed) subspecies.

The considerable size of the Adams Island colony was not discovered until 1972. Adams Island is a massive, brooding island lying athwart the southern end of the Auckland Islands group. It had long been known to hold Wandering Albatrosses but because of its size, difficult terrain and even more difficult weather, much of the eastern end, which requires a full day to reach from the usual landing place, was previously unknown. The 1972 party, which I was privileged to join, were determined to rectify the situation. What a day those who crossed the island had! When they finally broke through the cloud on the other side of the island, they found themselves in a huge, tussock-clad basin packed with Wandering Albatrosses — over a third of the total world breeding population. Adams Island is a superb albatross island; as well as the Wanderers, it holds Royal Albatrosses and Shy Mollymawks, and has hundreds of Light-mantled Sooty Albatrosses along the southern cliffs. These cliffs extend virtually unbroken for 20 kilometres. We went round them in a small boat, feeling, I may say, somewhat exposed in those southern swells. For their whole length they were simply alive with soaring albatrosses — a tremendous sight!

## The Royal Albatross

*Photos 20, 21, 22*

*Diomedea epomophora* 80–145 cm.

The Royal Albatross breeds only in the New Zealand region. There are 2 races: a large southern race (*epomophora*) breeding at Campbell Island and at Enderby, Adams and Auckland Islands of the Auckland group, and a smaller, northern race (*sanfordi*) breeding on the Sisters and the Forty Fours at the Chatham Islands, and at Taiaroa Head on the Otago Peninsula. This last colony is unique in that it is the only instance of an albatross breeding on an inhabited mainland.

The principal difference between the Royal and the Wandering Albatross is that, at all ages, the body plumage of the Royal Albatross is pure white. In the northern race, the upper wing remains entirely black throughout its life. In the southern race, the upper wing whitens progressively with age, eventually becoming entirely white except for the tips and trailing edge. Both races have horn-coloured bills and, like the Wandering Albatross, the bill can flush pink and turn blue in the cold. The cutting edge of the upper mandible is black, a useful distinction between the species at close range.

The life history of the Royal Albatross is now known in great detail. The birds spend the first 5 or 6 years of their life at sea, during which time they may circle the globe. Birds banded as chicks in New Zealand have been seen off South America. They then begin to visit their future breeding grounds in the same way as the

Wandering Albatross. Display procedures range from mutual preening and bill-clappering to 'ecstatics', with vertically pointed bills, fully extended wings and screaming calls.

Breeding commences when they are 9 or 10 years old. At Taiaroa Head, mature birds arrive in October, the males usually arriving first. Nests are built, or repaired — for the birds usually return to the same territories — and the single, large egg is laid in November. The egg is white, measures 125×75 millimetres and weighs about 450 grams. Incubation takes 78-80 days, in shifts of 5-10 days, or sometimes more. The chicks are covered in a dense coat of white down and are guarded for the first 4-6 weeks. Thereafter, like the Wandering Albatross, they are left on their own except for brief visits with food. These visits are very often brief indeed, a mere 10 or 15 minutes. They are fed daily at first, later at increasingly long intervals. Feeding is by regurgitation, the chick putting both mandibles inside and at right angles to the opened mandibles of the parent. Chicks are fed throughout the fledging period. The myth that for the last 2 or 3 weeks they are left to starve to encourage flight has now been discounted. The chicks eventually fly in September when 240 days old on average. The parents then spend a year at sea, during which they circle the globe via Cape Horn. The total breeding population of Royal Albatrosses is about 16,200 pairs. Of these some 8500 pairs breed at Campbell Island, 100 pairs at the Auckland Islands, 7600 pairs at the Chatham Islands, and some 20 pairs at Taiaroa Head.

## The Black-browed Mollymawk

*Photos 23, 24*

*Diomedea melanophris* c. 90 cm.

Mollymawks are small albatrosses with dark backs, colourful bills and more or less distinctive underwing patterns. The Black-browed Mollymawk has a wing span of about 220 centimetres. When adult, it has a bright yellow bill with a pink tip, a dark back and a dark grey tail. The wings are black above and white below, with broad black edges, the leading edge being broader than the trailing edge. Juvenile birds have dark greyish-green bills, an almost completely dark underwing, with only a small area of white in the centre, and a dark collar round the base of the neck.

There are 2 races of the Black-browed Mollymawk. The New Zealand race (*impavida*), which breeds at Campbell, has a pale honey-coloured eye. The nominate race, which breeds at South Georgia, Falkland, Kerguelen, Heard, Macquarie and Antipodes Islands (at Antipodes on Bollons Island), has a dark brown eye. Both races have a smudge of dark feathers behind the eye, giving them a rather frowning look.

In contrast to the 2 Great Albatrosses, the breeding cycles of mollymawks mostly occupy about 7 months and the birds normally breed each year. At Campbell Island, the Black-browed Mollymawk breeds on the ledges of sea cliffs in immense, densely-packed colonies in association with Grey-headed Mollymawks. Within this huge assemblage, each species tends to group with others of its own kind, though there is inevitably a degree of intermingling. Breeding commences in October. The nests, pedestals built up of mud and plant material, are added to each year so that eventually they grow to be substantial structures. They are placed close together, a fact that leads to much territorial remonstrance. The voice of this species — and of other mollymawks — is a sheep-like *baaa* and when large numbers of birds are displaying the noise is surprisingly like that heard from a mob of sheep.

Only 1 egg is laid and the incubation period is about 68 days. Both parents incubate and both feed the young. Feeding is by regurgitation in the same way as the Royal Albatross, and the young leave for the sea in March.

Black-browed Mollymawks disperse widely after breeding and regularly reach northern New Zealand waters. They readily follow ships. Their principal food is krill.

## The Grey-headed Mollymawk

*Photo 25*

*Diomedea chrysostoma* c. 80 cm.

The Grey-headed Mollymawk is about the same size as the Black-browed Mollymawk and has a similar wingspan. It is a beautiful bird, with a violet-grey head and neck sharply defined from the white underparts. The back and upper wing surfaces are black, the underwing is white with a black edging that is broader in front than behind, and the tail is grey. The bill is black with golden-yellow stripes on the upper and lower edges. There is a half-circle of white feathers just behind the eye. The species is very similar to Buller's Mollymawk, but may be distinguished from it by the completely grey head.

In the New Zealand region, the Grey-headed Mollymawk breeds at Campbell and Macquarie Islands. Elsewhere, it breeds at South Georgia, Marion, Prince Edward, the Crozets and Kerguelen Islands. At Campbell Island, it breeds in association with the Black-browed Mollymawks, building the same kind of pedestal nest, having similar displays, making the same *baaa*-ing noises but having longer incubation and fledging periods. The Grey-headed Mollymawk spends a longer time ashore before egg-laying and its chick takes longer to mature. Consequently, successful breeders take a year off before breeding again.

The displays of these 2 species are not quite so exuberant as those of the Wandering and Royal Albatrosses. Indeed, it is difficult to see how full-blown 'ecstatics', with their extended wings, could be tolerated in the tightly-packed communities in which these birds breed. When displaying, Grey-headed Mollymawks stand a few paces apart and stretch their bill towards each other till they touch. They then bow up and down and *baa*. At the same time, they erect and fan out their tails and perhaps sidle in a sort of shuffling dance. They then break off, only to go through the same performance a few minutes later. This activity will sometimes go on for hours.

After breeding, Grey-headed Mollymawks range widely but tend to keep south. They are not often seen in New Zealand coastal waters and unlike Black-browed Mollymawks they seldom follow ships. Their principal food is squid, whereas that of the Black-browed Mollymawk is krill.

## The Yellow-nosed Mollymawk

*Diomedea chlororhynchos* c. 74 cm.

This is a rare visitor to northern New Zealand waters. It breeds at Tristan da Cunha, Gough, Prince Edward and St Paul Islands and normally does not disperse further eastward than the Tasman Sea. In 1975, one landed briefly on the Sisters at the Chatham Islands and it has been seen at sea off North Cape and the islands of the Hauraki Gulf. It is the smallest of the mollymawks and has a conspicuously long, black bill with a yellow stripe on the upper surface, deepening to orange-red at the tip. The underwing is white with a narrow black margin, broader on the leading edge. Immatures have an all-dark bill but are easily distinguished from immature Black-browed Mollymawks by the white, not dark, underwing. Yellow-nosed Mollymawks soon learn to follow fishing boats and are easily enticed alongside with fish offal.

## Buller's Mollymawk

*Photo 28*

*Diomedea bulleri c.* 84 cm.

Buller's Mollymawk breeds only in the New Zealand region. There are 2 populations, one of which breeds at the Chatham Islands (on the Sisters and Forty Fours), the other at the Solander Islands and the Snares. The 2 populations have different breeding times; those at the Chatham Islands lay their eggs in early November and have the young fledged in April, while those at the Solanders and Snares lay their eggs during late January and February and have the young fledged in August. Both populations tend to remain in New Zealand waters all year, though there have been reports of birds off the Pacific coast of South America.

Buller's Mollymawk has a grey head and hindneck (darker in Chatham Island birds) and a white forehead. The bill is black with golden-yellow stripes on the upper and lower surfaces. The underwing is white with a narrow black border, slightly wider on the leading edge. There is a half-circle of white feathers behind the eye. Buller's Mollymawk is distinguished from the Grey-headed Mollymawk — which looks very similar — by the white forehead. Generally speaking, the ranges of the 2 species do not greatly overlap and Buller's is the one usually seen in inshore waters.

Buller's Mollymawks breed both on cliff ledges and on level ground, in colonies, and build the same type of pedestal nests as other mollymawks. The incubation period is 69 or 70 days and the chicks fledge when about 5 months old.

Buller's Mollymawks eagerly follow fishing boats and are readily enticed alongside with fish offal. They dive surprisingly well, thrusting themselves down with their wings, and will even disappear out of sight if sufficiently determined to catch up on a rapidly sinking fish head.

## The Shy Mollymawk

*Photo 32*

*Diomedea cauta cauta c.* 100 cm.

Also known as the White-capped Mollymawk, this species acquired the name 'Shy' from its reputed reluctance to follow ships. While this is indeed true of its 2 strong subspecies, the Grey-backed Mollymawk and the Chatham Island Mollymawk, it is by no means true of the Shy Mollymawk itself. Shy Mollymawks can be as eager and greedy for scraps as any Buller's and, being larger, more often than not get the lion's share of the loot.

The Shy Mollymawk is the largest of the mollymawks, with a wingspan of about 2.25 metres. Apart from a grey wash on the cheeks and the usual mollymawk dark back and upper wing surfaces, the bird is almost entirely white, including the underwing which has only a narrow black border round the edges. The bill is pale greenish-grey and has a lemon tip. The subspecies are quite different and are treated separately below. One feature common to all is the underwing pattern: pure white with a narrow black border all round and a small triangle of black feathers where the leading edge joins the body. This last is diagnostic of the Shy Mollymawk group.

The stronghold of the Shy Mollymawk is Disappointment Island of the Auckland group, with an estimated 60,000 pairs — a staggering sight from the sea; the island appears almost totally covered with evenly spaced white dots. The Shy Mollymawk also breeds on the main Auckland Island and on Adams Island. In Australia it breeds on Albatross Island in Bass Strait and on Mewstone and Pedra Branca Islands off southern Tasmania. The breeding cycle is akin to that of other mollymawks. After breeding, nominate Shy Mollymawks (but not the subspecies) disperse widely over the Southern Ocean.

## The Grey-backed Mollymawk

*Photo 27*

*Diomedea cauta salvini* 75 cm.

This subspecies of the Shy Mollymawk is also known as Salvin's Mollymawk and as the Bounty Island Mollymawk. It is a smaller bird than the nominate Shy and has much greyer cheeks and neck, and a grey, not black back. The bill is dark grey and has pale lemon upper and lower surfaces. Its stronghold is the Bounty Islands but it also breeds on the Western Reef of the Snares. It is not interested in following ships and can rarely be enticed to fishing boats. At the Bounty Islands it breeds all mixed up with the Erect-crested Penguins, which are in apparent millions (actually *c.* 115,000 pairs) and with Fulmar Prions that seem to occupy every crevice. Its life history presumably resembles that of other mollymawks but, because of the difficulty of access to and the inhospitability of its remote breeding sites, details are yet to be acquired. It may be of interest that this mollymawk and the Chatham Island Mollymawk both nest on bare, rocky islands totally devoid of vegetation, whereas the Shy Mollymawk nests on tussock-covered slopes. The Bounty Island population numbers *c.* 76,000 pairs.

## The Chatham Island Mollymawk

*Diomedea cauta eremita* 70 cm.

This is considered by many to be a distinct species. It is slightly smaller again and distinctly different in appearance. This race has a dark grey head and neck, and a bill that is bright yellow all over. It apparently feeds mostly on krill. It takes absolutely no notice of fishing boats. I remember having a brief visit to Pyramid Rock — the isolated stack to the south of the Chathams which is its only breeding place — and trying to attract the birds with generous quantities of fish offal and bait so as to get photographs, as we did not have enough time to make a landing. In no time at all, we collected 30 or 40 Buller's Mollymawks but, though there were hundreds of Chatham Island Mollymawks on the Pyramid and circling overhead, not one paid the slightest notice. This bird is seldom seen away from the Pyramid, even at the Chathams. Apparently it ranges east rather than north and west. The total population is about 4600 pairs.

## The Black-Footed Albatross

*Diomedea nigripes* 70 cm.

There is a single New Zealand record of this North Pacific species: Dusky Sound, 1884, Reischek collection.

## The Light-mantled Sooty Albatross

*Photos 29, 30, 31*

*Phoebetria palpebrata* 70 cm.

Without doubt, this is the most beautiful of all albatrosses. All albatrosses are admired for their mastery of the air, but Light-mantled Sooty Albatrosses are superb. They have a precision and perfection of gliding flight, especially when sweeping round the cliffs in tandem display, that is sheer joy to behold.

Light-mantled Sooty Albatrosses have been aptly described as having the subtle colouring of a Siamese cat. The body is pearly-grey shading to chocolate on the head. The upper back (mantle) is pale ash-grey and the wings are dark brown. The bill is black, with a pale blue line along the side of the lower mandible and there is a half-circle of white feathers behind the eye. The tail is long and tapered, giving the bird a balanced and elegant outline that other albatrosses, with their square tails, seem to lack. The call note is a long, drawn-out *peeee-o*. Heard floating down from misty crags, it is surely the most haunting and evocative of all sounds in the Southern Ocean.

Light-mantled Sooty Albatrosses are true subantarctic birds, breeding only on the more southerly islands and rarely ranging to warmer seas in the north. In the New Zealand region they breed at Antipodes, Auckland, Campbell and Macquarie Islands; elsewhere, at South Georgia, Marion, Prince Edward, Crozet, Kerguelen and Heard.

Light-mantled Sooty Albatrosses mostly nest alone or in small groups of 2 to 4. Sometimes, as at the Auckland Islands, ledges may be seen occupied by a dozen or more pairs, but this is uncommon and seems to be more a result of pressure on living space than a desire for company. The birds nest on inland cliffs as well as coastal ones and they are usually in places impossible to reach without the use of ropes. I think the sites are related more to their type of flight than to any need for inaccessibility. I think that below a certain and fairly fast speed — faster than that of the mollymawks and the great albatrosses — Light-mantled Sooty Albatrosses are unable to sustain lift and they need the updraughts of cliff faces to make accurate landings. Should it be possible actually to get to a Light-mantled Sooty Albatross nest, the birds do not object. Indeed, there is no other bird I have seen that can look right through you with such devastating effect; you might just not be there!

Light-mantled Sooty Albatrosses build low pedestal nests and display at the nest site by bowing and bobbing, and by throwing the bill vertically while giving their haunting *peeee-o* call. The single egg is incubated for 65-70 days and the chick fledges at 140-150 days.

## **Fulmars, Petrels, Prions, Shearwaters** Procellariidae

Pelagic birds highly adapted to life at sea. Come to land only to breed. Wings long and narrow. Tail short. Bill covered in horny plates and hooked at the tip. Nostrils in dorsal tubes. Legs set far back. Progress on land difficult (except Giant Petrel). Feet webbed. Sexes similar. Males larger than females though this is conspicuous only in the Giant Petrel. Swim and dive. Mostly fly close to the sea in long gliding arcs, using the updraught off waves to give lift. Most species nocturnal on land and nest in burrows; a few diurnal and nest on the surface. Feed on fish, squid, plankton and krill and drink sea water, excreting the excess salt through nasal glands. Life history of all species similar. Spend their immature years at sea. Return usually to place where reared to form pair bonds. Normally mate for life and breed annually, remaining faithful to nest site. All species colonial. Lay 1 egg, not replaced if lost. Have long incubation and fledging periods. Young fed by regurgitation. Vulnerable on land to introduced predators such as cats, rats, and Wekas; at sea to pollution by oil and pesticide residues. Except for Giant Petrel, mostly indifferent to man. Sixty-two species in 4 groups: the fulmarine petrels, the gadfly petrels, the prions, and the shearwaters. Forty-four species on the New Zealand list, of which 32 breed in the region, 10 of them endemically.

**16** The Southern Crested Grebe.
Photographed on Lake Fergus, Eglinton Valley.

**17** The Australian Little Grebe.

**18** A Wandering Albatross with its almost fully-fledged young, Disappointment Island.

**19** An Antipodes Island Wandering Albatross.

**20** A Northern Royal Albatross, Taiaroa Heads, Otago Peninsula.

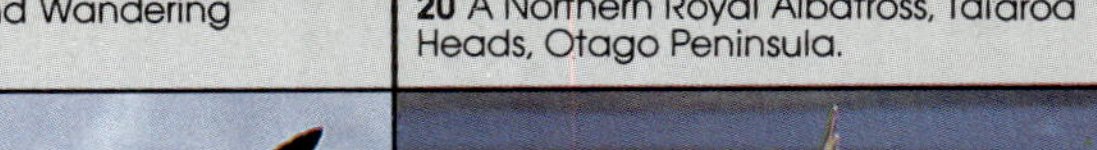

**21** A Southern Royal Albatross.

**22** Southern Royal Albatrosses displaying in a small gam at Campbell Island.

**23** The Black-browed Mollymawk. This is the Campbell Island race, which has a honey-coloured eye.

**24** A juvenile Black-browed Mollymawk at sea. Note the dark bill, the almost totally dark underwing and the collar of dark feathers around the neck.

**25** Grey-headed Mollymawks photographed at Campbell Island.

**26** The Bull Rock Mollymawk colony of Campbell Island, photographed in early February.

**27** The Grey-backed Mollymawk photographed at the Bounty Islands.

**28** Buller's Mollymawk.

**29** Light-mantled Sooty Albatrosses displaying.

**30** The Light-mantled Sooty Albatross.

**31** A Light-mantled Sooty Albatross at the Auckland Islands.

**32** Shy Mollymawks photographed at Disappointment Island, their principal breeding station.

**33** The Northern Giant Petrel photographed at Antipodes Island.

**34** The White-headed Petrel.

**35** A dark phase Kermadec Petrel, Meyer Island.

**36** A light phase Kermadec Petrel photographed on Meyer Island of the Kermadec group.

**37** The Mottled Petrel photographed on Big South Cape Island.

**38** The Antarctic Prion. This species comes ashore well after midnight, especially where there are skuas. Photographed at the Auckland Islands.

**39** Fulmar Prions at the Bounty Islands.

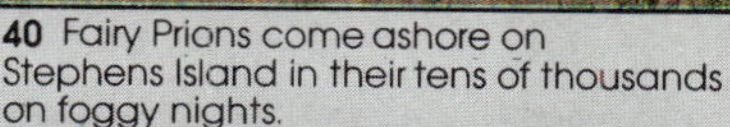

**40** Fairy Prions come ashore on Stephens Island in their tens of thousands on foggy nights.

**41** The Broad-billed Prion.

**42** A Fairy Prion on Stephens Island that fell prey to a tuatara.

**43** The Black-winged Petrel.

**44** The Grey Petrel.

## The Fulmarine Petrels

These are essentially cold-water birds of the Southern Hemisphere with 1 species in the Arctic and Subarctic. Unlike the majority of petrels, they nest on the surface and come ashore in daylight (those nesting in Antarctica, of course, having no option). Possibly as a corollary, all have a well-developed ability to squirt foul-smelling oil at predators. All are scavengers when the opportunity arises. All follow ships and can be attracted alongside with scraps. All are light in weight and so sit high on the water and dive poorly. Seven species; 6 on the New Zealand list, 5 breeding, possibly 6.

## The Northern Giant Petrel

*Photo 33*

*Macronectes halli* 84–92 cm.

Giant Petrels are the vultures of the petrel clan. Huge, scavenging and predatory birds that collect in numbers at carcases, they squabble and tear at the rotting flesh, covering themselves with filth and gorging to the point of being unable to fly. They play an important role in refuse disposal, but they are hardly endearing. They are the only petrels that stand and walk well, and the only petrels that feed on land. Wary and suspicious, they flee from man.

Giant Petrels are the size of an albatross, with a wingspan of about 215 centimetres, but are unprepossessing birds with none of the graces of the albatross clan. Their outstanding characteristic is the massive, pale, horn-coloured bill surmounted by large and conspicuous nasal tubes. In flight they have a hunchbacked look, require strong winds for gliding flight without flapping and frequently show a rather ragged rear edge to the wing, with a notch between the primaries and secondaries.

There are two species of Giant Petrel. The birds of the Northern species are predominantly dark brown and there are no white-phase birds. As they age, they develop white mottling on the face and foreneck but not, as in the Southern species, over the whole head and neck. The leading edge of the wing remains brown and the tip of the bill is reddish. The eye, initially brown, turns a baleful pale grey, almost white, and the look in this eye as you approach is enough to remind you — as if you were not already only too aware — that Giant Petrels can squirt foul-smelling oil at least 2 metres.

In the New Zealand region, the Northern Giant Petrel breeds at Chatham, at Antipodes, Auckland, Campbell and Macquarie Islands. Elsewhere it breeds at Gough, Marion, Crozet and Kerguelen Islands. It does not breed at Snares but occasionally does so at Port Pegasus, Stewart Island.

Northern Giant Petrels normally nest on their own or in small groups hidden in tussock and scrub. On the Forty Fours at the Chatham Islands, however, on an area of 14 hectares which is shared with 2500 pairs of Royal Albatross and 24,000 pairs of Buller's Mollymawks, is a colony of 1500 pairs on open ground. This is quite out of character and, so far as is known, unique for the species.

Northern Giant Petrels nest early. Most birds have eggs by the end of August and the incubation period is about 60 days. The chick is guarded for 2-3 weeks and fledges when about 115 days old. After breeding, Northern Giant Petrels disperse widely and are said to follow ships more readily than the Southern Giant Petrel.

## The Southern Giant Petrel

*Macronectes giganteus* 84–95 cm.

This species breeds on the Antarctic Continent, the islands of the Scotia Arc and at Falkland, Bouvet, Marion, Crozet, Heard and Macquarie Islands. It differs from the Northern Giant Petrel in that it has 2 plumage phases: one entirely white (at all ages) except for a scattering of dark feathers, the other much as the Northern Giant Petrel except that the whole head and neck, not just the face and throat, became pale with age. The leading edge of the wing also becomes pale and the tip of the bill is greenish, not reddish. The eye turns pale but apparently not as pale as in Northern birds. This species breeds some 2 months later than the Northern one and breeds in large colonies on open ground. The differences are notable on those islands where both species occur — Marion, Crozet and Macquarie. After breeding, the species disperses widely and ranges to New Zealand waters.

## The Cape Pigeon

*Daption capense* 40 cm.

Cape Pigeons are the opportunists of the petrel clan and are quick to take advantage of man's activities. Their usual food is plankton and small fish obtained from the surface, but they also scavenge and so freely collect at freezing works' outlets and other sources of offal. They readily follow ships, and have been known to do so for hundreds of kilometres, not only for garbage, but for the surface plankton stirred up by the propellers, much as gulls follow a plough. On the water, they sit high and skitter about like paper boats. Noisy and quarrelsome, they bicker over scraps with petulant cries.

Cape Pigeons are the easiest of petrels to identify. No other has the Cape Pigeon's chequered black and white pattern. There are 2 races: the New Zealand race (known as the Snares Cape Pigeon) breeding at Snares, Bounty, Antipodes, Auckland and Campbell Islands, and the Antarctic race breeding on Antarctica, the islands of the Scotia Arc, South Georgia, Bouvet, Crozet, Kerguelen, Heard and Macquarie Islands. This race is larger and distinctly whiter on the back.

Cape Pigeons breed on cliffs, often where inaccessible. The incubation period is 45 days and the fledging period 50 days. At the Snares Islands, eggs are laid in October and the chicks depart in late March.

## The Antarctic Fulmar

*Fulmarus glacialoides* 45 cm.

Also known as the Silver-grey Petrel, this is an Antarctic species that breeds only south of the Antarctic circle. Recently it has become a regular straggler to New Zealand waters. It is silver-grey above and white below and has a dark-tipped, pink bill with blue nostril tubes. In flight, it resembles a gull rather than a petrel and has a conspicuous white flash on the wings. It is closely related to the Common Fulmar of the Northern Hemisphere. It nests on cliff ledges and lays in December. The incubation period is 46 days and the young fledge at 50 days.

## The Antarctic Petrel

*Thalassoica antarctica* 45 cm.

This species breeds only on the Antarctic Continent and is one of only 3 species so confined, the others being the Emperor Penguin and the Antarctic Skua. It is only occasionally seen in New Zealand waters. In 1978, large numbers appeared in Foveaux Strait and were so tame that they could be picked up off the water after being enticed alongside the fishing boats with offal. The uppersurface is brown and the wings have a broad, white, rear edge. The undersurface is white. The tail is white, tipped brown. The Antarctic Petrel nests on rock ledges in colonies of up to one million birds. It is common in the Ross Sea, though breeding is not yet proven.

## The Snow Petrel

*Pagadroma nivea* 36 cm.

This is an Antarctic species breeding on the Antarctic Continent and neighbouring islands, including those of the Ross Sea; it is seldom seen north of the pack. A pure white species with beady black eyes and a stubby, black bill, its flight is erratic and bat-like. It nests on rock ledges and lays in December. The incubation period is 45 days and the fledging period is 42-50 days.

## The Gadfly Petrels

Gadfly Petrels are medium-sized birds notable for their fast, dashing flight with sudden, sweeping arcs that tower them high above the water. They are mostly solitary at sea and do not follow ships. They are light in weight, soft-plumaged and obtain their food from the surface. They do not dive well. On land they are docile, more vulnerable than most to introduced predators and they are easily handled. Most are dark above and white below, with a mottled forehead and a dark eye-patch. Many have a W-shaped marking across the back and wings. All have short, stubby bills. Twenty-nine species; 17 on the New Zealand list, of which 12 breed in the region, 5 endemically.

## The Grey-faced Petrel

*Pterodroma macroptera gouldi* 40 cm.

A common North Island species, this petrel is dark brown all over, with a pale grey area round the base of the bill extending on to the face. It has long, narrow wings and is also known as the Great-winged Petrel. In New Zealand it breeds on most islands and some headlands from the Three Kings Islands to East Cape. Elsewhere it breeds at Tristan, Gough, Marion, Prince Edward, Crozet and Kerguelen Islands and on islands off Western Australia. It breeds in winter in small, scattered colonies, often in short burrows or simply under a rock or twisted tree root. Eggs are laid in May, the young hatch in August and they depart in December.

## The White-headed Petrel

*Photo 34*

*Pterodroma lessoni* 43 cm.

A chunky, white-bodied subantarctic relative of *macroptera* with a white head and dark wings and a dark patch round the eye. The underwing is dark. It breeds at Antipodes, Auckland and Macquarie Islands and also at Kerguelen and Possession (Crozet). Eggs are laid in late November. The young hatch January-February and they depart in May. This species breeds in burrows in soft, peaty soil in small, loosely grouped colonies. After breeding, it ranges widely south of the subtropical convergence.

## The White-naped Petrel

*Pterodroma externa cervicalis* 43 cm.

This is a subtropical species now breeding only at Macauley Island of the Kermadec group, having been exterminated on Raoul by cats and rats. It is grey above and white below, has a black cap and a conspicuous white collar round the hind neck between the black cap and the grey back. It has a W-shaped pattern across the back and wings. The underwing is mostly white. It returns to Macauley Island in October, eggs are laid in December and the young depart in June. After breeding, the birds disperse into the central Pacific. Another race, the Juan Fernandez Petrel (*Pterodroma externa externa*), which breeds at Masafuera, has been recorded once in New Zealand, in 1971.

## The Bird of Providence

*Pterodroma solandri* 40 cm.

The Bird of Providence acquired its name at Norfolk Island during the early years of settlement when the colonists were frequently hard-pressed for food; vast numbers were taken but the bird's final extinction at Norfolk Island was apparently caused by domestic pigs allowed free range through the colony sites. The Bird of Providence today breeds only at Lord Howe Island. It is a winter breeder, returning in March. Eggs appear in May and hatch in July and the chicks fledge in November. The oceanic range of this species is unknown and there is only 1 New Zealand record despite the fact that it breeds so near. In appearance, the Bird of Providence is very similar to the dark phase of the Kermadec Petrel.

## The Phoenix Petrel

*Pterodroma alba* 38 cm.

The Phoenix Petrel is dark above and white below, with a broad, dark band on the chest and a dark underwing. There is only 1 New Zealand record, at Raoul Island (Kermadecs) in 1913. This is a tropical species breeding on atolls in the central Pacific and nesting on the surface.

## The Taiko

*Pterodroma magentae* 38 cm.

The Chatham Island Taiko was rediscovered in 1978 after a period of over 100 years during which no birds were seen and it was feared extinct. At the time of writing, occupied burrows have yet to be found. Not much is known about this bird except that it was once abundant, as evidenced by the remains in Moriori middens. It has a dark, brownish-black head and neck, a grey back and a white breast and abdomen. The underwing is grey and the undertail coverts are white, edged with grey.

## The Mottled Petrel

*Photo 37*

*Pterodroma inexpectata* 33 cm.

This species breeds only in the New Zealand region, principally on the islands around Stewart Island and at the Snares. A few breed in Fiordland. After breeding, it migrates to the North Pacific. It is a frosty-grey bird with a W-shaped pattern across the back and wings, a mottled forehead, a white face, a white throat and upper breast, a white underwing crossed by a conspicuous, broad, black diagonal line and a dark abdomen. It is a summer breeder, returning in late October and November. Eggs are laid from mid-December and the chicks depart in April.

## The Soft-plumaged Petrel

*Pterodroma mollis* 34 cm.

The Soft-plumaged Petrel was discovered breeding in the New Zealand region in 1978 when a colony, suspected since 1969, was confirmed at the Antipodes Islands. Elsewhere, the species breeds principally on islands in the Atlantic — Madeira, Desertas, Cape Verde, Tristan and Gough. It also breeds on Marion and Crozet Islands in the South Indian Ocean and possibly on Kerguelen, St Paul and Amsterdam Islands. It breeds in burrows and the breeding period is June-April. The species is pale slaty-grey above and white below, with a dark grey underwing and a grey band across the breast.

## The Kerguelen Petrel

*Pterodroma brevirostris* 33 cm.

A rare visitor to New Zealand waters, this petrel's plumage is slaty-grey all over. It flies fast and arcs high. It is a subantarctic species breeding September-March at Gough, Marion, Crozet and Kerguelen Islands.

## The Kermadec Petrel

*Photos 35, 36*

*Pterodroma neglecta* 38 cm.

The Kermadec Petrel is a tropical species breeding in the New Zealand region at the Kermadec Islands. Elsewhere, it breeds on Ball's Pyramid (Lord Howe Island) and at the Austral, Tuamotu, Oeno, Ducie and Juan Fernandez Islands. At the Kermadecs, it has been exterminated on the main island, Raoul, where it was once in vast numbers, by introduced cats and rats, but it is still plentiful on the vermin-free offshore Herald Islands. The Kermadec Petrel nests on the surface, comes ashore in daylight and has no set breeding season. Eggs may be found most months of the year, with a peak in February, and the incubation period is about 50 days.

Kermadec Petrels show a wide range of body plumage from dark brownish-grey all over, to almost pure white. In all forms, the wings are dark brown above and below and have a white patch at the base of the primaries. Kermadec Petrels fly very fast indeed and have a magnificent call.

## Cook's Petrel

*Pterodroma cooki* 30 cm.

Cook's Petrel is one of a group of small, very similar, gadfly petrels often referred to as the *cookilaria* petrels. Of the 6 on the New Zealand list, 3 have an all-white underwing (Cook's, Pycroft's and Stejneger's), and 3 have the white underwing crossed by a diagonal, black line (Black-winged, Chatham Island and Gould's). In good light, all show a W-shaped pattern across the back and upper wing surfaces. Three are very rare in New Zealand waters so, in practice, the problem at sea is to separate Cook's from Pycroft's. Cook's Petrel is paler than Pycroft's and slightly larger.

Cook's Petrel is an endemic breeder with 2 separate populations: one on Great and Little Barrier Islands, the other on Codfish Island. Both populations breed in burrows in dense forest towards the tops of the islands (and not near sea level), and both have been decimated by introduced predators — by cats (now eradicated) on Little Barrier Island and by Wekas on Codfish Island. The breeding season is October-April. After breeding, Cook's Petrel migrates across the Pacific to the west coast of the Americas.

## Pycroft's Petrel

*Pterodroma pycrofti* 28 cm.

Pycroft's Petrel is an endemic breeder with populations on Poor Knights, Hen and Chickens and Red Mercury Islands. It is a darker bird than Cook's Petrel and slightly smaller. It breeds in burrows in dense forest and mostly at low levels. The burrows are well separated and the populations are not large. The eggs are laid at the end of November. It is a strictly nocturnal bird, arriving only when the sky is fully dark and departing long before dawn. The oceanic range of this species is not known.

## Stejneger's Petrel

*Pterodroma longirostris* 28 cm.

A very rare vagrant to New Zealand waters from breeding grounds at Juan Fernandez Islands, it differs from all other *cookilaria* petrels in having a white forehead with no mottling.

## The Black-winged Petrel

*Photo 43*

*Pterodroma nigripennis* 30 cm.

The Black-winged Petrel is a species that, of recent years, has been extending its range to a quite notable degree. Originally known only from the offshore and outlying islands of the Kermadec group (on the main island, Raoul, it is predated by cats as soon as it lands), it has since colonised the Three Kings Islands, Norfolk Island (where again it is predated by cats but is established on the offshore islands and stacks), Lord Howe Island, New Caledonia and the Chatham Islands.

The Black-winged Petrel has a conspicuous, black, diagonal line on the underwing that makes identification easy. Unlike the other *cookilarias*, it comes ashore in daylight — except at the Chathams where the population of skuas is so high that the only safe course is to be truly nocturnal. Its call note is a high pitched *weet-weet*. The breeding season is October-April, with most eggs being laid in December. After breeding, the birds disperse towards the central Pacific.

The Black-winged Petrel's inclination for coming ashore in daylight is especially notable at the Kermadec Islands where, on the outer islands, their *weet-weet* calls, as they circle endlessly overhead, form a muted background of sound as soothing and unceasing as the murmur of surf. On Raoul, however, things are different, for there, cats await them. It was quite depressing. Pairs would be seen circling the grassy flat near our camp, hovering on the wind and calling to each other as they surveyed the ground beneath. We would get to know them over 4 or 5 days and then they would be missed. A brief search would reveal 2 fresh, cat-eaten corpses. On one occasion we found a heap of 42 of these petrels freshly killed — the work of a cat feeding kittens.

## The Chatham Island Petrel

*Pterodroma axillaris* 30 cm.

The Chatham Island Petrel is a very rare endemic breeder not yet recorded away from Chatham waters and is, so far as is known, confined to a small colony on South East Island. It is very similar in appearance to the Black-winged Petrel, but has black (not white) axillaries and its call note is deeper pitched. As with all petrels at the Chatham Islands (presumably because of the skuas), it comes ashore only on thoroughly dark nights.

## Gould's Petrel

*Pterodroma leucoptera* 30 cm.

This is a very rare vagrant to New Zealand waters. There are 2 races: one breeding on Cabbage Tree Island off New South Wales, the other breeding at New Caledonia. Examples of both races are recorded in New Zealand, washed up on beaches. This is the darkest of the *cookilarias* and has an underwing patten akin to that of the Black-winged Petrel but less clearly defined.

## The Blue Petrel

*Haloboena caerulea* 30 cm.

The Blue Petrel is a cold-water bird and resembles a prion with a white-tipped tail. It has the gadfly petrels' fast, erratic, twisting flight but is gregarious at sea rather than solitary. It breeds at Prince Edward, Kerguelen, Marion, Crozet and Heard Islands, and possibly also at Macquarie Island. The breeding season is September-March, with most eggs laid in early November and an incubation period of about 46 days. Most New Zealand records refer to birds washed up on beaches.

### The Prions

The prions are a specialised group of smallish petrels confined to the Southern Hemisphere. All are blue-grey above and white below and have a W-shaped pattern across the back and wings. The tip of the tail is black and the feet are blue. They feed on plankton, which they obtain by hydroplaning over the surface, filtering the water through specialised lamellae in the bill. The principle is that of the baleen whales, and prions were known to the early mariners as whale-birds. All prions breed in summer and can be incredibly abundant at their breeding grounds; there are colonies estimated to contain up to 10 million birds. All prions, with the notable exception of some populations of the Fulmar Prion, come ashore after dark and breed in burrows. They have incubation periods of about 56 days and fledging periods of about 50 days.

Prions are difficult birds to tell apart at sea. In the hand, they are distinguished by the size and shape of the bill, the amount of white on the face and the amount of black on the tail. There are 6 species, all on the New Zealand list, 4 of them breeding in the region.

## The Broad-billed Prion

*Photo 41*

*Pachyptila vittata* 28 cm.

The Broad-billed Prion is the largest of the prions and has an extraordinary, broad, steel-grey, flat bill with a violet-blue line down the side of the mandible. The head has a conspicuous pattern with a dark patch below the eye and a short, white eyebrow. The W-shaped pattern on the back and wings is prominent and the tail has a narrow black tip. The distribution of the species is along the subtropical convergence. In the New Zealand region, it breeds on the offshore islands around Stewart Island, at the Chatham Islands and at the Snares. Elsewhere, it breeds at Tristan da Cunha, Gough (an estimated 10 million) and St Paul Islands. It is sedentary and stays in the vicinity of its breeding grounds all year.

The voice of the Broad-billed Prion is a cooing yet rather rasping sound, interspersed with sudden, loud, staccato, squealing notes. On South East Island at the Chathams, where there is a substantial population of these prions, there is an old woolshed, long abandoned and now derelict and disintegrating, but still good shelter for working parties visiting the island. The noise at night from under the rotting floorboards of this old building has become a byword among those privileged to visit this fantastic island.

The bill of this species measures not less than 31×17-23 millimetres.

## Salvin's Prion

*Pachyptila salvini* 28 cm.

Salvin's Prion is also known as the Lesser Broad-billed Prion. It occurs in New Zealand waters only as a winter visitor from breeding grounds on Marion and Crozet Islands in the South Indian Ocean, and has a similar plumage pattern to the Antarctic Prion. The bill is bluish and typically measures 30×18 millimetres (26.6-34×12.5-20.5 millimetres).

## The Antarctic Prion

*Photo 38*

*Pachyptila desolata* 27 cm.

The Antarctic Prion has a wide breeding range in the colder waters of the Southern Ocean. In the New Zealand region, it breeds at Macquarie and Auckland Islands (and possibly on the Star Keys at Chathams); elsewhere, it breeds on Antarctica, including the islands of the Scotia Arc, South Georgia, Kerguelen and Heard Islands. This species has a distinct W-shaped pattern across the back and wings, a short white eyebrow, a black patch below the eye and a narrow tail bar. The bill is bluish, more or less straight-sided and typically measures 26.5×14 millimetres (25-29×12-16 millimetres).

## The Narrow-billed Prion

*Pachyptila belcheri* 25 cm.

The Narrow-billed Prion occurs in New Zealand waters only as a winter visitor from breeding grounds at Falkland, Kerguelen and Crozet Islands. It has a very narrow bill, a conspicuously white face with a black line under the eye and a pale pastel-blue upper surface, with the W-shaped marking narrow and poorly defined. The bill is bluish and typically measures 24×10 millimetres (23-27×9-12 millimetres). After breeding, this species disperses widely.

## The Fairy Prion

*Photos 40, 42*

*Pachyptila turtur* 23 cm.

The Fairy Prion is the common prion of New Zealand waters, where it breeds on many offshore islands from the Three Kings Islands southwards. It is abundant on Stephens Island in Cook Strait, at Stewart Island and at Chathams, and it also breeds at Snares and Antipodes. Elsewhere, it breeds on islands in Bass Strait, on Marion and Crozet and it has a small outlying population at the Falkland Islands (on Beauchene Island to the south of the group). The Fairy Prion has a very distinct, deep, black tip to the tail, a distinct W-shaped pattern across the back and wings, a plain face with no conspicuous markings and a short, robust, bluish bill measuring 20-25×10-12 millimetres. This is a sedentary species that remains in the vicinity of its breeding grounds all year.

## The Fulmar Prion

*Photo 39*

*Pachyptila crassirostris* 24 cm.

Apart from a population at Heard Island, the Fulmar Prion breeds only in the New Zealand region — on Pyramid Rock and the Forty Fours at Chathams, on the Snares Western Chain, and at the Bounty and Auckland Islands. At Bounty and Snares, where it nests in crevices in the rocks, it has the unique habit of coming ashore in daylight and it is notable that skuas are virtually absent from both these localities. In appearance, the Fulmar Prion closely resembles the Fairy Prion but has a more robust bill and an even more conspicuous tail bar. The species is unique in that it is the only prion in which the bill measurements differ between the sexes, the male's being larger. In consequence, average bill measurements (23×11 millimetres) are of less help in species separation than is the overall robust shape. Like the Fairy Prion, it is a sedentary species that remains in the vicinity of its breeding grounds all year.

### The Shearwaters

Shearwaters are medium-sized, long-winged petrels with long, slender bills, strongly hooked at the tip. Ecologically, they fall into 2 rather distinct groups: the light-weight, long-tailed, warm-water birds that obtain their food from the surface and dive poorly, and the heavier, short-tailed, cold-water birds that dive for their prey and use their wings under water to row themselves down, often to considerable depth and at remarkable speed.

Shearwaters have a fast, purposeful flight made up of a few rapid wing-beats followed by long, stiff-winged glides during which they skim the surface of the water. Most New Zealand shearwaters are migratory; those that are not either breed in winter, when the other petrels are away (the Little Shearwater), or they have the unusual arrangement whereby the juveniles migrate and the adults remain near the breeding grounds (the Fluttering Shearwater and Hutton's Shearwater). Shearwaters object strongly to being handled and bite hard.

Allied to the shearwaters are 4 species of large, subantarctic petrels with powerful bills that feed mostly on squid captured at the surface and which sometimes follow ships for offal. (In this they differ markedly from other shearwaters.) Shearwaters, with the single exception of the Flesh-footed Shearwater, show little interest in ships. Twenty species; 15 on the New Zealand list, of which 11 breed, 5 endemically.

## The Grey Petrel

*Photo 44*

*Procellaria cinerea* 48 cm.

The Grey Petrel is a cold-water species, grey above and white below with dark grey underwings. It has a rounded tail and a large, pale, horn-coloured bill with dark nostril tubes and a dark ridge. It freely follows small ships and can be attracted alongside fishing boats with offal. It flies powerfully, often wheeling high, and is usually solitary at sea. It dives more readily than the other *procellaria* petrels. The Grey Petrel breeds in winter, one of only 3 subantarctic petrels to do so. In the New Zealand region, it breeds at Antipodes, Campbell and possibly Macquarie Islands. Elsewhere, it breeds at Tristan, Gough, Marion, Crozet and Kerguelen Islands. Eggs are laid in May and the young leave in November.

## The Black Petrel

*Procellaria parkinsoni* 43 cm.

The Black Petrel is a New Zealand endemic breeding in late summer (December-May) on the forested tops of Great and Little Barrier Islands. It is an entirely black bird with a large, black-tipped, yellowish horn-coloured bill. After breeding, it migrates across the central Pacific to the Galapagos Islands and the east coast of Central America. At sea, it shows little interest in ships but will sometimes approach fishing boats and dive after offal.

## The Westland Black Petrel

*Procellaria westlandica* 51 cm.

The Westland Black Petrel is a New Zealand endemic breeding in winter (May-November) near Barrytown, Westland. In appearance, it differs from the Black Petrel only in its larger size. After breeding, it does not migrate but ranges the Tasman Sea to Eastern Australia. The incubation period is about 60 days and the fledging period 120 or more days, which is exceptionally long even for a winter-breeding petrel.

## The White-chinned Petrel

*Photo 49*

*Procellaria aequinoctialis* 51 cm.

The White-chinned Petrel is the subantarctic member of the Black Petrel group. By and large these 3 species have oceanic ranges with little overlap. The Black Petrel ranges (and migrates) into tropical waters, the Westland Black Petrel ranges the Tasman Sea and the White-chinned Petrel keeps to the Subantarctic, has a circumpolar distribution and seldom ranges to New Zealand inshore waters.

The White-chinned Petrel is a large and all-black petrel, except for some white feathers under the chin, not always present in the New Zealand populations. It has a large, pale bill with a black ridge. In the New Zealand region, it breeds at Antipodes, Auckland, Campbell and Macquarie Islands. Elsewhere, it breeds at Falkland, Tristan, Gough, South Georgia, Prince Edward, Marion, Crozet and Kerguelen Islands.

White-chinned Petrels dig enormous burrows, usually in the wettest, most saturated ground they can find, a behaviour unique among petrels. It is common to see a steady stream of water running out of the entrance. The nest itself, however, at the far end, is a low pedestal raised above the surrounding slosh.

The White-chinned Petrel was known to the early mariners as the Shoemaker. An apposite name, for early in the season these petrels come ahsore after dark and sit on top of the tussocks and call continuously, *taka-taka-taka-taka* — just like cobblers at a last. The breeding season is November-May with an incubation period of 50-60 days and a fledging period of 90-100 days.

## Cory's Shearwater

*Calonectris diomedea* 46 cm.

Prior to 1979, there was only a single New Zealand record of this North Atlantic species, a specimen washed up on the beach at Foxton in 1934. In 1979, 4 birds were seen at sea, attracted to a fishing vessel, off the east coast of Canterbury. This is a large shearwater, dark above and white below, with a yellow bill and a black tail.

## The Flesh-footed Shearwater

*Photo 48*

*Puffinus carneipes* 46 cm.

The Flesh-footed Shearwater is an overall dark brown, almost black petrel with a conspicuous dark-tipped, pale bill and flesh-coloured feet. It is a heavily built bird that dives well, and is the only shearwater regularly interested in ships, readily attracted to fishing boats with offal. In New Zealand it breeds on islands from the Hen and Chickens to Cook Strait. Its stronghold is Lord Howe Island where there are an estimated 17,500 pairs. It also breeds on islands off Western Australia and a few pairs have recently been discovered at St Paul and Amsterdam Islands. After breeding, it migrates to the seas around Korea and Japan. The birds depart in April and return in late September. Eggs are laid from late November to early December and the chicks hatch in late January.

## The Wedge-tailed Shearwater

*Photos 47, 51*

*Puffinus pacificus* 46 cm.

A rare visitor to New Zealand inshore waters, the Wedge-tailed Shearwater is the most abundant and widespread shearwater of the tropical Pacific and Indian Oceans, breeding on every major island group. In the New Zealand region, it breeds at the Kermadec Islands. It is an all-brown bird with a long, wedge-shaped tail, a slender, darkish bill and pale feet. It is light in weight and obtains its food from the surface. On uninhabited islands it comes ashore from midday onwards, otherwise it waits till dusk. At the Kermadec Islands, the burrows are cleared out in October and eggs are laid in December. The incubation period is 60-70 days and the fledging period about 100 days. Wedge-tailed Shearwaters are often silent in the air over their breeding grounds. Once ashore, however, they utter weird, moaning wails and screams that have been likened to the moans of Blue Penguins and the wails of fighting cats.

## Buller's Shearwater

*Puffinus bulleri* 46 cm.

Buller's Shearwater is a long-tailed, light-weight, surface-feeding, distinctively plumaged shearwater known to breed only at the Poor Knights Islands. After breeding, it migrates to the North Pacific. It is grey above and white below, with a dark cap, a W-shaped pattern across the back and wings and a long, wedge-shaped, dark brown tail. It has a long, slender, slate-grey bill and flesh-coloured feet with black outer sides.

The Poor Knights Islands were once overrun with wild pigs. At that time Buller's Shearwater was an extremely rare and little-known bird, for pigs are devastating in petrel colonies. When the pigs were finally eradicated in 1936, Buller's Shearwater was almost extinct, with virtually no occupied burrows. Today, occupied burrows are estimated to number 100,000 and Buller's Shearwater is now the common, large shearwater of the Hauraki Gulf.

Buller's Shearwater returns from migration in September and eggs are laid in late November. The chicks hatch in January and fledge in early April.

## The Sooty Shearwater

*Photos 45, 46*

*Puffinus griseus* 43 cm.

The Sooty Shearwater, the New Zealand Muttonbird, is the best known, most widely distributed and most abundant petrel of the New Zealand region. It breeds on many offshore islands around New Zealand north to the Three Kings, and on all outlying island groups except the Kermadecs and Bounty Island. Truly enormous numbers occur at the Snares and at the Titi (or Muttonbird) Islands off Stewart Island. Elsewhere, small numbers breed on islands off South-east Australia, at the Falkland Islands and on islands off South America. After breeding, the Sooty Shearwater migrates north — the New Zealand birds to the North Pacific, the South American birds to the North Atlantic.

Sooty Shearwaters return from migration in late September. They immediately repair to their last year's burrow where they reunite with last year's mate and re-establish the pair bond. This is a noisy and exciting period on the Muttonbird Islands, with thousands of voices giving tongue. After mating, the birds go to sea for about 3 weeks before returning to lay. The eggs are laid during a remarkably constant and compressed period of 2-3 weeks between the end of November and the middle of December. Both parents incubate, in shifts of 10-14 days, and the incubation period is around 56 days. The chick is fed daily for its first few days and thereafter feeds become less frequent but of greater quantity. Petrel chicks can withstand long periods of starvation but in good times they can take enormous amounts of food at a time and become very fat. This is the basis of the muttonbird industry and 'muttonbird' is a term applicable to the adults and chicks of many species. The chicks fly when about 100 days old, in late April or early May. They immediately migrate to the North Pacific and it is probable that many of them remain there for at least their first year. Thereafter, they return with the main mass of migration but they do not breed until about 6 years old.

Sooty Shearwaters are nocturnal on land and where numbers are great — as at the Snares and Titi Islands where they are estimated in millions — huge rafts of birds may collect out at sea, waiting for dark. The fall-in of such numbers plummeting through the trees is unforgettable. The drop starts with a scattering of birds, one here and one there, and then builds up very rapidly to an absolute bombardment, as birds plunge through the trees to thump to the ground beneath. Their direction finding is astounding. They will land within metres — centimetres, even — of their burrows. Once they are underground, loud wails and screams come from all sides, as bird greets bird. Birds career into one's line of vision with ungainly, stumbling runs, only soon to subside back into their normal squatting position. Overhead, the sky is filled with dark, sweeping shapes as the birds circle in fast arcs, fixing their position. After an hour, or a little more, the main drop is virtually all over and the island gradually becomes silent, only to break forth into renewed cacophony an hour or so before dawn, when the exodus occurs. To take off from land, petrels need a clear space from which to launch themselves into the air, and at this time of morning one sees long lines of birds shuffling along time-worn paths to cliff tops and other vantage points. To stand on one of these headlands and watch the dark shapes disappear into the dawn, is one of those indescribable experiences that takes one back through time.

The Sooty Shearwater is an overall dark brown bird with a dark bill, dark feet, and a pale patch in the central area of the underwing that shows up at sea at a surprising distance when the bird banks in the sunlight.

## The Short-tailed Shearwater

*Puffinus tenuirostris* 38 cm.

Just as the Sooty Shearwater occurs in millions in the New Zealand region and forms the basis of the New Zealand muttonbird industry, so the Short-tailed Shearwater occurs in millions in the Bass Strait region and forms the basis of the Australian muttonbird industry. The Short-tailed Shearwater is slightly smaller than the Sooty Shearwater and lacks the pale area on the underwing; otherwise it is very similar. It is not known to breed in New Zealand, though it is suspected a few may yet be found on Big South Cape Island. After breeding, it does a figure-of-eight migration through the North Pacific and many birds are storm-wrecked on the New Zealand west coasts, as they pass through the Tasman Sea. The breeding cycle of this species closely follows that of the Sooty Shearwater.

## The Christmas Shearwater

*Puffinus nativitatis* 35 cm.

There is a single New Zealand record (1976) of this rather small, dark-plumaged, wedge-tailed, tropical shearwater that breeds in the shade of bushes on atolls in the Central Pacific.

## The Manx Shearwater

*Puffinus puffinus* 35 cm.

This species breeds in the North Atlantic. It resembles and is related to the Fluttering Shearwater and has been recorded once in New Zealand (1972).

## The Fluttering Shearwater

*Photo 50*

*Puffinus gavia* 33 cm.

The Fluttering Shearwater is a small shearwater, brown above and white below, with a white underwing and a dark bill. It breeds in burrows on islands from the Three Kings to Cook Strait and also at New Caledonia and the New Hebrides (now Vanuatu). It is a common bird of New Zealand inshore waters. It requires a stiff breeze before it can shear and glide in stiff-winged flight and is most often seen flying low over the water, with fluttering wing-beats interspersed with short glides.

Fluttering Shearwaters are noisy birds at their breeding grounds, uttering prolonged, loud, staccato, crackling calls. They return to their islands in August, eggs are laid in September and the young depart in late December. After fledging, the young birds migrate across the Tasman to Australian waters where some evidently remain for at least their first year before returning. The adults, on the other hand, remain in New Zealand waters all year.

## Hutton's Shearwater

*Puffinus huttoni* 36 cm.

Hutton's Shearwater closely resembles the Fluttering Shearwater. It is a slightly larger bird and is darker above. In the hand, it can be seen that the feathers of the armpit — the axillaries — are long, dark brown and oval ended. In the Fluttering Shearwater, the axillaries are short, off-white and square-ended. The principal difference, however, between the 2 species, is in their breeding behaviour. Hutton's Shearwater breeds 2 months later than the Fluttering Shearwater in burrows at altitudes above 1200 metres on the Seaward Kaikoura Mountains where it contends with alpine weather and late-melting snowdrifts. The birds return in September and lay mostly in early November. The chicks hatch in late December and fledge February-March. After breeding, immatures migrate across the Tasman, while the adults remain in New Zealand waters.

## The Little Shearwater

*Puffinus assimilis* 30 cm.

In the New Zealand region, the Little Shearwater breeds on islands off the northern part of the North Island and at the Kermadec, Chatham, Antipodes and Auckland Islands. Elsewhere, it breeds at Norfolk and Lord Howe Islands, on the islands off Western Australia, at Tristan, Gough, Cape Verde and Canary Islands in the Atlantic and at Rapa Island in the Pacific.

The Little Shearwater is blue-back above and chalky-white below and has a black bill. It flies with rapid wing-beats, seldom gliding, and is one of the most nocturnal of petrels on land, coming ashore only in full darkness. It seldom arrives much before 11 p.m. and it leaves well before dawn. It is a winter breeder, with eggs laid mostly in May or June and the young fledged by the end of October. It is a species, however, that often has a smattering of late breeders, so that young may still be found ashore at the end of November. The birds breed in burrows, which are often short and placed in rocky ground, and the nests tend to be widely scattered. At the Antipodes Islands, where there is a densely packed colony of some tens of thousands on Bollons Island, they nest on a tussock-covered slope and they lay their eggs in spring (September), not in winter.

## Storm Petrels Hydrobatidae

Storm petrels are tiny seabirds of delicate and frail appearance, whose flight, erratic and flitting, has been likened to that of butterflies. In the hand they feel like thistledown. How they survive the screaming gales of the Southern Ocean is a source of wonder, even though reason tells us that the stronger the wind, the higher the waves and the more the shelter in the hollows between.

They have long, slender legs; nostril tubes united into a single opening. Their food is plankton, which they obtain from the surface of the sea while hovering and pattering over it as if walking on the water. From this behaviour the word 'petrel' is derived, by analogy with St Peter. Many follow ships for plankton stirred up by the propellors. All, with the notable exception of Galapagos Storm Petrel, strictly nocturnal on land. All nest under cover, lay a single egg which is incubated for 40-50 days; chicks have fledging periods of 60-70 days. All are very vulnerable to introduced predators. Twenty-one species; 6 on the New Zealand list of which 5 breed in the region.

## Leach's Fork-tailed Storm Petrel

*Oceanodroma leucorhoa* 19 cm.

This Northern Hemisphere storm petrel is a very rare straggler to New Zealand waters, with only 3 records prior to 1980. In November 1980 2 (not proved to be a pair) were found on the ground on Rabbit Island at the Chatham Islands. They were evidently prospecting for nest sites, for one was discovered in a burrow. A repeat visit to the island in April 1981 found no sign of successful breeding. This is the first record of Leach's Storm Petrel attempting to breed in the Southern Hemisphere.

Leach's Storm Petrel is an overall blackish-brown storm petrel with long wings, a white rump, short black legs and a forked tail. It is the only fork-tailed storm petrel on the New Zealand list.

## Wilson's Storm Petrel

*Oceanites oceanicus* 19 cm.

Wilson's Storm Petrel is a square-tailed, all-black storm petrel with a white rump, very long legs and feet with yellow webs. It breeds in Antarctica and on the islands of the Ross Sea, the Scotia Arc, South Georgia, Falkland, Kerguelen, Bouvet and Heard. After breeding, it migrates to the Northern Hemisphere, principally to the North Atlantic and Indian Ocean, rarely to the North Pacific, so, although it is thought to be the world's most abundant seabird, it is not common in New Zealand waters.

## The Grey-backed Storm Petrel

*Garrodia nereis* 18 cm.

The Grey-backed Storm Petrel is a bird of subantarctic waters, seldom seen away from the vicinity of its breeding islands. In the New Zealand region it breeds on most of the outer islands of the Chatham group, at the Antipodes and Auckland Islands and possibly on Dent Island at Campbell. Elsewhere, it breeds at Falkland, South Georgia, Gough, Crozet and Kerguelen Islands. It has a dark grey, almost black, head and neck, a grey back, a mostly white underwing and a white breast and abdomen. It has a square tail and a grey, not white rump. It breeds from October to February or March, usually in the centre of a tussock clump or a low-growing vegetation such as *cotula*, making tiny 'burrows' about 3 centimetres wide.

## The Black-bellied Storm Petrel

*Fregetta tropica* 20 cm.

The Black-bellied Storm Petrel is a circumpolar, subantarctic species that disperses north, after breeding, to reach New Zealand waters. It is a predominantly black bird, with a white rump, white axillaries, a whitish central area to the underwing and white flanks. It has a thin black line down the centre of the abdomen, difficult to see at sea. It has conspicuous, upstanding nostril tubes and an erratic zigzagging flight. It differs from Wilson's Storm Petrel by the white on the underwing, from the Grey-backed Storm Petrel by the white rump and from the White-bellied Storm Petrel by the black belly stripe.

In the New Zealand region, the Black-bellied Storm Petrel breeds at Antipodes and Auckland Islands; elsewhere, on the islands of the Scotia Arc, South Georgia, Crozet and Kerguelen. It is a late breeder, with eggs laid December-January, but details are little known.

## The White-bellied Storm Petrel

*Fregetta grallaria* 19 cm.

This is a subtropical relative of the Black-bellied Storm Petrel and differs from it in having a wholly white belly and less conspicuous nostril tubes. In the New Zealand region, it breeds at Macauley Island of the Kermadec group. Elsewhere, it breeds at Lord Howe, Tristan, Gough, Rapa and Austral Islands. After breeding, it disperses widely. It is a late summer breeder, with eggs laid in January and the young fledged by the end of May. Typically, the nest is in a crevice among rocks, with the entrance obscured by overhanging vegetation, but the bird will also burrow into soft soil, digging a tiny tunnel about 45 centimetres long.

## The White-faced Storm Petrel

*Photo 53*

*Pelagodroma marina* 20 cm.

The White-faced Storm Petrel is the common storm petrel of New Zealand inshore waters. It is unmistakable. It is the only storm petrel with a white face broken by a dark line through the eye, and a black cap. It has a very wide breeding distribution. In the New Zealand region, it breeds on selected islands from the Three Kings to the off-lyers of Stewart Island, and at the Kermadec, Chatham and Auckland Islands. Elsewhere, it breeds in Australia and Tasmania, on Tristan and Gough, and on the Cape Verde and Selvagens Islands where it is known as the Frigate Petrel. After breeding, it disperses widely, with New Zealand birds moving into the Central Pacific.

Some of the colonies of the White-faced Storm Petrel are so overwhelming in numbers as to be beyond comprehension. I recall especially an eerie, still, foggy night at South East Island at the Chatham Islands, when White-faced Storm Petrels materialised out of the mist like the floating flakes of a blanketing snowstorm. They were in their myriads, swirling down through the trees so thickly that to take a step was surely to crush one underfoot. Such mass arrivals are typical of this species; they arrive about an hour after full dark and normally the drop-in is all over in an hour.

The burrows of this species have tiny entrance holes about 3 centimetres across and when the birds come and go, they cover the entrance with fallen leaves and other litter. In daylight, you can walk over a White-faced Storm Petrel colony and have no suspicion at all of its existence.

White-faced Storm Petrels lay towards the end of October and have an incubation period of 55-67 days.

### **Diving Petrels** Pelecanoididae

Small, chunky birds confined to the Southern Hemisphere. Black above and white below, with blue feet, small wings, short legs, and stubby, compact bills. When disturbed at sea, they either dive promptly or patter rapidly along the surface to fly with whirring wing-beats for 100 or so metres before dropping back to the water and diving. Feed on plankton and small fish which they catch by diving and chasing in the manner of a penguin, using the wings for propulsion. In the hand, a diving petrel is identified by structure of the nostrils, which open flush, directly upwards, and side by side at the base of the upper mandible. Four species; 2 on the New Zealand list, both breeding.

## The Common Diving Petrel

*Photo 52*

*Pelecanoides urinatrix* 20 cm.

This species has a wide range in the Southern Ocean, breeding on almost every subantarctic island group. In the New Zealand region, it breeds from the Three Kings Islands south to Stewart, Snares, Auckland, Antipodes and Chatham Islands. It does not breed at Bounty or Macquarie Islands and its status at Campbell is uncertain.

Diving petrels are spring and summer breeders, the exact dates depending on location — early in the north, later in the south. They nest in burrows, usually in forest or in areas of dense tussock, and the incubation period is about 53 days. The chick is guarded for the first 10-15 days and fed nightly by each parent in turn; thereafter it is left on its own in the burrow while the parents are at sea. It fledges at

**45** Sooty Shearwaters at sea off the Auckland Islands.

**46** The Sooty Shearwater or New Zealand Muttonbird.

**47** The Wedge-tailed Shearwater.

**48** The Flesh-footed Shearwater.

**49** The White-chinned Petrel.

**50** The Fluttering Shearwater.

**51** The Wedge-tailed Shearwater.

**52** The Common Diving Petrel.

**53** The White-faced Storm Petrel.

**54** The Red-tailed Tropicbird.

**55** The Red-tailed Tropicbird.

**56** The Australasian Gannet.

**57** A Masked Booby and chick.

**58** The Little, or White-throated, Shag.

**59** The Pied Shag.

**60** The White-throated Shag.

**61** Australian Pelicans.

**62** The Auckland Island Shag.

**63** The Auckland Island Shag.

**64** Chatham Island Shags.

about 50 days. Diving petrels differ from all other petrels in that both adults often occupy the burrow at night during the incubation and early fledging periods.

## The South Georgian Diving Petrel

*Pelecanoides georgicus* 17 cm.

The 4 species of diving petrel are so similar that they can only be told apart when in the hand — and even then by recourse to complex measurements and minute details of plumage. Nevertheless, for the field worker the South Georgian Diving Petrel does show one distinct difference: it breeds in areas uncluttered by vegetation — on scree slops and in sand dunes. So far as is known, the South Georgian Diving Petrel in the New Zealand region today breeds only in the sand dunes of Codfish Island where there is a recently (1978) discovered colony of about 30 pairs. The species was previously known to breed in 2 sand dune locations at the Auckland Islands, but both those colonies have, apparently, subsequently been made untenable by sea lions. Elsewhere, this species breeds at South Georgia, Kerguelen and Heard Islands.

# PELECANIFORMES

Fish-eating birds with all 4 toes connected by a web (totipalmate). Six families: Tropicbirds, Pelicans, Gannets and Boobies, Cormorants, Darters, Frigatebirds.

## **Tropicbirds** Phaethontidae

Tropical seabirds pelagic between breeding seasons. Sometimes known as Bo'sun Birds from the shrill, trilling call of the Red-billed Tropicbird (*P. aethereus*) of the Atlantic, which resembles the whistle of a boatswain's pipe. Sexes similar. Plumage in all species predominantly white and with the central tail feathers greatly elongated. Bill stout and slightly down-curved. Legs very short. Unable to walk. On land they shuffle on the belly. Feet small, with all 4 toes united by a web. Fly with steady wing-beats 30 or so metres above the sea, seldom lower. Dive for food, which is principally flying fish and squid. Do not follow ships, but curious — will approach, circle perhaps once or twice and then disappear off to the horizon. Usually solitary at sea but gregarious at breeding stations. Breeding cycle long, as is the case for all pelagic birds. Lay a single egg which may be replaced if lost. Have long incubation and fledging periods. At the nest show no fear of man. Normally mate for life and remain faithful to nest site. Three species; 2 on the New Zealand list, 1 breeding.

## The Red-tailed Tropicbird

*Photos 54, 55*

*Phaethon rubricauda roseotincta* 46 cm. (86 cm. including tail)

The Red-tailed Tropicbird has a wide breeding range throughout the tropical Indian and Pacific Oceans, and in the New Zealand region breeds at the Kermadec Islands. It is an overall white bird with a heavy red bill, a conspicuous black line over the eye and 2 long, scarlet, central tail feathers. The plumage of breeding birds is suffused with a rosy flush and has a lustrous sheen. In sunlight they glow. Immature birds have black barring on the back and a black bill.

Red-tailed Tropicbirds return to the Kermadec Islands in early November and are soon circling and displaying near the cliffs, uttering their harsh, barking calls. Their aerial display is exciting to watch. First, one bird soars upwards to hover, with sharply depressed and sideways-twitching tail, directly over the back of another. Then, as it breaks away, the lower bird swings up to hover with twitching tail, and so on. The sight of one pair displaying excites others and soon the air is filled with their barking calls.

The nests are simple scrapes in the hollows of cliff faces and usually have overhead protection from the sun. They are sited where the birds can launch themselves directly into the air and, as a result, are usually inaccessible to predators and man. Like petrels, tropicbirds appear uneasy about putting foot on land, and early in the season circle round and round, time and again baulking at the final commitment of landing. After mating, the birds go to sea for some days before returning to lay. The egg is reddish and is heavily blotched with red-brown. Incubation takes about 40 days and both adults incubate, in shifts of 2-7 days, sometimes more. The chick is guarded when small and fledges when anything from 80 to 100 days old, depending on food supplies. The principal food is squid, which is collected from far out at sea and then fed to the chick by regurgitation. Many chicks die of starvation when food supplies fail, for, in comparison with subantarctic waters, tropical seas can be capriciously impoverished and the adults can have difficulty in obtaining their needs.

## The White-tailed Tropicbird

*Phaethon lepturus dorotheae* 30 cm. (78 cm. with tail)

There are 4 New Zealand records of this widespread tropicbird which breeds in all tropical seas and is common in the Pacific. It has white central tail feathers, a yellow bill and a conspicuous, broad black band across the base of the upper wings. Its nearest breeding grounds to New Zealand are New Caledonia, Fiji and Tonga, and it nests in the tops of tall forest trees as well as on cliffs.

### **Pelicans** Pelecanidae *Photo 61*

Pelicans are unmistakable. A cosmopolitan family of large, fish-eating birds with huge bills and distensible bill-pouches. Rather clumsy on land, with a waddling gait, they swim with grace, fly strongly and soar with ease. Eight species; New Zealand 1, a straggler: 4 records (1 of at least 3 birds) of the Australian Pelican (*Pelecanus conspicillatus*).

### **Gannets and Boobies** Sulidae

Large, fish-eating, exclusively marine birds with long, pointed wings, long, stout, conical bills without external nostrils, and long, wedge-shaped tails. In flight, they look streamlined and cigar-shaped. They walk with a waddling gait like a goose and their food is obtained by spectacular, plunging dives from a height — mostly school fish (gannets) or flying fish (boobies) but both (especially boobies) take squid. Sexes alike except that boobies show differences of bill and facial skin colour in the breeding season. Voices of gannets are similar in both sexes; of boobies different. Gannets are birds of colder waters; boobies are tropical. Boobies especially show little fear of man; hence the name. All are slow to mature, mate for life, are faithful to their nest sites and breed in colonies. Eggs are incubated between the feet (no brood patches) and the young hatch black, blind, naked and helpless. Nine species; 3 on the New Zealand list, 2 breeding.

## The Australasian Gannet *Photo 56*

*Sula serrator* 90 cm.

The great majority of Australasian Gannets, some 32,000 pairs, breed in New Zealand. Only a relative few breed in the Bass Strait region and Tasmania. Three or 4 pairs also breed at Norfolk Island, on Philip Island near one of the Masked Booby colonies.

With their overall white plumage, golden-buff head and neck, long, white, black-tipped wings and long, white-edged, black tail, Gannets are unmistakable and familiar birds of North Island coastal waters. In the south they are less well known, for of some 14 breeding places, only 2 occur off the South Island: the Nuggets and Little Solander Island, each with about 40 pairs. The largest colony is on White Island (5800 pairs) and the most famous is at Cape Kidnappers (4700 pairs).

Gannets have clearly defined breeding seasons and breed in densely packed colonies with the nests in serried ranks, each just out of reach of its neighbours. Most birds return in August, the males returning first, and most have eggs in October (the dates vary according to location). Only 1 egg is laid and it may be replaced (about 5 weeks later) if lost. Both parents incubate and the period is 42-44 days. The chick is hatched black, blind, naked and helpless but soon acquires a coat of white down. It flies at about 15 weeks. As a juvenile, its plumage is spotted and streaked with black on the upper surface and about 4 years are required for it to obtain the immaculate adult plumage. After fledging, the young birds migrate to Australia; the adults on the other hand remain in New Zealand waters. Australasian Gannets first breed when 4-7 years old and are estimated to live 25-30 years.

## The Brown Booby

*Sula leucogaster plotus* 74 cm.

The Brown Booby is widely distributed in tropical seas but does not range far from its breeding grounds and so occurs in the New Zealand region only as a straggler to northern waters. Its nearest breeding places are the islands of the Coral Sea and Fiji. The head, neck, back, breast, wings and tail are chocolate brown. The lower breast and abdomen are white. The clear cut line of demarcation across the breast is diagnostic. The underwing is brown with white coverts. The bare skin of the face is blue in males, yellow-green in females.

## The Masked (Blue-faced) Booby

*Photo 57*

*Sula dactylatra personata* 86 cm.

The Masked Booby occurs and breeds on islands in all tropical oceans. In the New Zealand region, it breeds at the Kermadec Islands. It is the largest of the boobies, the size of a gannet, and at first sight may be mistaken for one. The Masked Booby has a pure white body plumage. There is no ochre-yellow on the head and neck. The wings have black tips and a black rear edge extending their whole length. The tail is black. The bare skin of the face is blue-black, the eye is yellow and the bill is yellow in the male, yellow-green in the female. At their breeding grounds, male Masked Boobies whistle while females grunt. Juvenile birds are mottled greyish-brown on the head and upper surface.

Masked Boobies plunge-dive as spectacularly as gannets and their principal food seems to be flying fish. They breed in colonies on open, flat ground, spacing their nests well apart. The cycle for a particular pair occupies about 6 months, but as pairs may commence breeding almost any month of the year, the colonies are occupied continuously all year round, with the various pairs at varying stages of the cycle, from site occupation to fledging young. Two eggs are laid, the second 5 days after the first, and incubation commences with the first egg. Consequently, by the time the second chick hatches, if it does, the first chick has a 5-day start and progressively elbows its sibling out of the way with the result that the sibling eventually starves and dies. Should food supplies fail during the 5 days between hatchings, then, theoretically, the second chick survives if the first does not. Either way, Masked Boobies rear only 1 chick at best. The incubation period is 43-44 days and both parents incubate. Newly hatched chicks are ugly, black, naked and reptilian, but they soon grow a coat of long, white, fluffy down and at a month old are very attractive. They are fed by regurgitation by both parents. They have to be able to withstand periods of starvation, for tropical seas do not have the reliable abundance of marine life that is associated with the nutrient-rich waters of the subantarctic. The young fledge at 120 days and are fed by the parents for a further 6-8 weeks after they fly.

## **Cormorants or Shags** Phalacrocoracidae

Medium to large, mostly black, black and white or grey and white, fish-eating, surface-diving birds with long, slender, sharply hooked bills, long, flexible necks, fairly long tails and large feet with all 4 toes connected by a web. In breeding condition, the bare skin of the face is often colourful and many develop ornamental plumes. Sexes similar. Swim low in the water with the back awash and the bill tilted at an upward angle. Feed on fish, eels and crustaceans captured by underwater pursuit, propelling themselves by thrusting both feet together. Legs set far back. Stand upright. Can perch in trees. Walk with a waddle. Those with black feet often seen perched with wings extended as if out to dry — though whether this is the correct explanation is open to doubt. Both fresh and salt water. The marine species are coastal, seldom ranging out of sight of land. Fly low over the water and require a long series of jumps, both feet together, to become airborne. Inland species may soar high on thermals. Breed in colonies, remaining faithful to sites. Eggs, usually 3-5, laid 2 days apart and incubated from the first, on the feet (no brood patch), by both sexes for about 30 days. Hatch asynchronous and chicks therefore of different ages and different sizes. The last to hatch often succumbs. Chicks hatch black, blind, naked and helpless. Fed by regurgitation by both parents. Fledging periods about 50 days.

In New Zealand all cormorants are known as shags; the terms are interchangeable. Nevertheless, a distinction can be made between shags, which are entirely marine, nest on the ground or on rock platforms and cliff faces facing the sea and fly with the head and body at the same level, and cormorants, which inhabit both fresh water and salt, nest mostly in trees and fly with the head and body at a slightly uptilted angle. All New Zealand species are to some extent marine and all but 4 exclusively so. The family is exceptionally well represented in the New Zealand region with 16 distinct forms of 8 species. They may be divided into 3 groups: those with black feet that associate with both fresh and salt water, nest mostly in trees and often perch with wings extended as if to dry; those with pink feet and blue eye-rings (*Leucocarbo*) and those with yellow feet and a spotted and plumed plumage (*Stictocarbo*). *Leucocarbo* and *Stictocarbo* are strictly marine, nest only on rock platforms and cliffs facing the sea, and do not perch with wings extended as if out to dry. Thirty species; New Zealand 8, all breeding, 3 endemic.

## The Black Shag

*Phalacrocorax carbo novaehollandiae* 88 cm.

The Black Shag is the Common Cormorant of the Old World with a wide, if broken, breeding distribution that includes parts of Australia, Tasmania, China, Japan, Central Asia, India, Ceylon, Africa, Europe, Iceland, Greenland and Labrador. In New Zealand it is principally an inland, freshwater species and occurs the length of the country. It is also resident at the Chatham Islands. Where marine, it keeps to sheltered inlets and does not normally venture out to the open sea. Nevertheless, it has straggled to Snares, Campbell and Macquarie Islands.

The Black Shag is overall black with an oily-green sheen. In breeding plumage, it has a black crest and some white feathers on the chin and flanks. The bare skin of the face is dirty yellow, the bill is dark, the eye is green and the feet are black. It is a wary bird, difficult to get close to. It breeds in colonies, often in trees but also on the inaccessible cliffs of river gorges and on the tops of niggerheads (*carex*) in isolated and undisturbed swamps. The nests are bulky structures of sticks and are re-used year after year. In the North Island, eggs may be found most months of the year. In the South Island, most are found in October. The usual clutch is 3 or 4 and the eggs are laid at 2-day intervals. Incubation commences with the first egg and takes about 30 days. The chicks are of different sizes and are fed on regurgitated fish and eels. They fledge at about 50 days.

The Black Shag has a bad reputation with the fishing fraternity. In truth, it is possible that more good is done by its capture of eels than harm by its capture of small trout. Generally speaking, game fish, except when small, are too fast for shags. Shags go for easier prey.

## The Pied Shag

*Photo 59*

*Phalacrocorax varius* 80 cm.

The Pied Shag occurs in New Zealand and Australia. In New Zealand, it is marine and rarely moves inland, except along tidal waters, whereas in Australia it is both freshwater and salt. In New Zealand, its distribution is discontinuous and, for practical purposes, is restricted to 3 regions: Northland to East Cape, the Marlborough Sounds and Stewart Island. It has straggled to Snares, Lord Howe and Norfolk Islands.

The Pied Shag is a large and quite approachable, elegant bird. The uppersurface is glossy black, the undersurface white and on the head the demarcation line is above the eye. The eye is green, surrounded by a ring of blue, and there is a diagnostic, bright yellow patch of bare skin between the eye and the base of the bill. The bill is dark horn and the feet are black.

Pied Shags nest in trees overhanging water, building substantial nests of sticks and debris that are added to year after year. They nest in colonies and have an extended breeding season in that individual pairs may commence to lay almost any month of the year and, as a consequence, Pied Shag colonies are occupied continuously. The clutch is 2 to 4 and both parents incubate. The chicks are fed by regurgitation — an uncomfortable-looking and rather inelegant procedure. As soon as a parent returns to the nest, all the chicks' heads rise up on long, writhing necks to the accompaniment of unceasing, wheezing, whining noises, while they peck at the parent's bill. When the bill opens, the nearest chick immediately thrusts it head inside as far as it will go — which is completely out of sight — and when the bolus of regurgitated food is exhausted, the parent has literally to shake the chick loose from its gullet. Until the chicks are reasonably well grown, one parent stays at the nest on guard while the other goes for food. If the chicks are hungry, as they mostly are, the bird at the nest, like as not, has nothing to give them. The chicks then whine and wheeze and writhe and sway — and they go on and on and on. They are relentless. There is a rather nice story of one of the subantarctic shags — all shag chicks behave like this — to the effect that the exasperated parent finally, and in desperation, stuffed its offspring with grass in order to keep it quiet. One can sympathise.

## The Little Black Shag

*Phalacrocorax sulcirostris* 60 cm.

In general appearance, the Little Black Shag is a small edition of the Black Shag. In breeding condition, it grows a few white feathers on the sides of the head but does not develop white flank patches. The eye is emerald green, the bare skin of the face is black (not yellowish) and the bill and feet are black. It frequents lakes and tidal estuaries and in New Zealand is most common in the Waikato and Bay of

Plenty districts of the North Island. Elsewhere, it occurs in Australia, New Guinea, New Caledonia, Indonesia and Borneo. It has straggled to Norfolk and Lord Howe Islands.

Little Black Shags breed in colonies, sometimes with other black-footed shags, usually in trees overhanging water, and probably also on offshore rocky stacks. Little Black Shags have the habit of forming flocks and hunting in packs. They will settle on the water in compact groups of up to 100 or more birds, and swim rapidly after shoaling fish, the birds in front diving, the birds at the rear taking short leapfrogging flights to the front to dive in their turn.

## The Little Shag

*Photos 58, 60*

*Phalacrocorax melanoleucos brevirostris* 56 cm.

The Little Shag is a small and distinctive, though variable, shag with a short, yellow bill and a long tail. It is a wary bird and seldom stays long once it has seen you. It associates with other black-footed shags, especially Pied Shags. It has 2 main plumage phases: a dark phase, known as the White-throated Shag, which is black all over except for white cheeks, face and throat; and a pied phase, known as the Little Pied Shag, which has the face, foreneck and entire underparts white. Between the two extremes, various intermediates occur. In New Zealand, most birds are of the White-throated form, especially in the south. Over the rest of its range — Australia, New Caledonia, New Guinea, the Solomon Islands, Indonesia and Malaysia — only the Little Pied form occurs. The bird has straggled to Snares and Auckland Islands and a small colony established itself on Six Foot Lake at Campbell Island about 1967. Strangely, these were of the Little Pied, not the White-throated form.

The Little Shag is a common species of both inland and coastal districts. It nests in trees overhanging freshwater lakes and on coastal cliffs and offshore stacks where the nests may be in low bushes or on the ground. The usual clutch is 3 or 4 and most birds have eggs in October. In display, Little Shags erect the feathers of face and head like a ruff, an act which has given rise to the colloquial name of frilled shag.

## The New Zealand King Shag

*Leucocarbo carunculatus carunculatus* 76 cm.

The various pink-footed, blue-eyed, subantarctic shags of the New Zealand region are classified into 3 species groups — the New Zealand King, Stewart Island, Bronze and Chatham Island Shags under *carunculatus*, the Campbell Island, Bounty Island and Auckland Island Shags under *campbelli* and the Macquarie Island Shag under *albiventa*. All these shags are sedentary, of restricted distribution and entirely marine. None, to my knowledge, hold out their wings as if to dry in the manner so common with the black-footed shags and they all have a pot-bellied look in flight.

The King Shag is confined to the Marlborough Sounds and is the rarest of the group, with a population of some 300 birds. It is glossy green-black above, including most of the head. The throat, foreneck and underparts are white. There is a white bar on the wing and a white patch on the scapulars. The bare skin of the face is reddish-brown and the ring round the eye is bright blue. The bill is dark and has conspicuous orange-yellow caruncles at the base. The eye is hazel and the feet are pink. This subspecies has no crest.

The King Shag breeds in compact colonies on the rock platforms of North Trio, Sentinel Rock, Duffers Reef, Bushy Island and White Rocks, building substantial nests of seaweed and debris. The White Rocks colony has been in occupation for more than 200 years; it was recorded by J. R. Forster in 1773, during Cook's second voyage. The birds are usually winter breeders, with eggs in May and well-grown young by August, but the onset of breeding may vary from year to year and from colony to colony. The clutch is 1 to 3 and the full cycle takes about 5 months.

## The Stewart Island Shag

*Leucocarbo carunculatus chalconatus* 68 cm.

The Stewart Island Shag has 2 plumage phases. In the pied phase it differs from the King Shag in having a well-developed crest when breeding and in lacking the conspicuous orange caruncles at the base of the bill, having instead a few reddish-orange papillae. It also lacks the patch of white feathers among the scapulars. The dark phase, known as the Bronze Shag, is uniformly greenish-black all over, with a bronze sheen. It is crested and has the same small papillae on the bill instead of conspicuous caruncles.

Stewart Island and Bronze Shags interbreed freely and the 2 phases come true. There are 2 principal breeding populations: 1 based on Otago Peninsula, the other on Stewart Island. The Otago birds are larger and heavier and have more robust papillae on the bill than the others. The Otago birds breed on Goat Island, Taiaroa Head, Gull Rock and Green Island. The Stewart Island birds breed on Papa-Kaha (Bluff Harbour), Centre Island (Foveaux Strait) and Kanetetoe, Jackey Lee, Whero, Zero Rock and Codfish Islands. Nests are re-used year after year and eventually build up to become substantial pedestals. The clutch is 2 or 3 and the birds evidently have an extended laying period. In October, nests have been seen at all stages from fresh eggs to large young.

## The Chatham Island Shag

*Photo 64*

*Leucocarbo carunculatus onslowi* 63 cm.

Similar in general plumage characters to the King and Stewart Island Shags, the Chatham Island Shag makes the others look dull by comparison. It is an altogether more colourful bird with cleaner and brighter metallic reflections from its plumage and a more conspicuous, white alar bar. The bare skin of the face is red and the blue eye-ring is brilliant. The caruncles at the base of the bill are large and are red rather than orange. This shag is confined to the coastal waters of the Chatham Islands and its breeding stronghold is the Star Keys. It also breeds on the cliffs of the main Chatham Island and on Rabbit Island. Little is known of this bird's annual cycle, but it presumably falls in line with the others of the species.

## The Bounty Island Shag

*Leucocarbo campbelli ranfurlyi* 71 cm.

The Bounty Island Shag resembles the Stewart Island Shag in size and general plumage. It has bright red facial skin and is crested in the breeding season, but has no caruncles on the bill or even papillae and the blue eye-ring tends towards violet. In other words, it shows features of *carunculatus* on the one hand and *campbelli* on the other. The New Zealand *Checklist* puts it with *campbelli.*

The bird is confined to the Bounty Islands and is not numerous. There is a record for the Antipodes Islands when 2 shags were seen there in 1950, but none have been seen there since. Not much is known about the bird, for the Bounty Islands are seldom visited, difficult to land on and inhospitable in the extreme. There is no shelter, no water and no vegetation, just bare rock covered with mollymawks and penguins. Most visits, therefore, have been brief. In 1978 the New Zealand

Wildlife Service established a party ashore for 2 weeks (which was somewhat more than they had bargained for, but that is what the weather dictates down there), and this is the only occasion, since the sealing days of the early 1800s, that anyone has stayed ashore for more than a few hours.

Bounty Island Shags breed on the cliffs, building nests of seaweed and laying 3 eggs. The population is estimated to be about 460 pairs, which is not great, considering the abundance of food in these waters. It is thought that the limiting factor may be the lack of breeding space; all the flat ground is taken up by mollymawks and penguins.

## The Auckland Island Shag

*Photos 62, 63*

*Leucocarbo campbelli colensoi* 63 cm.

The Auckland Island Shag is glossy black above and white below and has pink feet, as do all the *leucocarbo* shags. The facial skin is red, the eye-ring violet, the bill dark horn and there are no caruncles or papillae. The head is crested in breeding plumage and there is a white alar bar. Some birds have a complete black collar across the lower foreneck; in the majority, the collar is incomplete. The bird is common at the Auckland Islands and large rafts containing some hundreds of individuals collect on sheltered waters in the lee of the islands. It breeds on the cliffs, mostly where inaccessible, and in totally inaccessible places on the main island where pigs, released by early visitors, destroy all that can be reached. The most accessible colony is the one spread out on top of one of the cliffs of Enderby Island. The nests are substantial structures of seaweed and grass cemented together with guano and the usual clutch is 2 or 3. Incubation takes about 30 days and most pairs have young in January.

## The Campbell Island Shag

*Photo 66*

*Leucocarbo campbelli campbelli* 63 cm.

The Campbell Island Shag resembles the Auckland Island Shag but has a completely black head and neck, except for a white throat patch. The facial skin is deep red and the eye-ring is purple. There are no caruncles or papillae on the bill. The head is crested in breeding plumage. This shag is confined to Campbell Island and the offshore stacks, breeding on the sheer, volcanic cliffs facing the sea. So far, no easily accessible colony has been found and consequently little has been recorded of its breeding cycle. After the breeding season, these shags collect in rafts on the water, as do the Auckland Island birds.

## The Macquarie Island Shag

*Leucocarbo albiventer purpurascens* 71 cm.

I have not seen this species. It is glossy blue-black above and white below and has pink feet. The base of the bill has large, conspicuous, yellow caruncles, the facial skin is brown, the eye-ring brilliant blue and the head crested. There is a white alar bar. The white of the throat extends much further up the sides of the head than with the others of the region, almost to the level of the eye.

The Macquarie Island Shag is confined to Macquarie Island and the outlying stacks, such as the Bishop and Clerk Rocks. It breeds on rock platforms and cliffs, building a substantial nest, and lays up to 3 eggs in November. Other subspecies occur at the Crozet, Marion and Falkland Islands and on the islands and coasts of Patagonia.

## The Spotted Shag

*Photo 65*

*Stictocarbo punctatus punctatus* 73 cm.

The Spotted Shag is one of 3 closely related, totally marine shags with spotted plumage and orange-yellow feet, confined to the New Zealand region. They breed on cliffs facing the sea and I have yet to see any of the group perched with wings in heraldic posture, as if to dry. The Spotted Shag's distribution is centred on breeding sites in the Hauraki Gulf, the Auckland west coast, Wellington Harbour, the Marlborough Sounds and the east coast of the South Island — especially Banks and Otago peninsulas. On the west coast of the South Island and at Stewart Island, it is replaced by the Blue Shag.

In full breeding plumage, the Spotted Shag is one of our most handsome species. The bare skin of the face is emerald green and the throat is royal blue. The eye is surrounded by a ring of blue, studded with emerald green beads, and there are two forward-curving black crests on the head. The neck is black with a metallic gloss and a broad white stripe runs down each side. In full plumage, the neck is profusely ornamented with white plumes and these plumes also appear on the back and thighs. The backs of the wings are greyish and each feather is spotted with black. The underparts are white and the legs and feet are a rich orange-yellow. Unfortunately, this exotic plumage is transitory in the extreme and by the time eggs are laid, the birds are well on the way to reverting to their normal dull, drab, everyday garb in which all ornamentation and colour are lost.

Spotted Shags breed on the ledges of vertical cliffs facing the sea. They are especially fond of cliffs pockmarked with hollows and overhangs, for they like to place their nests where there is overhead protection. Some colonies are dense, with serried ranks occupying every available space, while others are more scattered. The cliffs of the Marlborough Sounds, for example, are studded with punched-out hollows that are much admired by the Spotted Shags. They take them up as residences, liberally splatter the surrounds with white droppings and, thus ensconced, peer out with sinuous necks and suspicious mien at every passing launch.

Spotted Shags display by standing at the nest site, facing inwards so that the full benefit of the plumage is seen by incoming birds. They erect the tail, tremble the wings, raise each white plume at right angles and throw back the head. The display is very brief and is apparently done in silence. The nests are made of seaweed and the clutch is normally 3. Incubation takes about 32 days and the young are fed on regurgitated fish. As a rule, Spotted Shags breed early in the season, but they are unpredictable and erratic birds and at any given site, eggs may appear in August one year and in October the next.

## The Blue Shag

*Stictocarbo punctatus steadi* 73 cm.

This subspecies replaces the Spotted Shag at Stewart Island and along the west coast of the South Island. It is a darker bird and has a narrower white line down the side of the neck; otherwise it looks identical. It is often a solitary nester, tucking its nest up among the overhanging roots of trees at the top of low coastal cliffs in sheltered inlets, and it seems to breed later in the year than the Spotted Shag. About this, however, there is as yet insufficient information. The spotted shags, as a group, are unpredictable and it is evident that there is much yet to be discovered about their annual cycles.

## The Pitt Island Shag

*Photo 68*

*Stictocarbo punctatus featherstoni* 63 cm.

The Pitt Island Shag is a sedentary shag confined to the Chatham Islands where it breeds on South East, Mangere, Pitt and Star Keys Islands. It is darker again than the Blue Shag. It has no white stripe down the neck and the white plumes are restricted to a sparse scattering on the head and neck. (The bird in the illustration is almost as richly endowed as this species becomes.) The bare skin of the face is green, the eye-ring is purple and the legs and feet are orange. It nests on vertical cliffs facing the sea, in small colonies of a dozen or so pairs, placing its nests in the pockets of volcanic rocks. Its season is evidently irregular. Eggs have been recorded in August and I have seen fresh (unstained) eggs in early November. No doubt the cycle resembles the rather unpredictable and irregular cycles of the other spotted shags.

## **Darters** Anhingidae

Cormorant-like, freshwater birds with long, dagger-like bills, long, thin, kinked necks, slim bodies and long tails. There is a single record, Hokitika 1874, of the Australian Darter *Anhinga melanogaster rufa* straggling to New Zealand.

## **Frigate Birds** Fregatidae

Large, piratical, tropical seabirds with wonderful dexterity of flight. Wings long, black and angular. Tail long and deeply forked, opened and closed with a scissor-like action as they manoeuvre. Legs very short and feet small. Unable to walk. Never settle on the sea. Should they accidentally do so, they have great difficulty getting off again and soon become waterlogged. Seldom far from land and return at night to roost. Roost and nest on trees and bushes because of the difficulty of taking off from a flat surface. Remain near breeding grounds all year. Bill long and hooked. Sexes differ in plumage and size. Females larger. Feed on fish, squid and refuse, which they pick off the surface of the water. Harass other seabirds, especially boobies, forcing them to disgorge their catch, which the frigates then snatch as it drops. Prey on the eggs and young of seabird colonies. Nest in colonies on bushes near or among the colonies of the other seabirds on which they prey. Males display by inflating their scarlet throat pouches like balloons. Clutch 1. Incubation, by both sexes, 40-50 days. Fledging period about 5 months. Chicks dependent on parents for a further 4-6 months after fledging. At best, Frigate Birds rear 1 chick every 2 years. Five species; 2 on the New Zealand list, both stragglers.

## The Greater Frigate Bird

*Fregata minor* 100 cm., wingspan 2 m.

The male is entirely blackish with the distensible, red throat pouch small when not breeding. The female is black with a grey throat, white breast and black abdomen. This is a rare straggler (about 12 records) to northern New Zealand waters. It breeds in all tropical seas and the nearest breeding grounds to New Zealand are Christmas Island in the Indian Ocean and the atolls of the Central Pacific.

## The Lesser Frigate Bird

*Fregata ariel* 80 cm., wingspan 1.90 m.

The male is entirely black except for white armpits and the red throat pouch is small when not breeding. The female is black with a white throat. This is a rare straggler to New Zealand (about 20 records), mostly following tropical storms. The nearest breeding grounds to New Zealand are the islands of the Coral Sea and Fiji.

# CICONIIFORMES

Principally birds of marshlands and waterways. They have long legs, long necks and long bills. Seven families; 2 in New Zealand: Herons and allies; Ibises and Spoonbills.

## **Herons, Egrets, Night Herons, Bitterns** Ardeidae

Medium to large birds with long legs, long necks, long straight bills and long, unwebbed toes, 3 forward and 1 back. Mostly birds of freshwater swamps and marshes, but the Reef Heron is marine and the White-faced Heron and Cattle Egret are commonly on dry pasture land. All fly with deliberate wing-beats with the head tucked back and the legs projecting beyond the tail. They stand upright and walk sedately. Sexes are similar. All have specialised feathers known as powder downs that are not shed and which fray continually at the tips to produce a powder used for preening. Most species nest in colonies, often with other water birds. Eggs mostly 3 to 5, with incubation from the first or second and so the hatch is asynchronous and the chicks are of different sizes. The young are fed by regurgitation. Sixty-four species; New Zealand 10.

## The White-faced Heron *Photo 70*

*Ardea novaehollandiae* 67 cm.

Prior to 1940, the White-faced Heron was known in New Zealand only as a rare straggler from Australia. About that time, the birds became permanently established and since then their increase has been little short of explosive. They now occur throughout the country wherever suitable habitat exists. The range of this species includes Australia, New Guinea, New Caledonia, the Lesser Sundas and the Celebes. It has recently colonised Norfolk and Lord Howe Islands and, since its arrival in New Zealand, the Chatham Islands. It straggles to the Kermadecs and Fiji, and to Campbell and Macquarie Islands.

The White-faced Heron is an elegant, slim, blue-grey heron with a white face and yellow legs. The bill is black and the eye yellow. There are some rusty feathers on the breast and in breeding condition long, pale grey plumes grow on the back. In flight it shows a contrasting pattern of pale grey against dark flight feathers. Its voice is a harsh *crark*.

White-faced Herons occupy open habitats from coastal mudflats to inland pastures. Their food is principally water-related — fish, frogs, crabs and other crustaceans, insects and insect larvae — but they will take lizards and even small birds, given the opportunity.

White-faced Herons normally nest high in trees and in New Zealand favour introduced pines. They tend to nest early and to nest alone, unlike most herons, which require the stimulus of a colony to breed successfully. Presumably this solitary habit has been a factor in their rapid expansion over the country. The clutch is usually 3 to 5, the incubation, by both parents, lasts 25 days and the fledging period about 45 days. The young stay with the parents till the start of the next breeding season. At the Chatham Islands, they have been found nesting under rocks just above the high tide mark in the manner of a Reef Heron.

## The White-necked Heron

*Ardea pacifica* 90 cm.

The White-necked Heron is an Australian species that rarely strays beyond the confines of that continent. There are 2 New Zealand records: 1952 and 1978. The combination of white head, neck and breast with a dark blue-grey body and wings is diagnostic. In flight, it shows a white patch halfway along the leading edge of the wing. The bill and legs are black and the eye yellow.

## The White Heron

*Photo 67*

*Egretta alba modesta* 90 cm.

White Herons, better known as Great White Egrets, occur on all continents and are common in Australia. In New Zealand they are rare: 81 were counted during a census in 1977.

The White Heron is an all-white heron with black legs and a yellow bill. It has a very long neck, characteristically kinked in the middle. The eye is yellow and the black line of the gape extends back behind the eye. In breeding plumage, the White Heron develops long filamentous plumes that cascade over the back, and the bill temporarily turns black. Outside the breeding season, White Herons are mostly solitary birds, typically seen standing quietly in shallow water, waiting for prey, or stalking with slow and deliberate tread. White Herons do not dash rapidly about like Little Egrets. They feed on fish, frogs, crustaceans, aquatic insects and insect larvae.

The only known breeding colony of White Herons in New Zealand is at Okarito on the West Coast where they breed in association with Royal Spoonbills and Little Shags. They nest in spring, with eggs in September and October, and the young are mostly fledged by the end of December. The clutch is 3 to 5, the incubation period 25 days and the fledging period about 42 days.

## The Plumed Egret

*Egretta intermedia* 65 cm.

A very rare straggler to New Zealand, with 2 records: 1972 and 1979. This is a tropical species of Northern Australia, southern and eastern Asia, India and Africa. It is very like a small Great White Heron, with similar black legs and yellow bill, but the bill is proportionately stubbier and the black line of the gape ends below the eye and does not extend behind the eye as it does in the White Heron. It feeds in the same deliberate manner as the White Heron.

## The Little Egret

*Egretta garzetta immaculata* 60 cm.

The Little Egret has a wide distribution over the Old World. In New Zealand it is rare (the 1977 census found 22) and is apparently only a vagrant from Australia. Of recent years, it has appeared with some regularity at certain favoured localities, which led to the suspicion that there might somewhere be an undiscovered breeding colony. That now seems less likely, for Australian research has shown that juveniles tend to be dispersive and that some cross the Tasman each year.

The Little Egret is a small, white heron with a black bill and black legs. It is a very active feeder, dashing about the shallows after its prey in a manner quite different to the sedate stalking of the White Heron and Plumed Egret. It has a high stepping gait and associates with other herons.

## The Reef Heron

*Egretta sacra* 66 cm.

The Reef Heron is entirely coastal, seldom venturing even short distances inland, and is a bird of rocky rather than sandy shores. It occurs principally in the north and is absent from much of the South Island coast. It has straggled to the Chatham Islands. Its range includes much of the south and central Pacific, Australia, South-east Asia and Japan. It is essentially a warm-water bird and New Zealand is at its southernmost limit.

The Reef Heron is a stockier bird than the White-faced Heron, which now shares its habitat, and has a heavier bill and shorter legs. It has a hunched appearance in comparison to the White-faced Heron's slim, elegant outline. Its overall plumage is dark slaty-grey. There is a small streak of white on the throat but this is difficult to see in the field. The bill is brownish-yellow, the legs yellowish-green and the eye yellow. In the tropics, the Reef Heron has a white phase but this does not occur in New Zealand.

Reef Herons stalk their prey, crouching low and keeping the body in a more horizontal attitude than other herons. They are mostly seen alone and they nest as solitary pairs in crevices and caves and under the overhang of jumbled boulders on offshore islands and rocks, mostly not far above high water mark. They have an extended breeding season, with eggs recorded from August to February. The normal clutch is 2 or 3 and the incubation period 25-28 days. The eggs are laid 2 days apart and the hatch is asynchronous. The chicks fledge at about 5½ weeks.

## The Cattle Egret

*Photo 69*

*Bubulcus ibis coromandus* 50 cm.

About 1930, Cattle Egrets, previously confined to Africa and Asia, began a world-wide extension of range and are now found on all continents. They reached Australia about 1940 or earlier and New Zealand in 1963. Since then, they have built up in New Zealand to become the commonest white egret in the country; 300 were recorded during the 1977 census.

The Cattle Egret is a small, white egret with a yellow bill, yellowish legs and yellow eyes. The bill is short and stubby and a prominent tuft of feathers under the chin gives a characteristic deep-jowled appearance. At rest, the bird appears hunched-up and stocky. In breeding condition it grows orange-buff plumes from the head, breast and lower back, the bill and legs turn red and the eye orange-red.

Cattle Egrets are gregarious and are normally seen in flocks associating with grazing animals, especially cattle, feeding on the insects the animals disturb.

Cattle Egrets breed in colonies, often with other species. No nest has yet been seen in New Zealand, but a pair with young were seen at Paretai, Otago, in 1972. Their usual clutch is 3 or 4, the incubation period 24 days and the fledging period about 30 days.

## The Nankeen Night Heron

*Photo 73*

*Nycticorax caledonicus* 56 cm.

Night Herons are gregarious birds that roost by day in leafy trees and feed at night. The Nankeen Night Heron of Australia, New Guinea, New Caledonia and islands north to the Philippines and Carolines, is a rare straggler to New Zealand, recorded intermittently since 1856. An unsuccessful attempt was made to introduce the species in 1852. Breeding may have occurred near Blenheim 1957-59. The Nankeen Night Heron is chestnut above and creamy white below. The crown of the head is black and, in breeding plumage, 2 long, white plumes grow down over the back of the neck. Juveniles are entirely different and look rather like bitterns, with their overall pale brown plumage streaked brown and white on the head and neck, and spotted with white on the wings.

## The Australasian Bittern *Photo 71*

*Botaurus poiciloptilus* 70 cm.

The Australasian Bittern is a secretive bird that inhabits dense reed beds and swamps. It occurs throughout New Zealand wherever suitable habitat occurs and is also found in Tasmania, south-east and south-west Australia and New Caledonia. It is a large, brown bird cryptically marked with streaks of darker brown, black and ochre and mottled above with buffy-yellow. The throat is cream and the feathers of the neck are dense and elongated. The legs and feet are green and the sexes are alike.

Bitterns are well known for their booming calls — one of the most far-carrying of all bird sounds — and for their habit, when alarmed, of drawing themselves upwards to their full extent and freezing, with the bill pointed skywards. The eyes are swivelled forwards to give them binocular vision of the intruder, while relying on their camouflaged plumage to melt them into the background. On windy days, they even sway to match the movement of the reeds.

Bitterns are skulking, secretive, partly nocturnal, essentially solitary birds, seldom seen out in the open. They walk deliberately and clamber easily through the reeds. In flight, they are broad-winged and they fly with the head retracted in the manner of all herons. They feed on fish, frogs and aquatic life generally, including insects and their larvae, but will take lizards, if opportunity presents, and even small birds.

Bitterns nest solitarily on or close to the ground in dense cover surrounded by water and lay 3-5 eggs at 2-day intervals. These are incubated by the female only. Incubation takes 25 days and commences with the first or second egg, so the chicks hatch over a period of days. So far as is known, they are brooded and fed only by the female.

At the nest illustrated, photographed with a friend many years ago near Queenstown, the first egg hatched on 18 December, the remainder on the 20th, 21st and 23rd. So, by the time the last chick hatched, the first was 6 days old and growing rapidly. Feeding was by regurgitation. The Bittern would silently arrive at the nest and, after a few moments, would commence regurgitating contractions. A green frog would appear, to be slid down the bill and deposited on the nest. This frog would be followed by another — dull this time and partly digested — then another — and then finally a pultaceous lump recognisable as a frog only because of what had gone before. This last would be picked up by a chick and swallowed, with much gulping. As the chicks grew bigger, the largest became very demanding, grasping the parent's bill in a crosswise manner as soon as she returned to the nest, and pulling and tugging till she started to regurgitate. The first frog to appear would be followed down the bill by this chick and caught as it reached the tip. The next chick would claim the next frog and so on down the line to the smallest chick, which would thus receive the most digested offerings more suited to its smaller swallowing capacity.

As the chicks grew, feeding and brooding became less and less frequent, and we began to spend long hours in the hide with no sight of the parent bird at all. The quaint, golliwog chicks, however, provided a never-ending source of amusement. They would shuffle round the nest making quiet bubbling noises — like blowing

**65** A Spotted Shag in full nuptial plumage.

**66** A Campbell Island Shag photographed in February.

**67** The Great White Egret, or White Heron.

**68** The Pitt Island Shag.

**69** Cattle Egrets.

**70** The White-faced Heron.

**71** The Australasian Bittern.

**72** The Australian White Ibis.

**73** The Nankeen Night Heron.

**74** The Royal Spoonbill.

**75** The Whistling Tree Duck. A very rare straggler to New Zealand. Photographed in Australia.

**76** The Australian Cape Barren Goose. The photograph is of a captive bird.

**77** The introduced Australian Black Swan.

**78** The introduced Mallard.

**79** Paradise Shelducks.

**80** The introduced Canada Goose.

**81** The male New Zealand Shoveler.

**82** The Australian Wood Duck has been recorded twice as a straggler to New Zealand. Photographed in Australia.

**83** The Australian Mountain Shelduck.

**84** The New Zealand Scaup.

**85** The Auckland Island Flightless Duck.

**86** The Grey Duck.

**87** The female New Zealand Shoveler.

**88** The Blue Duck.

**89** The New Zealand Falcon.

**90** The Harrier.

**91** The introduced Grey Partridge.

**92** The introduced California Quail.

**93** The introduced Chukor.

air through water — but instantly freezing, with bill perpendicular, to watch with binocular eyes every Harrier that lazily floated overhead. They were careful to excrete their droppings over the edge of the nest into the water, backing in an ataxic and precarious manner to the nest edge and teetering on wobbly legs, a performance harrowing to watch for fear one of them would overbalance and fall in.

They also began to explore round and through the niggerheads forming the base of the nest. The front and sides of the nest plunged straight into deep water, but at the rear further rushes and niggerheads abutted, through which devious routes led to other parts of the swamp. Once this exploratory period commenced, we realised that our time was drawing to a close, for shortly the Bittern chicks would be fed away from the nest and out of sight. As it happened, this period coincided with the end of our free time. Much as we would have liked to continue our observations, we were unable to do so and we considered ourselves fortunate indeed to have seen as much as we had.

## The New Zealand Little Bittern

*Ixobrychus novaezelandiae* 30 cm.

The New Zealand Little Bittern is a problem species, with only 20 records, mostly from Westland. None have been seen this century. Museum specimens differ from both *minutus* of Australia, with which it has been classified, and *exilis* of South America. The New Zealand *Checklist* now gives it full specific rank. The Little Bittern is (was?) a tiny bittern with the secretive, solitary, nocturnal habits of the clan. The crown and nape are black, the back and scapulars are dark brown, the hindneck chestnut and the undersurface streaked dark brown over buff. The bill and legs are green. No nest has ever been seen.

## Ibises and Spoonbills Threskiornithidae

Large, principally freshwater birds with long legs, long necks and long, distinctive bills — spatulate in spoonbills, down-curved in ibises. Sexes similar. Males have longer bills. Gregarious and breed in colonies. Fly strongly in long lines and 'V's. Thirty species; New Zealand 4, 1 breeding.

## The Glossy Ibis

*Plegadis falcinellus* 56 cm.

This cosmopolitan species is known in New Zealand only as an irregular visitor from Australia, though often in small flocks. For an ibis, it is a small bird and at a distance looks like a dark curlew. In good light, the rich, glossy bronze and greenish plumage is conspicuous. The bill and legs are brown. It flies fast with the neck extended and drooping, and the legs trailing beyond the tail. It frequents wetlands and swampy places and is usually in the company of others of its kind.

## The Australian White Ibis

*Photo 72*

*Threskiornis molucca* 72 cm.

A large ibis with the head and neck naked and black, its plumage is entirely white except for black tips to the flight feathers which show clearly as the bird passes overhead. At rest, with the wings folded, these black tips give the appearance of a black tail. In fact, the tail is white. The bill is long, black and down-curved and the legs are black. White Ibises fly with alternating wing-beats and glides, and flocks tend to do so in unison. It is a rare straggler to New Zealand, sometimes in flocks, and it can be tame and approachable. The natural range of this species is Australia, New Guinea and the Moluccas.

## The Royal Spoonbill

*Photo 74*

*Platalea leucorodia regia* 78 cm.

The Royal Spoonbill is an Australian species (extending to New Guinea and Indonesia) that colonised New Zealand about 1950 when pairs were discovered breeding at the White Heron colony at Okarito, South Westland. Numbers have slowly built up over the intervening years and in 1979 another colony was discovered near Blenheim, where they nested in association with Pied Shags, using their old nests. The present New Zealand population is thought to be about 50 birds.

The Royal Spoonbill is a distinctive bird with an overall immaculate white plumage. The bare skin of the face is black, as are the legs and long spatulate bill. There is a red spot on the forehead and the eyelids are conspicuously yellow. In breeding plumage, Royal Spoonbills develop white plumes from the back of the head.

Spoonbills feed by wading through the water, sweeping the bill from side to side with a scything action. Fish, frogs and freshwater insects are their main food. They are gregarious throughout the year and freely associate with other species.

The Royal Spoonbill nests in trees, building a shallow nest of sticks. The clutch is 2 to 4 and incubation, by both sexes, takes about 24 days. Incubation is from the first egg, so the hatch is asynchronous and the chicks are of different sizes. The fledging period is about 45 days.

## The Yellow-billed Spoonbill

*Platalea flavipes* 90 cm.

There is a single New Zealand record of this Australian endemic, in 1976. It has a yellow bill and yellow legs and its plumage is white.

# ANSERIFORMES

Waterfowl. Cosmopolitan. Two families, 1 represented in New Zealand: Swans, Geese and Ducks.

## **Swans, Geese and Ducks** Anatidae

A distinct and easily recognisable family of web-footed, aquatic birds with short legs and flat bills (except *mergus*). All, except the Magpie Goose of Australia, are flightless during the moult. Form flocks after breeding. Eggs plain and unspotted. Nests lined with down. Chicks downy and active soon after synchronous hatching. One hundred and forty-five species; New Zealand 17, of which 5 endemic, 5 introduced and 1 extinct.

### The Grass Whistling Duck *Photo 75*

*Dendrocygna eytoni* 42 cm.

There have been 4 records of this rare straggler to New Zealand from Australia. An unmistakable, brown duck with long, flat, pale yellow plumes projecting upwards from the flanks. Its bill and legs are pink. The sexes are alike. A grasslands bird, seldom spending much time on water. Also known as Whistling Tree Duck.

### The Mute Swan

*Cygnus olor* 150 cm.

The Mute Swan was introduced from Britain in the 1860s as an ornamental bird and is now feral in small numbers in scattered localities, notably at Lake Ellesmere near Christchurch and on the lakes of Hawke's Bay. It is an all-white swan with an orange bill that has a black knob at the base. The sexes are alike, with males larger. The Mute Swan is not mute in the sense of being dumb; its voice is a trumpet but is infrequently used and rather hoarse.

Mute Swans can be savage when nesting. They build an enormous pile of raupo and other plants and lay 5-7 eggs. Incubation is from the last egg and takes about 38 days. The chicks hatch together and leave the nest soon afterwards. They mature at about 120 days or more and remain with the parents over the winter.

### The Black Swan *Photo 77*

*Cygnus atratus* 100 cm.

Introduced from Australia during the 1860s, the Black Swan has proved a successful colonist and is now abundant and widespread. From New Zealand, it was introduced to the Chatham Islands and it has proved equally successful there.

The Black Swan is all black, except for white flight feathers. The bill is red and is crossed near the tip by a white bar. The extreme tip of the bill is also white. The legs and feet are black. Its voice is a far-carrying, musical trumpet.

Black Swans nest both in colonies and alone. Where numerous, they nest in colonies that can be immense. At Lake Ellesmere, for example, the colony extends along the lake shore almost as far as the eye can see. The clutch is usually 4 to 6 and incubation, by both parents, takes 37 days. The downy chicks soon leave for the water and they mature at about 5 months. The food of Black Swans consists mostly of water plants which they reach by dipping down with their long necks.

## The Canada Goose *Photo 80*

*Branta canadensis* 100 cm.

The Canada Goose was first introduced, from North America, in 1876. The first successful introduction, however, was not till 1905. Since then, Canada Geese have become well established in Canterbury and Otago, occupying especially the tussock grasslands dotted with small ponds that are such a feature of the broad, flat valleys that flow east from the Southern Alps. Elsewhere in New Zealand, Canada Geese appear mostly as stragglers.

The Canada Goose is a large, brown goose with a black head and neck conspicuously marked by white cheek patches. It feeds mostly by grazing, but also by upending in shallow water, and it forms large flocks when not breeding. Its voice is a musical honking.

Canada Geese breed in spring and most have eggs in October. The nests are placed near water and almost invariably on small islands of grass or swamp vegetation, if these are present. They nest both in scattered colonies and alone. The clutch is usually 4 to 6 and incubation, for 28 days, is by the female only. The young stay with the parents throughout the winter and until the families break up at the commencement of next year's breeding season.

## The Cape Barren Goose *Photo 76*

*Cereopsis novaehollandiae* 85 cm.

The Cape Barren Goose is endemic to Australia and is a rare bird, occurring principally on the islands of Bass Strait. It was introduced to New Zealand in 1915 but did not establish. Rare sightings from Fiordland suggest that it may occasionally arrive here as a wind-blown straggler. It is a large goose-like species (it is not a true goose), pale grey in colour with pink legs and black feet. The black of the feet extends a short way up the legs and, as a result, the birds look as if they have just walked through black, sticky mud. The bill is black and almost entirely covered by a large and conspicuous lemon-yellow cere (a soft fleshy covering over the base). They are grazers, eating mostly grass, of which they require large quantities.

## The Paradise Shelduck *Photo 79*

*Tadorna variegata* 62 cm.

The Paradise Shelduck is a New Zealand endemic widespread over both islands. It is a bird of open spaces that adapts readily to man-made pasturelands and is one of the most conspicuous birds of the immediate approaches to the Southern Alps.

The Paradise Shelduck is a large, goose-like duck that walks well and feeds both by grazing and by upending in shallow water for weed and animal life. The sexes differ in appearance. The female has a conspicuous white head and neck and a predominantly chestnut body, while the male has a black head glossed with green and a predominantly dark body. Both show a conspicuous white patch on the wing in flight. The voice of the female is a loud, carrying, discordant, trumpeting clamour, most unattractive when heard close by but, when softened by distance, possessing a wild character that accords well with the wild scenery of mountain valleys. The voice of the male is a guttural *glink-glink*. Both birds are ever alert and only too ready to give voice. At first sight of an intruder, they take wing, circle overhead, fly to the far end of the river flat, return and recircle, all the time making a clamour to wake the dead and leaving no doubt that their preserve has been invaded. They are not popular with deer shooters.

Paradise Shelducks mate for life and are always seen as pairs. The pairs stay together not only when on territory (which they jealously guard), but also during autumn and winter when, with the onset of winter snows, they retreat out of the back country to assemble on the lagoons of the plains in flocks that may number a hundred or so birds.

Paradise Shelducks nest in holes — in the ground, in trees, under logs, in dense clumps of flax or tussock. Nests in dead trees may be at a considerable height — up to 8 metres. The usual clutch is 5 to 8 and incubation is by the female only. The nest is well lined with down and the eggs are well covered each time the female leaves. The incubation period is 30 days. The drake is attentive to his duck and, while she is incubating, stations himself nearby. When the duck comes off to feed, she joins him and the 2 birds feed together. When she returns, the drake accompanies her. The birds fly back in tandem; the duck peels off to pitch at the nest, the drake carries on, circles and returns to his waiting place.

The ducklings are cared for by both parents. Should danger threaten, the parents attempt to distract the intruder by pretending a broken wing. Squawking loudly, the bird flounders over the tussocks as if wounded, though always carefully just beyond reach. Sometimes both birds distract; at other times one distracts while its mate leads the young to safety.

## The Mountain Shelduck *Photo 83*

*Tadorna tadornoides* 65 cm.

A recent straggler to New Zealand, the Australian Mountain or Chestnut-breasted Shelduck was first seen here in January 1983, following a period of westerly winds. In all, 38 individuals were recorded throughout the country. The natural range of the species is southern Australia and Tasmania where, contrary to its name, it is more a bird of coastal, brackish lakes than a bird of the mountains. Males have a black head and neck glossed with green, a white collar at the base of the neck, a chestnut breast and the rest of the plumage mostly black except for white shoulders, green secondaries and chestnut tertiaries. Females are similar but for rings of white circling the eyes and the base of the bill. Like Paradise Shelducks, Mountain Shelducks mate for life and remain paired all year, so with the numbers recorded, establishment of the species in lowland, swampy regions would seem a distinct possibility.

## The Mallard *Photo 78*

*Anas platyrhynchos* 58 cm.

The Mallard is a widespread Northern Hemisphere duck first introduced from Britain in 1867, but not established till 1930 when extensive liberation was carried out, including birds of American stock. It is now the dominant duck of all settled districts and has successfully established itself at the Chatham Islands. It has recently appeared at Norfolk and Lord Howe Islands and it is thought more likely that these birds have come from New Zealand than from Australia (where it has also been introduced). It has straggled to Antipodes, Auckland, Campbell and Macquarie Islands and may now be established at Campbell Island.

The Mallard drake, in breeding plumage, has a glossy green head and a thin, white collar, a yellowish bill, a chestnut breast, creamy-grey flanks, a violet speculum, orange feet and a curly tail. In eclipse plumage, into which it moults after breeding, it loses the bright colours and comes to resemble the female. The female Mallard resembles a Grey Duck but is browner and lacks the clear-cut cream stripes on the head. The bill is greenish-yellow, the speculum violet and the legs and feet orange. Mallards hybridise with Grey Ducks — especially where both occur in city parks, not so much in the wild — to produce birds with mixed characteristics.

Mallards accept a wide range of habitats and are very tolerant of human activity. They tend to be sedentary and in New Zealand have not yet spread much beyond the settled districts.

In common with all dabbling ducks, Mallards feed by dabbling at the water's edge and by upending in the shallows. When taking flight, they leap off the water with a single spring. They nest from August to January and lay larger clutches than the Grey Duck, usually 12 to 15. Incubation is by the female only and takes 28 days. The males take no part in the care of the young.

## The Grey Duck *Photo 86*

*Anas superciliosa* 55 cm.

The Grey Duck has a wide distribution. It occurs and breeds throughout New Zealand and it also breeds at the Kermadec, Chatham, Snares, Auckland, Campbell and Macquarie Islands. Elsewhere, it breeds from Australia and New Guinea east to the islands of the central Pacific and north to Java and Sumatra.

The sexes of the Grey Duck are alike. The overall plumage is grey-brown and there are two conspicuous, horizontal, pale stripes on the head, bordering a black line through the eye. The bill, legs and feet are a dark slaty-green and the speculum is green.

In settled areas, Grey Ducks are now outnumbered by Mallards and in parks and city gardens hybridise with them. In back country and mountain areas, Grey Ducks remain the dominant dabbling duck. They lay smaller clutches than the Mallard, usually 6 to 10, and, as with all dabbling ducks, incubation (28 days) is by the female only. They feed by dabbling at the water's edge and by upending in the shallows, and they also eat such items as grain, acorns, grass seed and berries. They fly fast and spring off the water with a single leap.

## The Grey Teal

*Anas gibberifrons gracilis* 42 cm.

A common bird in Australia, where it is highly nomadic, the Grey Teal has been known to breed in New Zealand for at least 60 years, but only recently has it become widespread, following further irruptions from across the Tasman.

At first glance, the Grey Teal resembles a small Grey Duck, but it has a more uniformly marked and rounder head, a crimson eye and is creamier in colour. In flight, it has a conspicuous, triangular white patch on the uppersurface of the wing and it has a peculiar, hoarse quack.

The Grey Teal will nest anywhere but usually does so in holes in trees, in rabbit burrows and in dense vegetation on the ground. The usual clutch is 5 to 9 and the incubation period 24-26 days. The drake remains attentive to his duck and both birds may be seen shepherding their brood of young.

Grey Teal are dabbling ducks that feed by dabbling and upending. They take wing in a single leap. As well as Australia, this species also breeds at New Caledonia, New Guinea, the Lesser Sundas, Java, Andaman and Christmas Islands (Indian Ocean). It straggles regularly to Macquarie Island and may now be resident there.

## The Brown Teal

*Anas aucklandica chlorotis* 48 cm.

This now rare New Zealand endemic, once widely distributed, is today reduced to populations in Northland, Great and Little Barrier Islands and Fiordland. None have been seen at Stewart Island since 1971 and the total population is estimated at about 1000. Allied to it are 2 flightless forms: one at the Auckland Islands, the other at Campbell Island.

The Brown Teal has an overall plumage of warm brown. The male has a dark brown head with greenish reflections, a white collar on the foreneck, a chestnut breast, vermiculated sides and a white patch on the flanks. The female is duller and lacks the white collar and white flanks.

The Brown Teal is both a fresh and saltwater bird and is largely crepuscular and nocturnal. It feeds on both animal and plant life and it dives well. The nominate form flies strongly but the 2 subantarctic forms are flightless, and have been so for a long time; their wings are small, their flight muscles are degenerated and they have only a small keel on the breast bone.

Brown Teal are strongly territorial. They nest in dense cover with a clutch of 5 to 7, but the nest is difficult to discover and little has been recorded about their breeding history in the wild. They respond well to captive breeding, however, and over the last few years numbers of captive birds have been released in suitable areas in an endeavour to save the species from extinction.

The Auckland Island and Campbell Island flightless forms are entirely marine. They, too, are largely nocturnal, spending their days skulking under cover, but they may be seen out in the daytime, paddling about on the bull kelp, though keeping a wary eye out for skuas, their principal and traditional predators.

## The Auckland Island Teal (Flightless Duck) *Photo 85*

*Anas aucklandica aucklandica* 43 cm.

This bird differs from the Brown Teal in that the male has no white collar. The wings are puny but the legs are robust and it runs over the rocks and kelp with great agility. It feeds on small animal life and algae such as sea lettuce. It is strongly territorial and some furious fights may be seen. Its call note is a reedy whistle. Skuas are the main enemy of Auckland Island Teal, and it is interesting to see their prompt reaction when one appears. Let a Giant Petrel or shag fly overhead and they take no notice; let a skua appear and they promptly dive. If caught in the open, they make all speed for the water, where they are safe, as both they and the skuas know. Skuas, incidentally, have a habit of standing quietly in the shadows of the forest edge, waiting for the unwary, and this may be how most are caught. Skua pellets and middens often contain skulls of these small endemic ducks.

On the main Auckland Island, the flightless teal is now extinct, exterminated by cats. It is still in good numbers on Adams, Disappointment, Ocean, Ewing and Rose Islands and there are a few on Enderby Island.

## The Campbell Island Teal

*Anas aucklandica nesiotis* 43 cm.

This subspecies was for long feared extinct, a victim of the substantial rat population of Campbell Island. In 1975, it was rediscovered by officers of the Wildlife Service, who managed to land on Dent Island — one of the offshore stacks. Its population is unknown.

## The New Zealand Shoveler

*Photos 81, 87*

*Anas rhynchotis variegata* 48 cm.

The New Zealand Shoveler is a race of the Australian Shoveler and is a dabbling duck, specialising in filtering out small animals from water by means of lamellae in the bill, on the same principle as that used by prions. The bill is large and spatulate and the bristle-like lamellae are easily seen along the edges. Shovelers eat insect larvae, snails, shrimps, pond weed and fine seeds. They do not eat grain or other large seed and they do not feed on pastures. Predominantly freshwater, they also frequent the coast and are quick to learn that salt water is normally a safe place to go during the shooting season.

In full breeding plumage, the Shoveler drake is a resplendent bird. The head is black glossed with green and there is a curved white line in front of each eye. The undersurface is chestnut and there is a white patch on the flanks. The upper wing coverts are powder-blue, the speculum green and the legs and feet orange. The female, except for the blue wing coverts, resembles a small Mallard.

Shovelers fly very fast indeed and a pair in tandem display flight — rocketing round and across a pond, twisting and banking, colours flashing in the sunlight — is a sight to see. Shovelers have a characteristic whistle of the wings in flight that makes them instantly identifiable.

Shovelers are silent birds; they do not quack, though when displaying on the water, they make *took-took* noises as they swim side by side, pumping their heads up and down as they go. They nest on the ground in damp situations, in short but dense cover. The clutch is 9 to 13 and the incubation period is 25 days. The drake remains attentive to his duck and, while she is incubating, may be seen quietly swimming on the pond not too far away. He escorts her back to the nest when she returns after feeding and when she comes off the 2 birds feed together.

## The Northern Shoveler

*Anas clypeata* 50 cm.

A very rare straggler from the Northern Hemisphere, there are 3 records of this duck in New Zealand — in 1968, 1969 and 1971. All were males in breeding plumage, with the head dark green, the breast white, the abdomen chestnut and the forewing pale blue.

## The Blue Duck

*Photo 88*

*Hymenolaimus malacorhynchos* 53 cm.

The Blue Duck has evidently been isolated in New Zealand for a very long time. It is a unique species with no obvious relationship to the ducks of other parts of the world. Slightly larger than a Grey Duck, it has an overall bluish-grey plumage, spotted on the breast with chestnut-red. The eye is yellow. The bill is off-white, contains filtering lamellae and has a black, flexible membrane at the tip. The bill is evidently well supplied with blood vessels, for, should you accidentally surprise a bird, the bill often flushes bright pink, much as the bill of an albatross will in a similar situation. The sexes are alike, except that the male is slightly larger and has brighter chestnut spots on the breast. Unlike other ducks, Blue Ducks can see directly forward. Where, for example, a Mallard will look first with one eye and then, if unsure, with the other, a Blue Duck will often gaze directly, in the manner of a Harrier.

The Blue Duck's home is the cascading, forest-fringed mountain stream. They prefer streams of medium size, avoiding the small and shallow side creeks and, also, especially if open country is involved, the wider rivers of the lower reaches. Blue Ducks like to be hemmed in by gorge and forest; not for them the open, tussock head basins or the grassy riverflats so fancied by the Paradise Duck. Blue Ducks demand fast, clear, highly oxygenated, fresh water.

Strongly territorial, Blue Ducks take over selected sections of their chosen streams and allow no other Blue Ducks into their domain. Over much of their range, no other kinds of ducks or other waterbirds occupy this particular habitat and, consequently, Blue Ducks usually have these mountain rivers entirely to themselves. Even in autumn and winter, when other ducks mostly congregate in flocks, Blue Ducks remain as pairs and family groups. They have their own favourite stretches of river and, should you at any time see a pair in a particular place, you can usually expect, months or even years later, on revisiting that place, to be greeted by a Blue Duck's whistle.

The whistle of the Blue Duck is one of the most nostalgia-arousing sounds of the New Zealand backblocks. Just as recollection of the Kea's clear, echoing cry evokes rocky bluffs and misty tops, so the recollection of the Blue Duck's whistle evokes bush-clad gorges, quiet pools and tumbling mountain streams. The whistle is the call of the male; females have a rattling note. When calling, both sexes stretch the head and neck forwards and downwards in a characteristic posture.

When they so desire, Blue Ducks can fly at speed, skimming in tandem with short, rapid wing-beats, low over the water. As a rule, however, they are reluctant to take wing, for they are the tamest of waterfowl. When disturbed, they usually simply swim out into the current and allow themselves to be swept into the rapids whence they tumble downstream to the next quiet pool. Once again in quiet water, they clamber out onto a rock in mid stream, wiggling their dumpy tails, whistling and rattling disapproval of the intrusion.

Blue Ducks dive expertly in the swift water gushing through small rapids, and much of their food — caddis fly larvae and the like — is obtained in this manner. Most of their feeding is done at night. During the day they spend much of their time hidden. Nests of the Blue Duck are hard to find and few have been reported. The usual clutch is 5 to 8 and incubation takes about a month. The ducklings take to the water soon after hatching and, from an early age, bob competently about in the swirling rapids. They dive with ease and, if harried, can remain submerged for a remarkable length of time, clinging with their feet to irregularities of the rocks. Blue Ducks with young have none of the tricks of distraction seen with other ducks: no broken-wing displays or floundering runs across the water. To escape danger, they simply lead the young into fast water and rapidly disappear downstream.

## The White-eyed Duck

*Aythya australis*

The White-eyed Duck is an Australian species with the habit of dispersing widely in times of drought. During these dispersals, it has colonised New Guinea, New Zealand and other islands, but these outlying colonisations have never proved to be permanent. After a few years, the birds dwindle in numbers and eventually disappear. At the present time, the White-eyed Duck, from being resident during the late 1800s, has become a rare straggler to these shores. It is a diving duck that dives for food in deep water and patters along the surface when taking wing. Its overall colour is brown and the male has a conspicuous white eye. Both sexes have a white rump, a white wing bar and a white underwing. The bill is dark and crossed near the tip by a whitish bar.

## The New Zealand Scaup *Photo 84*

*Aythya novaeseelandiae* 40 cm.

Often known as the Black Teal, the New Zealand Scaup is an alert, chubby, diving duck common on many clean, freshwater lakes and ponds in both the North and South Islands. It is a sociable bird, usually seen in small flocks or rafts of a dozen or more, chattering musically among themselves as they swim from one part of a pond to another. This species is specialised for diving and has large feet set well back. Consequently, it walks poorly and seldom ventures far from the water's edge. It flies with rapid wing-beats and patters along the surface when taking wing.

The male Scaup has a black head glossed with green and purple, an orange-yellow eye and a white bar on the wing. The body of the bird is a dark brownish-black. Females are duller and the eye is brown. New Zealand Scaup nest in dense cover near water and they sit very tightly indeed. In fact, until almost trodden on, they do not usually flush and so the nests are hard to find. The eggs are remarkably large for the size of the bird and the usual clutch is 5. The eggs are laid on alternate days and incubation, which commences with the last egg, takes 28 days. The male continues to attend his duck and, while she is incubating, may be seen floating quietly on the water nearby. The ducklings can dive as soon as they leave the nest, which is about 24 hours after hatching.

## The Australian Wood Duck *Photo 82*

*Chenonetta jubata* 45 cm.

A very rare straggler to New Zealand from Australia, there are 4 New Zealand records — 1910, and 3 in 1944 — of this beautiful duck. The sexes differ; the male has the head and neck brown, the body grey with fine lines on the flanks and the breast mottled brown and white; the female has the head brown with a white patch surrounding the eye, the body mottled brown and white and the wings grey.

## The Auckland Island Merganser

*Mergus australis* 58 cm.

A marine species confined to the Auckland Islands and now presumed extinct. Mergansers are fish-eating ducks with narrow saw-toothed bills and belong principally to the Northern Hemisphere. The Auckland Island Merganser has not been seen since 1905 and only about 20 specimens are known. It inhabited sheltered, coastal waters and the lower reaches of rivers and its extinction is presumably related, at least in part, to the liberation of cats and pigs. The sexes were similar: the head reddish-brown with a backward crest, the body grey with a white wing patch and the bill and feet orange-yellow.

# ACCIPITRIFORMES

Diurnal birds of prey. Two families: Hawks, Falcons.

## **Hawks and Eagles** Accipitridae

Diurnal birds of prey with hooked bills and powerful, grasping talons. Nostrils open through an unfeathered cere. Wings broad. Sexes alike. Females larger. Food entirely animal — alive or as carrion. Build own nests. Incubation by the female. Chicks downy. Eggs incubated from the first so the chicks are of different ages and the elder may persecute the younger — the so-called 'Cain and Abel conflicts'. *C.* 220 species, New Zealand 1.

### The Australasian Harrier *Photo 90*

*Circus approximans* 60 cm.

Harriers are long-winged, long-tailed, long-legged hawks, typically seen quartering the ground with lazy, soaring flight on upswept wings. The head is small and the feathers of the face are arranged in a disc, as in owls, to aid hearing. The Australasian Harrier occurs throughout New Zealand and also at the Chatham Islands. Elsewhere, it occurs in Australia, New Guinea, New Caledonia, the New Hebrides (Vanuatu), Loyalty, Fiji, Wallis and Tonga, and has been introduced to Tahiti and the Society Islands. It straggles to Samoa, Kermadec, Norfolk, Lord Howe, Auckland and Campbell Islands.

The overall plumage of the Harrier is brown. The undersurface is streaked, the tail is barred and the rump, in adults, is white. The legs and feet are yellow and the eye is brown in juveniles, yellow in adults. Eye colour is not a sex difference as once thought. As they grow older, Harriers become paler in plumage and truly old birds may be quite grey. Females are larger than males and have heavier and more powerful feet.

The Harrier, as an open country bird, has benefited greatly both from man's clearance of land and from his introduction of rabbits, mice, opossums, hedgehogs and other aliens which have increased its food supply, especially as roadside carrion. Harriers are catholic in their choice of animal food: insects, lizards, frogs, tadpoles, small birds and their eggs and nestlings are all among the items recorded.

Harriers nest on the ground towards the centre of dense stands of vegetation. Originally, no doubt, they nested principally in swamps and bracken fern, but in these days of intensive agriculture, they often do so in fields of wheat and other crops. Harriers are exceptionally shy and timid at the nest, deserting at the slightest provocation, so details of their nesting cycle have proved difficult to acquire.

Early in the season, Harriers may be seen displaying over their future nest sites, soaring and sweeping and calling with mewling notes. By September, many birds are carrying nest material. Harriers build a rough nest, little more than a collection of sticks and debris. The eggs are laid at irregular but usually 2-day intervals, though in this respect Harriers are totally unpredictable. I have known further eggs to appear after incubation has been in progress for a fortnight. The clutch varies from 3 to 7 and incubation begins with the first or second egg. It is rare to see more than 4 eggs hatch because by the time the fourth hatches, if it does, the eldest chick is some 8 days old and the parent is now concerned more with chicks than with eggs. As the chicks grow, the older chicks elbow their younger siblings away from food and the smaller chicks gradually disappear.

For the first 24 hours, Harrier chicks are weak and helpless and have difficulty even in lifting up their heads. During the first week, they are fed some 5 or 6 times a day and, from the start, the larger chicks obtain the lion's share of the food. At the end of the first week, the oldest chicks start to clamber over the side of the nest into the surrounding cover. They cannot yet stand but shuffle about on their tarsi. Although the youngest may have only just hatched, the parent now leaves the nest for longer and longer periods and at this time the youngest chick usually succumbs. During the second week, the chicks shuffle off the nest platform as soon as they are left unattended. Each has its own tunnel into the surrounding vegetation. They will attempt to feed themselves off scraps left at the nest platform but they lack the strength and have little success. Wing stretching movements are commenced. By the third week the oldest chick can stand and walk but it is clumsy and it falls frequently. Feathers are appearing and the chick spends much time nibbling at them. Feeding is now much less frequent and a meal will last a chick a good 12 hours. By the fourth week, the remaining 1 or 2 chicks are large. Their covering consists more of feathers than of down and they spend a great deal of time preening. They find the area at the back of the neck difficult to get to and attempts are made to stand on one leg so that they can scratch with the other, but they nearly always fall over. Flying movements of the wing begin.

By the fifth week, practically all down has disappeared and the chicks appear fully feathered, though the tail is still short. They can stand on one leg and can lift themselves momentarily into the air as they exercise the wings. For how long the chicks then remain dependent on the parents is not known.

## **Falcons** Falconidae

Diurnal birds of prey with hooked bills and grasping talons. Nostrils open through an unfeathered cere. Upper mandible toothed, lower notched. Sexes similar. Females larger. Wings long and narrow. Capable of great speed in stooping flight. Food animal, not taken as carrion. No true nest building. Incubation by female. Chicks downy, of different ages, but Cain and Abel conflicts absent. *C.* 60 species; New Zealand 2, 1 endemic.

## The New Zealand Falcon

*Photo 89*

*Falco novaeseelandiae* 45 cm.

The New Zealand Falcon, an endemic species, occurs in the central and southern parts of the North Island, over most of the South Island back country, and at Stewart Island. An isolated population occurs at the Auckland Islands and it is presumably from here that birds occasionally straggle to Campbell Island. A recent survey put the total population at between 3000 and 4500 pairs.

New Zealand Falcons vary greatly in size and plumage and not just because of differences between the sexes. Those birds inhabiting forest areas are generally smaller and darker than those that live in the open tussock valleys east of the Southern Alps. Females are always larger than their mates. The upperparts are black, barred with brown, the underparts ochre and buff, barred and striped with reddish-brown. The feathers of the thighs are rufous and there is a well-marked, black moustachial stripe. The legs and feet are yellow.

New Zealand Falcons are predators, principally on small birds. They nest mostly on the ground — under logs and overhanging rocks — but also on cliffs and on naturally occurring platforms of debris in trees. They make no true nest, merely a hollow which may look as though it has had material carried to it but apparently never has. They are totally fearless in defence of their nest and some sort of head protection is necessary when investigating them. More than one person has had his scalp opened by the raking hind claw of an infuriated falcon as it hurtled past.

The clutch is usually 4 and incubation (for 30 days) and care of the young is by the female only; she is fed during this period by her mate. The young hatch over a period of some days and so are of different ages. When small, they are fed bill-to-bill by the female who tears up the prey brought by her mate and offers pieces to each chick in turn. The gentleness of the hen bird with her chicks is delightful. Only the choicest pieces of prey are offered. Feathers and sinew — at least during the early days — are cast aside or eaten by the hen herself. She will hold out a small piece of liver or breast, her head so held that the chick can easily see and reach the titbit, and will then wait, with interested gaze, until the chick has quite finished, before offering the next piece. Among the chicks there is no ill-mannered demanding of attention; no elbowing of weaker siblings out of the way as there is with Harriers. Each gets its share.

As they get older, the chicks gradually become able to dismember prey for themselves. They fledge at about 6 weeks and are dependent on their parents for some time after they leave the nest (for how long I don't know), while they learn to hunt for themselves.

## The Nankeen Kestrel

*Falco cenchroides* 33 cm.

The Nankeen Kestrel is an Australian bird that has, over recent years, extended its range to colonise Lord Howe and Norfolk Islands. At the same time, stragglers appeared with increasing frequency in New Zealand and it was hoped that the bird might establish here also. So far that has not happened. Should it do so, it would be a welcome addition, for this is an attractive species. The uppersurface is 'nankeen' cinnamon brown and the undersurface white or pale buff. The tail of the male is pale grey, of the female russet, and in both there is a black bar near the tip. The legs and feet are orange-yellow.

Kestrels are also known as 'windhovers', from their supreme ability to hover on the wind as they scan the ground below. Should nothing be seen, they fly with a few rapid wing-beats for 30 or 40 metres to hover again. If prey is sighted, they drop by stages, hovering between each step, until a few metres above ground and the sudden final pounce. Food consists principally of lizards, mice, small birds and large insects, which last are usually immediately taken aloft to eat on the wing, held in one foot while the bird is hovering. Most of their hunting is done over open country, so the New Zealand pastoral scene should suit them well.

# GALLIFORMES

Game birds. Six families, 3 introduced to New Zealand: Partridges, Quails, Pheasants; Guineafowl; Turkeys.

## **Partridges, Quails, Pheasants** Phasianidae

A diverse group of birds noted for their eating qualities and traditionally hunted by all peoples. New World quails have bills with serrated edges, are usually crested. Old World quails, partridges, pheasants and allies lack serrated edges to the bill, often have spurs on the legs. All feed on the ground and eat both animal and vegetable matter. Most are gregarious. Nest on the ground; most lay large clutches. Incubation by the female. Young are downy, precocious and feed themselves. Egg-shells left in the nest. One hundred and seventy-four species; New Zealand 8, 7 introduced, 1 native now extinct.

### The Chukor

*Photo 93*

*Alectoris chukar* 33 cm.

Introduced in the 1920s, the Chukor is now widely distributed over the arid country east of the Southern Alps. Its natural range is from Manchuria and the Himalayas west to the Aegean. It is a species adapted to climatic extremes and rugged terrain, and in New Zealand is mostly found at higher altitudes, on rocky slopes clad with scattered scrub and tussock.

The Chukor is conspicuously marked on the flanks with chestnut and black bars over a cream background. A black line runs through the eye, down the neck and across the breast. The cheeks and throat are creamy-white, the top of the head is grey and the uppersurface is grey-brown. The bill and legs are bright red.

It is a characteristic of Chukor that they go uphill on foot and downhill on the wing. When startled, they go downhill like bullets. They nest on the ground, usually under a tussock, and the clutch ranges from 8 to 16. Only the female incubates. The incubation period is 22-24 days and the young are active soon after hatching. They stay with the parents over the winter.

### The Grey Partridge

*Photo 91*

*Perdix perdix* 30 cm.

Large numbers of Grey Partridges were liberated in 1962, but they did not establish, except perhaps in Southland where a few may still survive. The natural range of this species is Europe and Western Asia. The Grey Partridge is a plump, grey-brown bird with a reddish head and a grey neck. All males and some females have an inverted, russet-coloured, horseshoe-shaped mark on the breast. The upperparts are streaked and the flanks are barred. The bill and legs are blue-grey. Partridges are birds of varied country with woods and hedgerows. They do not take kindly to barbed-wired fences and intensively cultivated ground.

### The New Zealand Quail

*Coturnix novaezealandiae* 15 cm.

Extremely abundant in the early days of settlement, the New Zealand Quail became extinct about 1870. Why it should have disappeared so quickly is not clear. It is subspecifically related to the Australian Stubble Quail (*coturnix novaezealandiae pectoralis*), a species that is given to nomadic movements, and so the possibility of stragglers of the Australian race reaching New Zealand has to be kept in mind. The Stubble Quail is dark brown above, mottled with paler markings, and each feather has a conspicuous cream stripe down the centre. The throat is chestnut in the male and the breast and belly are white. The eye is red.

## The Brown Quail

*Synoicus ypsilophorus* 18 cm.

The Brown Quail is an Australian species (extending to New Guinea and the Lesser Sunda Islands) and was introduced during the 1860s. It is now widespread over the northern part of the North Island and has colonised a number of offshore islands from the Three Kings to the Aldermans. It is a bird of swamp margins and dense grass. The upperparts are brown, barred with black, each feather with a pale, thin, central stripe; the underparts are buff, barred with zigzag black bars. The eye is red and the bill blue-black. The Brown Quail nests on the ground and lays about 10 eggs. Incubation is by the female and the young are precocious and fly at an early age.

## The Bobwhite Quail

*Colinus virginianus* 23 cm.

Large numbers of this North American quail were liberated throughout the country in 1898–99. Few pockets, if any, have survived and there have been no confirmed sightings since the 1950s (Wairoa, Hawke's Bay). It is a small, plump quail with a conspicuous white eyebrow, white throat, chestnut crown and rufous breast. It gets the name Bobwhite from its call note.

## The California Quail

*Photo 92*

*Lophortyx californica brunnescens* 25 cm.

Introduced from North America during the 1860s, the California Quail has proved a successful colonist and is now a widespread and familiar bird in both the North and South Islands. Full description of its plumage is complex and, for recognition purposes, largely unnecessary, for the black, perky, forward-bobbing crest is diagnostic. It has a black face and throat, bordered by a white necklace, a grey breast, brown head, brown back, streaked flanks and a chestnut abdomen. Females are duller and have shorter crests.

California Quail are birds of scrublands with scattered trees and adapt well to man's activities. They freely enter gardens and are commonly seen when driving along country roads. They run fast on twinkling legs, taking off only at the last moment to rise with a whirr and then glide on stiff wings, seldom further than is necessary to reach cover. In autumn, very large coveys may occur. In spring their cheerful, 3-syllable, *Dick Vercoe* call has become a familiar sound.

California Quail nest on the ground, laying clutches of up to 16 eggs. Incubation is by the female and takes 22 days. The chicks are active soon after hatching and remain with their parents until the coveys break up after the winter.

## The Pheasant

*Phasianus colchicus* male 85 cm., female 60 cm.

Pheasants have been liberated as game birds in New Zealand since the 1840s. Generally speaking, they do not thrive well in this country and so the numbers are periodically boosted by the release of stock raised in game farms. Male pheasants are colourful and unmistakable. The head and neck are bottle green, as are the ear tufts, and the bare skin and wattles round the eye are red. The body plumage is basically chestnut, all the feathers scalloped with black. The tail is long and most birds have a white ring round the neck. Females are drab and brown and have shorter tails. Pheasants are woodland birds that dislike cold, wet, windy weather. They nest on the ground and the males are polygamous. Incubation and care of the young is by the female only. The clutch varies from 7 to 15 and the incubation period is 23-25 days. As with all members of the family, the young can fly from an early age, long before they are fully grown.

## Peafowl

*Pavo cristatus* 75 cm. plus tail of 1 m.

Native to India and Sri Lanka, Peafowl have been introduced to New Zealand as ornamental birds since the 1840s. Feral populations have established in Northland, Wanganui, Hawke's Bay and Gisborne districts. Little is known about these wild birds, for though easily domesticated, Peafowl in the wild state are shy and wary. They roost in trees and the males are polygamous. The nest is on the ground, the clutch is 3 to 5 and incubation is by the female.

## **Guineafowl** Numididae

Of African origin, the Tufted Guineafowl (*Numida meleagris*) has long been domesticated. In New Zealand, domestic escapes occurred from the early days of settlement and there are now a number of feral populations in both islands. Guineafowl are globular birds with thin necks, small, unfeathered heads and an overall grey plumage covered with white spots. They are gregarious and noisy and run well. They roost in trees at night and are extremely wary in the wild state.

## **Turkeys** Meleagrididae

Turkeys (2 species) belong to North and Central America. One species (*Meleagris gallopavo*) has long been domesticated. As with the Guineafowl, domestic escapes occurred in New Zealand from the earliest days of settlement. Most of these feral populations have since died out and the present position of wild turkeys in New Zealand is unclear.

# GRUIFORMES

A diversified group of mostly marshland birds. Eleven families, 2 represented in New Zealand: Cranes; Rails, Gallinules and Coots.

## **Cranes** Gruidae

Tall, stately, long-legged birds of open plains, noted for their dancing displays and trumpeting voices. The Australian Brolga, *Grus rubicunda*, 110 centimetres, has been recorded twice (1947 and 1968) as a wind-blown straggler to New Zealand. An overall grey bird with an area of naked, red skin on the head, it closely resembles the Sarus Crane, *Grus antigone*, now also in Australia. In the Sarus Crane, the naked, red skin of the head extends down to include the upper part of the neck. At a distance, the 2 species are very difficult to tell apart, so there is some recent doubt as to which species has actually been seen here.

## **Rails, Gallinules and Coots** Rallidae

Mostly marshland birds. All can swim and dive. Many are agile climbers. Most fly well though all seem reluctant to do so. Rails have reached most of the world's remote islands, where many have subsequently become flightless. All cock their tails as they walk. Sexes are alike. Many are largely nocturnal and most are vocal at dusk. They nest on or close to the ground. Both sexes incubate and both care for the young. The chicks are downy and the down in all species is black. They are fed bill-to-bill by the parents. Rails are mostly secretive and skulking, with laterally compressed bodies for slipping through dense vegetation, and are cryptically coloured in browns and greys. Gallinules have the bill extended to form a frontal shield and very long toes to support them on floating vegetation. Coots also have frontal shields, are aquatic, dive for their food and have the toes lobed like grebes. Coots form large flocks in winter and, when taking wing, patter along the surface of the water like Scaup. One hundred and thirty-two species; New Zealand 11, 3 endemic, 1 extinct.

### The Banded Rail

*Photo 95*

*Rallus philippensis assimilis* 30 cm.

In New Zealand, the Banded Rail is most often reported from northern North Island coastal regions, including some offshore islands, from the coastal saltings of Nelson and Golden Bay and from those Muttonbird Islands off Stewart Island that are Weka-free. Wekas are predators of ground-nesting birds' eggs and soon eradicate species such as Banded Rails and Fernbirds from small islands. Elsewhere, Banded Rails occur in Australia and South-east Asia and on islands in the south-west Pacific east to Samoa. Well-marked races once inhabiting the Chatham Islands and Macquarie Island are now extinct, following the introduction of cats, rats and Wekas.

The Banded Rail is a colourful bird. It has a grey throat, a chestnut band through the eye and another across the chest. The upperparts are brown and the underparts conspicuously marked with alternating white and black transverse stripes. The Banded Rail is most often seen at dusk, feeding on the mudflats of mangrove inlets. On the Muttonbird Islands, it may be seen at any time of day fossicking about in the leaf litter of the forest floor. A very wary and suspicious bird, it bolts at all speed for the nearest cover at the first hint of danger. It nests in dense vegetation, with a clutch of 5 or 6, and the incubation period is 25 days. The chicks are clothed in black down and leave the nest when a few hours old.

## The Auckland Island Rail

*Rallus pectoralis muelleri* 21 cm.

This is a subspecies of the variously named Pectoral, Lewin or Slate-breasted Rail of New Guinea, Eastern Australia and Tasmania. The Auckland Island race has been seldom seen, the last occasion being in 1966, when one was brought back alive to the Mount Bruce Native Bird Reserve. It is smaller and darker than the Banded Rail and lacks the chestnut band on the breast. The crown and nape are chestnut, the uppersurface black and brown, the throat and breast grey and the abdomen black, barred with thin, white lines.

## The Chatham Island Rail

*Rallus modestus*

Formerly found on Mangere and Pitt Islands in the Chatham Islands, this rail was extinct by 1900 owing to the introduction of cats and to overzealous collecting.

## The Weka

*Photo 94*

*Gallirallus australis* 50 cm.

There are 4 races of this well-known, flightless, endemic rail. All are about the size of a domestic fowl and have an overall brown plumage streaked with black. The wings are rudimentary but the legs and feet are strong and the bill powerful. Their voice is a far-carrying *coo-eet, coo-eet*. The North Island Weka has more grey on the underparts and brownish rather than reddish legs, and, with the exception of liberations in North Auckland and Coromandel, is found only near Gisborne. In the South Island, the principal subspecies, the Western Weka, occurs west of the divide and in South Westland and Fiordland and has a black phase. East of the divide there was once a race known as the Buff Weka. It is now extinct over its original range, but in 1905 was introduced to the Chatham Islands where it is now plentiful. Efforts are at present being made to re-establish the bird in Canterbury, by liberations from the Chatham Island population. Finally, at Stewart Island there is a small race, also with a black phase. This race was introduced to Macquarie Island where it thrives and is a pest.

Wekas walk with measured pace and flicking tail and are tame, curious and larcenous. They run fast and can swim. They have a keen eye for strange and shiny objects, and around campsites and habitations will make off with everything movable that takes their fancy. They eat a great variety of vegetable and animal food, including the eggs and young of any ground-nesting bird they may find. Wekas introduced onto offshore islands have decimated and often exterminated local breeding species, and their presence is often one of the major problems in managing offshore island sanctuaries.

In suitable localities, Wekas will breed all the year round and have 4 clutches a year. They nest on the ground in a variety of situations but usually under dense cover. The usual clutch is 3 to 5 and the incubation period about 25 days. The chicks leave the nest soon after hatching and when small are attractively covered in jet black down. They are looked after by both parents for about 2 months and are then driven away when the parents commence to nest again.

## The Spotless Crake

*Porzana tabuensis plumbea* 20 cm.

Also known as the Sooty Rail, the Spotless Crake is widespread throughout the south-west Pacific, Australia and New Zealand. In New Zealand, it occurs from the Kermadec Islands to Stewart Island, and at the Chatham Islands. It is a small, slate-coloured bird with white barring under the tail and a brilliant red eye. It is secretive and seldom seen, though its clicking and rattling call notes may be heard at dusk from swamps. It nests in dense swamp vegetation, usually *carex* or raupo, and it starts nesting in August. A number of nests are built, one of which is eventually used for laying. The incubation period is 22 days and the young leave the nest when a few hours old. Nests have been found from August to February, so possibly 2 broods are reared.

At the Kermadec Islands, the place where I have had most success at finding these crakes, they were to be seen on the offshore islets in every imaginable variety of habitat, both by day and by night. On the main island, Raoul, they have been exterminated by cats. On Meyer Island, they were to be seen running deftly along the branches of trees to obtain insects from around the nests of Noddy Terns and from the crevices of the bark. They explored petrel burrows without hesitation, whether occupied or not. They took insects from the tide wrack and from the litter of the forest floor, and they collected the spillage around the nests of Grey Ternlets after the chicks had been fed. Indeed, they made use of every possible source of food. They were always alert and wary and, at one's slightest movement, vanished like wraiths. They were most difficult birds to come to terms with and even in the confines of a small island, they managed to keep their breeding places hidden.

In the North Island, Spotless Crakes nest in swamps from August to December. They build a substantial structure of grass and sedge, often at some height above water level. The usual clutch is 2 or 3 and the incubation period about 23 days. The chicks are covered in black down and are cared for by both parents.

## The Marsh Crake

*Porzana pusilla affinis* 18 cm.

This small crake is also widespread throughout New Zealand (and much of Europe, Africa, Asia and Australia) and is, if anything, even more secretive than the Spotless Crake. It may be found in many swampy areas — I once saw 10 in an afternoon along the raupo belt of Lake Hayes — but is so retiring that not until 1974 was a nest discovered and described in New Zealand.

The Marsh Crake is the smallest of the New Zealand rails and is a beautifully marked species. The bill and legs are yellowish-green and the eye is red. The upperparts are rufous, the head and underparts blue-grey and the flanks are barred with white and black.

This species swims well and scuttles up and down raupo leaves like a mouse. Its call note is a 'click' but it has also been described as having notes similar to the croaking of frogs.

As mentioned, the nest of the Marsh Crake has only once been described in New Zealand, with a clutch of 7. Elsewhere, the clutch is 5 to 7 and the incubation period 20 days. Most nests are placed in clumps of rush in shallow water. The chicks have black down like other rail chicks and fly at about 7 weeks. Over the rest of the Old World this species is known as Baillon's Crake.

## The Pukeko

*Photo 98*

*Porphyrio porphyrio melanotus* 51 cm.

Under various names, but especially Purple Swamphen, this brilliantly coloured bird occurs throughout most of the Old World. In New Zealand, it is one of the species that has benefited from man's clearance of land for agriculture and is now widespread over most of the country. Although at first sight quite unlike the typical rails, the bird betrays its relationship by its tail-flicking walk, its black downy chicks and many aspects of its daily and breeding behaviour. The overall plumage of the Pukeko is royal blue, shading to black on the head, wings, abdomen and thighs. The bill and shield are scarlet; the legs and feet orange-red. The under-tail coverts are white and are conspicuously flirted with every step the bird takes.

The Pukeko is omnivorous, eating a wide variety of plant and animal foods. It holds rush stems in one foot, in the manner of a parrot, while it eats the ends and it will eat the eggs of ground-nesting birds, especially ducks, should it stumble across them. Most of its food is vegetable but insects, frogs, worms and other aquatic animals are taken.

Pukekos are ungainly birds yet remarkably competent in what they undertake. They look clumsy on water, yet swim well. They look ridiculous in flight, yet can fly great distances and have turned up as stragglers on many outlying islands. They run well, in a shambling manner, and can perch in trees.

The breeding behaviour of the Pukeko is complex. They breed as conventional pairs but also in groups that may number up to 5 or 6 birds. Pukekos are strongly territorial. At the end of winter, pairs and groups begin to form and the swamps become noisy with unmusical screams as territorial boundaries are established and vigorously contested. Within group territories, social hierarchies are established and by August or September most groups have begun the construction of nest platforms. Pukekos breed throughout the summer, rearing 2 broods.

Those birds nesting as conventional pairs lay from 3 to 7 eggs. The eggs are laid daily and the incubation period is about 24 days. Incubation commences about halfway through laying, so the chicks hatch over a period of 2 or 3 days. Both parents incubate.

Those birds nesting as groups lay from 3 to as many as 18 eggs, with eggs being laid by 2 or 3 females. These may be deposited all in the same nest or in 2 separate nest-bowls situated side by side. All adults of the group may take at least some part in the incubation, though most is done by the dominant birds.

The chicks are covered with black down and leave the nest when about 24 hours old. They are shepherded and fed by their parents — or various members of the group — for about 2 months, and separate nest-like platforms are often made to brood the chicks at night. When the young are about 2 months old, the adults usually nest again and when this second clutch hatches, the young of the first brood may help in feeding those of the second.

## The Takahe

*Photo 101*

*Notornis mantelli* 63 cm.

The rediscovery of the Takahe in the Murchison Mountains of Fiordland in 1948 is one of the dramatic stories of New Zealand ornithology. Prior to that, only 4 specimens were known and the bird had not been seen for 50 years. The present population of Takahe is about 200 birds, a dangerously low figure for birds in a marginal environment competing against introduced herbivores and predators.

The Takahe is flightless and resembles a massive Pukeko. It has a very strong, red bill and sturdy, red legs and feet. Its colouring is brilliant: iridescent blue on the body, green on the wings and back.

Except when forced to lower levels by the snows of winter, the Takahe lives above bushline. It is vegetarian and its principal food is snow tussock which it pulls out and holds in one foot, like a parrot, eating the succulent base and discarding the rest. The resultant heaps of discarded ends have a character diagnostic of the presence of the bird. In winter it is largely reliant on the rhizomes of the water fern, *Hypolepis*.

The Takahe is strongly territorial and requires a large area to breed successfully. Territories have been measured ranging from 3 to 70 hectares. Eggs are normally laid from mid-October to late December and the usual clutch is 2. The incubation period is 30 days and both sexes incubate. The chicks are covered in jet black down and are active soon after hatching. They are cared for by both parents but their winter survival is low, principally because deer have so browsed the upper levels of the bush and adjacent tussock that little accessible food remains to the birds when they are forced into the bush by snow.

Efforts to rear the Takahe in captivity have run into many problems. In the long term, the answer must lie in the provision of good habitat; given that, the birds will look after themselves. To that end, birds have been transferred to Maud Island in Cook Strait and efforts are being made to eradicate or at least reduce the number of deer in the Murchison Mountains, for it is now proved that one of the main threats to Takahe over their present range is competition by deer for winter food, in particular, 2 varieties of snow tussock. Also being tried is topdressing of selected areas with fertiliser so as to increase the nutrient value of the plants.

## The Dusky Moorhen *Photo 97*

*Gallinula tenebrosa* 37 cm.

A very rare straggler from Australia, the Dusky Moorhen has been recorded once in New Zealand, at Lake Hayes in 1968. It looks rather like a small, dull, slate-coloured coot with a red bill and a red shield. The bill has a yellow tip.

## The Black-tailed Native Hen *Photo 100*

*Gallinula ventralis* 35 cm.

There have been 2 certain records (1923 and 1957) of this very rare straggler from Australia. The upperparts are bronzy-brown, the underparts blue-grey, the upper mandible and shield pea green, and the lower mandible red, green at the tip. The legs and feet are red and the eye golden yellow. This is a nomadic species that could well colonise the country.

## The Australian Coot *Photo 96*

*Fulica atra australis* 40 cm.

The Australian Coot is one of the many Australian species that have found living space in New Zealand during recent years. It was first reported breeding (on Lake Hayes) in 1958 and since then has become firmly established in many parts of the country.

Coots are aquatic birds that spend most of their lives on still waters. The Australian Coot has a black plumage, a conspicuous white bill and shield and olive-green legs. It swims well, bobbing its head back and forth with each thrust of the legs. It dives with ease and much of its food is obtained in this manner. It flies strongly and patters along the water when taking wing.

Coots are territorial birds, brooking no trespass by other coots, and are aggressive to other species. The nest is a platform of weed and debris constructed just above water level and their normal clutch is 5 to 7. Incubation, by both sexes, takes about 21 days and commences before the clutch is complete, so the chicks hatch over a period of some 48 hours. During their first few days of life, coot chicks have a striking appearance. The bill is white, the base of the bill and shield is scarlet, the crown of the head is blue and the down of the face, neck and upper chest is orange. The rest of the down is black. These colours are soon lost, and when a few days old the chicks are jet black all over. The chicks can swim soon after hatching but, unlike scaup, are unable to dive in their downy plumage. They are dependent on their parents for 4 or 5 weeks.

The Australian Coot is a race of a species widespread over Europe, India, Asia and Australia. Where numbers are large, coots form flocks of considerable size in winter, often occupying ornamental lakes in city gardens and becoming remarkably tame. Their voice is a loud, explosive *kut* (hence the name), sounding at a distance rather like wood being hit with an axe. They are birds of lowland waters and feed on both vegetable and animal matter.

# CHARADRIIFORMES

Waders, Skuas, Gulls, Terns and allies. Sixteen families, 8 represented in New Zealand.

## **Oystercatchers** Haematopodidae

Conspicuous black or black and white birds with red legs and bills. The bills are flattened from side to side and are used to pry off and lever open cockles, mussels and other bivalves (including, occasionally, rock oysters). Cosmopolitan; 6-8 species, depending on the classification adopted; New Zealand 3, 2 endemic.

### The South Island Pied Oystercatcher

*Photo 102*

*Haematopus ostrelagus finschi* 46 cm.

During the breeding season, South Island Pied Oystercatchers are one of the most conspicuous birds of South Island riverbeds and pastures east of the Southern Alps. After breeding, the birds move to the coast and also migrate north to form huge flocks on the tidal estuaries of Nelson and the North Island.

This oystercatcher has a clear-cut plumage pattern that does not vary. It has a black head, neck, upper back, wings, tail and chest, with a white wing bar, a white lower back and white underparts. The bill and eyes are red and the legs and feet pink.

South Island Pied Oystercatchers are one of the first of the local migrants to return inland in spring and they show great faithfulness to remembered sites, returning to the same places each year and making the riverbeds ring with their piping parties and *kleeping* calls. Oystercatcher piping parties are a display peculiar to the family and usually involve 3 birds: with bills pointed to the ground and shoulders hunched, the birds run together, veering this way and that, all the while uttering long, trilling calls. After a few minutes, the party breaks up and the odd birds flies away.

The nest is a simple scrape on open, flat, not too cluttered ground, usually next to a piece of driftwood or a conspicuous stone, and is lined with a few bits of broken stick and debris. Most eggs are laid in September and October and the normal clutch is 2 or 3. The eggs are laid on alternate days and incubation, by both sexes, takes 25-30 days. The chicks take about 48 hours to chip out of the egg and are active soon after hatching. When they are small they are dependent on the parents for food but soon learn to fend for themselves. They grow rapidly and are independent at about 5 weeks.

Oystercatchers with small young react noisily to human approach. With eggs, their response varies. Some sneak off while you are still some distance away, to run or walk 30 or 40 metres before hiding behind an old log or other projection, while keeping an eye on proceedings. Most, however, react noisily, running up and displaying with dragging wing and fanned, depressed tail. If this does not have the desired effect, they often then turn away, as if giving up all intention of dissembling, and shuffle down in some likely place, as though settling on a nest — all the while keeping a calculating eye on the intruder to assess whether or not he is impressed. If not, they get up and try a different place. False brooding can be a most realistic performance.

The South Island Pied Oystercatcher is classified as a race of an oystercatcher that occurs also in Europe, Asia and Australia and, like it, probably does not breed until 3 years old. Immatures remain in flocks in northern harbours for at least their first year, before returning to establish territories on South Island breeding grounds.

## The Variable Oystercatcher

*Photo 99*

*Haematopus unicolor* 48 cm.

The Variable Oystercatcher is a larger bird than the South Island Pied Oystercatcher and is purely coastal. It has 2 main plumage phases: an all-black phase and a pied phase. Between the 2 are various intermediates. The black phase is black all over and has a red bill, red eyes and pink legs, and is the dominant form in the south. The pied phase resembles a South Island Pied Oystercatcher but the demarcation line on the breast between black and white is indistinct, as is the wing bar. Intermediates show varying degrees of black mottling on the undersurface, ranging from mostly white to almost entirely black. Females are larger than males and have longer bills.

Variable Oystercatchers are sedentary. They flock after breeding but do not migrate. They are more approachable birds than South Island Pied Oystercatchers and they breed later. They occur on both rocky and sandy coasts, nesting not far above high tide mark among beach debris or on rocky outcrops, and sometimes on small rocky islets just offshore. The clutch is normally 3 and they rarely nest before November or December. At Stewart Island, the black-phased birds behave like Chatham Island Oystercatchers, nesting under the cover of rocky overhangs and in shallow caves.

## The Chatham Island Oystercatcher

*Photo 103*

*Haematopus chathamensis* 48 cm.

This is one of the world's rare birds with a total population of 25-30 pairs. It has the South Island Pied Oystercatcher's plumage pattern — though showing less white — and the Variable Oystercatcher's approachable, non-migratory, late-nesting behaviour. It has a heavier and shorter bill than the mainland forms and heavier feet. Juvenile birds have lavender-grey legs and a conspicuous black tip to the bill.

Chatham Island Oystercatchers breed successfully only on the outer islands of South East, Mangere and Star Keys. On the main island and Pitt Island, the eggs and young fall prey to introduced Wekas and cats. They nest mostly under cover — under bushes or overhanging rocks and in caves — but also among beach debris. Possibly, the tendency to nest under cover is related to the drop-in of petrels at night and to the high density of skuas, for it is notable that the Shore Plover (which is also a member of a family that normally nests in the open) nests in similar situations.

The normal clutch is 2 or 3 and, like the Variable Oystercatchers, they nest late in the season, with eggs in November or December.

## **Plovers and Dotterels** Charadriidae

A cosmopolitan family of small to medium-sized waders with the bill shorter than the head and slightly swollen at the tip. Plumage boldly patterned. Sexes alike. Gregarious when not breeding. Many are migratory. Those migrating to New Zealand from the Northern Hemisphere have distinct breeding and non-breeding plumages; the former colourful, but rarely seen in this country, the latter nondescript. Sixty-three species; New Zealand 14, 4 endemic.

### The Spur-winged (Masked) Plover *Photo 104*

*Vanellus miles novaehollandiae* 38 cm.

The Australian Spur-winged Plover colonised New Zealand about 1930 when stragglers, blown across the Tasman, successfully established in Southland. Since then, they have gradually spread northwards and now occupy most of the open country of the South Island and much of that of the North Island.

The Spur-winged Plover is brown above and white below, and has a black crown and hindneck and a black collar. It has a yellow bill, conspicuous yellow wattles on the face, long, red legs and a yellow spur at the bend of the wing. The tail is crossed at the tip by a black bar and the flight feathers are black, giving a distinctive wing pattern in flight. The sexes are alike. Unlike most wading birds, Spur-winged Plovers do not moult into an eclipse plumage but retain the same pattern all year. They have a buoyant, rather heron-like flight and often suddenly 'tumble' in the air. They are alert and noisy, with harsh, rattling calls, and may often be heard flying about and calling at night.

Spur-winged Plovers are birds of open country, especially short grasslands near water. In New Zealand, they found a vacant niche on agricultural pastureland and are now a common and conspicuous farmland bird, especially in Southland and Otago where numbers have become substantial. They are essentially sedentary birds, staying close to their chosen grounds all year, though collecting in flocks in autumn, and their spread up the country has been mostly by contiguity rather than by leapfrogging.

Spur-winged Plovers often nest early. In Southland, many have eggs in July. The nest is a depression in the ground lined with dry grass and the normal clutch is 4. Both parents incubate and the period is 28 days. The young are shepherded by both parents. In Australia, Spur-winged Plovers resort readily to broken-wing distraction displays and may make diving attacks on man, but in New Zealand, neither behaviour is seen to any extent, though the birds mob Harriers and Magpies at all times of the year.

### The Pacific Golden Plover

*Pluvialis fulva* 25 cm.

The Pacific Golden Plover breeds in north-east Siberia and western Alaska and, after breeding, migrates to the Pacific, New Zealand, Australia and Malaysia. In New Zealand, it may regularly be found at favoured coastal localities from Parengarenga to Bluff, and it has reached the Chatham and Auckland Islands. It is a plump, alert bird with an upright stance, a rounded head, a high forehead and a short bill. In breeding plumage, it is black below and spangled gold above. In winter plumage as seen here (except for occasional individuals just after arrival or just before departure), it is mottled brown above and fawn below, shading to white on the belly. It has a white eyebrow but no wing bar.

On the shoreline, Golden Plovers tend to keep to themselves and are seen as small parties in straggling lines along the water's edge. They have the habit of moving off the estuaries to feed on adjacent pastures and may here be joined by Turnstones. They fly rapidly and with dash and are talkative in flight, calling to one another with clear musical whistles — hence 'Whistling Plover'. They delight in fast, precision manoeuvres in which they twist and turn and dive together with sudden changes of direction on slim, pointed wings. Golden Plovers are seldom vocal on the ground and, when they touch down, it is noticeable that all sound abruptly ceases. Wary and difficult to approach, they are the fourth most common migrant wader to reach New Zealand.

## The Grey Plover

*Pluvialis squatarola* 28 cm.

The Grey Plover breeds throughout the Arctic and, on migration, reaches all continents. In New Zealand, it is a rare bird nearly always seen alone. It is similar in stance, shape and winter plumage to the Golden Plover, with the same high forehead, but is larger and has a bigger bill. In flight, it shows a black patch on the underwing — the axillaries — which is diagnostic, a white wing bar and a white rump. In breeding plumage, it turns black below and spangled silver above. Unlike the Golden Plover, this species is unlikely to be seen away from the shoreline.

## The New Zealand Dotterel

*Photos 112, 114*

*Charadrius obscurus* 27 cm.

The New Zealand Dotterel is an endemic species with a curiously discontinuous distribution. One population inhabits the sandy beaches of Northland and some offshore islands, the other the bleak, windswept, tundra-like tops of the central high country of Stewart Island. The species collects in flocks in autumn and winter, but it does not migrate. Counts of these winter flocks indicate a population of about 1200 birds in the north, 250 at Stewart Island.

In breeding plumage, New Zealand Dotterels are brown above and chestnut-red below, the females duller. In winter they turn whitish underneath. They have no breast bands. At all times, New Zealand Dotterels are remarkably and conspicuously tame. Winter flocks may be approached to within a few metres, while nesting birds are so completely fearless as to make broken-wing displays actually at one's feet.

At Stewart Island, where my photographs were taken, their nesting habitat is inhospitable in the extreme. A few birds breed on the sandy stretches of Mason Bay on the western coast, but most are found in the mountains above bushline. This is bleak, windswept country characterised by granite outcrops interspersed with tarns, stunted scrub and bog. Few details of the life history of these southern birds have been recorded, owing to the remoteness of their habitat. The nests we found (early October) were in the lee of a tussock and were well formed, using more material than one normally expects of dotterels. The clutch was 3 and we saw both sexes incubating. My wife and I twice visited the nesting area, which was a good 2 hours' climb from our camp, spending about 5 hours there each time. On neither occasion did any of the off-nest birds appear, so the birds evidently sit for long hours at a stretch. The off-nest birds, we later discovered, congregated on the tidal mudflats of Cook's Arm some 5 kilometres distant, the only mudflats in the area.

In the North Island, the nests are mostly in sand dunes and eggs have been found from September to January, with a normal clutch of 3 and an incubation period of 28–31 days. Both sexes incubate and the young become independent when 6 or 7 weeks old.

## The Red-kneed Dotterel

*Erythrogonys cinctus* 18 cm.

The Red-kneed Dotterel is an Australian endemic of the arid inland and has been recorded in New Zealand once, in 1976. It has a black head, a white throat, a black breast band and white abdomen. The uppersurface is brown and the legs grey with red 'knees'. It is an alert bird, difficult to stalk. The chances of it turning up again in this country are remote.

## The Ringed Plover

*Charadrius hiaticula* 19 cm.

The Ringed Plover breeds across northern Eurasia and Greenland, and migrates to Africa and Southern Asia. There is one New Zealand record, at Miranda, 1970–71. This is a small plover with the diagnostic combination of orange legs and a black-tipped orange bill. The undersurface is white with a black breast band (poorly defined or incomplete in winter), and in flight it shows a white wing bar.

## The Red-capped Dotterel

*Charadrius ruficapillus* 15 cm.

The Red-capped Dotterel is an Australian endemic, closely related to the widely distributed Kentish Plover (*C. alexandrinus*). In 1947, a female was found mated with a Banded Dotterel on the Ashley riverbed near Christchurch. The eggs were fertile and the chicks showed characters of both parents. Red-capped Dotterels have been seen since on the Ashley and also in Manukau Harbour. It is a small dotterel, pale brown above and white below. The forehead is white and the top of the head and the nape are rusty red. There is a black line from the bill through the eye and the bill and legs are black. Females are duller and without the chestnut colour on the head.

## The Banded Dotterel

*Photos 105, 107*

*Charadrius bicinctus* 18 cm.

The endemic Banded Dotterel is the common dotterel of New Zealand, found the length of the country in both inland and coastal habitats. It breeds at the Chatham Islands and a distinct race inhabits the Auckland Islands. During the breeding season it is most common in inland South Island districts east of the Southern Alps. After breeding, inland Banded Dotterels move to the coast where they form flocks. Some stay in the South Island but most move north and others migrate across the Tasman to Australia, where flocks of up to 1000 birds have been seen. Of recent years, they have occurred regularly at Fiji and they are seen on passage at Norfolk and Lord Howe Islands.

In breeding plumage, Banded Dotterels are instantly identified by the diagnostic presence of 2 bands across the lower neck and breast: the upper one narrow and black, the lower one broad and chestnut. The uppersurface is brown and the undersurface white. The forehead is white and there may or may not be a white eyebrow. The bill is black and the legs and feet are greenish. Males are more richly coloured than females and slightly larger. In winter plumage, the breast bands disappear or become much faded; juveniles have no bands.

Banded Dotterels return to their breeding grounds in August, and in inland South Island districts, where winters can seem never-ending, they are a welcome sign of spring. They are faithful to remembered territories and I have one instance of a pair that used the identical nest-scrape 3 years in succession. They nest on dry ground where visibility is unobstructed and, on riverbeds, prefer those parts that have for many years been undisturbed by flood and are settled and overgrown with carpet plants and stunted grasses. In such places, they excavate a hemispherical cup roughly the size of half a tennis ball. The eggs are laid on alternate days to a clutch of 3 and, as each is laid, tiny stones and pieces of lichen or other dry vegetation are packed around so that when the clutch is complete, the eggs are contained in a cavity that has been half or three-quarters filled with packing. A few days later, the packing is flush with the surface and only a very small segment of the upper curve of each egg remains exposed. The end result is a marvellous example of protective camouflage. Not all nests are as well made as these and on stony places or coastal beaches they simply make a scrape with a little material added.

Banded Dotterels nest from August to December, but October is the main breeding month. Both sexes incubate and the incubation period is normally 25 days. As incubation advances, the male takes a larger and larger share and he is usually at the nest when the chicks hatch. The chicks can chip from the egg at great speed. I remember arriving one afternoon at a nest I had under observation to find 2 wet, recently hatched chicks and an egg with a tiny, barely discernible, pinhole 'star'. Twelve minutes later, the chick was hatched, and the adult carried the eggshells away. Once hatched, the chicks find their feet almost as rapidly and the parent has a bumpy time indeed as the youngsters heave and wriggle underneath it. Most chicks make wobbly forays after an hour. At 2 hours, they are ranging in ever-widening circles. At 3 hours, they are off down the beach on twinkling legs.

The subspecies at the Auckland Islands is a larger and heavier bird, weighing about 80 grams as against 60 grams. It breeds on the higher ground of Adams Island and possibly on the main island (though the presence of cats on the latter has to be considered). After breeding, it moves north to Enderby Island where it spends the winter on the Derry Castle Reef. The total population is about 150 birds.

## The Mongolian Dotterel

*Charadrius mongolus* 19 cm.

The Mongolian Dotterel breeds in eastern Asia and migrates south as far as Australia. In New Zealand it is a rare straggler; only 1 or 2 a year. In breeding plumage, this is a most elegant dotterel, with a chestnut nape, a black face and a broad chestnut breast band, edged black above. In eclipse plumage, as seen here, it looks very like a winter- or immature-plumaged Banded Dotterel, differing only in its slightly heavier and longer bill, darker legs and whiter face, with a dark patch below and behind the eye.

## The Large Sand Dotterel

*Charadrius leschenaulti* 22 cm.

This species breeds in central Asia from Mongolia west to Turkey and winters south to Africa and Australia. In New Zealand, it is a rare but regular straggler. In breeding plumage, it is similar to the Mongolian Dotterel. While in eclipse plumage, it looks very like non-breeding Mongolian and Banded Dotterels. It is larger than the Banded Dotterel, has longer legs, a white forehead, a heavier bill and a blackish patch in front of the eye. The underparts are white with a grey or slightly tawny wash at the sides of the neck.

## The Oriental Dotterel

*Charadrius veredus* 25 cm.

The Oriental Dotterel breeds in North China and Mongolia and winters south to northern Australia where it is common. In New Zealand, it is a very rare straggler of irregular occurrence. It is a notably long-legged bird in comparison with the other dotterels and, at rest, its wing tips cross over above the tail. In breeding plumage, it has a broad chestnut breast band edged black below. In winter plumage, it resembles other winter-plumaged dotterels, except for its stance and long, yellowish legs. It prefers inland habitats to coastal ones.

## The Black-fronted Dotterel

*Photo 106*

*Charadrius melanops* 18 cm.

The Black-fronted Dotterel, an Australian endemic, was first recorded in New Zealand in 1954, near Napier. Since then, it has become firmly established on the riverbeds of Hawke's Bay, the southern part of the North Island and the northern South Island. By 1980, it had spread south to Central Otago and in 1981 was found nesting near Alexandra. It is a small dotterel with distinctive markings. The uppersurface is brown and the undersurface white, crossed by a conspicuous, black, V-shaped breast band. A black line runs through the eye, and the eye is surrounded by a bright-red eye-ring. The bill is scarlet with a black tip and the legs are pink. Unlike most waders, it does not have a dull eclipse plumage but retains the same dress all year.

Black-fronted Dotterels are birds of stony riverbeds, over which they run at great speed. They have a peculiar jerky and dipping flight and when courting indulge in fast aerial chases, uttering churring call notes. They bob the head frequently when standing, and have a habit, when they do not wish to be seen, of hunching up and turning back towards you, whereupon they vanish into the background. They nest on the ground, usually near the water's edge, making a scrape lined with small stones, and the normal clutch is 3. In New Zealand, nests have been found from September to January. Both sexes incubate and they display freely with broken wing when approached. Black-fronted Dotterels do not flock to great extent after breeding, but mostly remain on their chosen grounds all year. They have large eyes and in their native Australia they are often active at night after the heat of the day is past.

## The Shore Plover

*Photo 109*

*Thinornis novaeseelandiae* 20 cm.

The Shore Plover is a New Zealand endemic once present in small numbers on the main islands, but now confined to South East Island of the Chatham group, where it numbers about 100 birds. In plumage pattern, it recalls the Black-fronted Dotterel and no doubt represents an early colonisation by that stock; both retain the same plumage pattern all year and are without dull eclipse plumage, and both have red bills with black tips, red eye-rings, red legs, black head and face markings and white head bands. The Shore Plover, however, lacks the Black-fronted Dotterel's distinctive V-shaped breast band. Males are readily distinguished from females by their brighter colouring. Juveniles have white faces and for some reason (it is an optical illusion) the bill appears to be slightly down-curved.

On South East Island, the Shore Plover is very much a bird of the shore, though areas of low-growing turf and ice plant short distances inland are sometimes used. Most of the Shore Plovers occur on the northern and eastern parts of the island. This segment of the coast is characterised by a series of flat platforms of volcanic rock covered with colourful seaweeds and broken up by rocky headlands. So smooth and level are some of the platforms that the island was once used as a shore whaling base and traces of this activity can still be seen. (How, with all this activity, South East Island managed to escape the rats, cats and Wekas that have plagued the other islands of the group is a mystery, but something to be thankful for.)

My first visit to South East Island was in November 1970. At the time of our arrival most of the plovers were still at an early stage of the breeding cycle, with males holding territories but leaving them to join in communal displays on the rock shelves at certain times of the day.

Feeding seemed to take place mostly in the early mornings and evenings, when 10 or a dozen birds could be seen together among the seaweed and at the edges of the rock pools. When feeding, the birds would often stand on one foot and extend the other forward to vibrate it rapidly on the weed. This would be followed by a quick run forward to snap up the disturbed animal, and the action would then be repeated.

Most nests were found just above high tide mark and the common denominator of all sites was overhead cover, a frequent finding on bird islands, especially if there is a heavy downpour of petrels at night. Nevertheless, it was a surprise to see it demonstrated by the plovers (and oystercatchers) which are generally confirmed breeders of wide open spaces. We found 10 nests, all at the ends of tunnels in dense masses of rushes and grass. They have also been found under logs and boulders and even in deserted petrel burrows. The nest itself is a substantial cup woven out of grass, and trial nests may be made before one is finally selected. The usual clutch is 3 and both sexes incubate.

Shore Plovers have a most interesting communal display performed on the neutral ground of the rock shelf feeding areas. This display is quite unlike anything I have seen with other small New Zealand plovers and is more akin to the piping parties of oystercatchers. Up to 6 or 8 birds may be involved. In an ever-moving pattern the birds form and reform in rough circles, all facing inwards, with heads lowered and shoulders hunched, taking short runs towards one another. Birds will break off to run after others, only to return and rejoin the circle. All the time, a continuous prolonged chittering note is kept up. The display will continue for perhaps 5 or 10 minutes before the birds disperse, perhaps to regroup a short time later on a different part of the shelf. Sometimes the displays were triggered off by invasion of nearby nesting territories; at other times they seemed to arise spontaneously. Tandem display flightings, with the male chasing the female, were also frequent, as were display flights with slow, deliberate wing-beats akin to those performed by South Island Pied Oystercatchers.

The guarding of territories and nest sites was very much the province of the male. He would, in fact, even give broken-wing displays for an empty nest before eggs were laid. Once eggs were laid the birds sat tightly and became exceptionally tame.

About midday, Shore Plover activity on the rock shelves diminished markedly. Afternoons were for siesta and the birds would be found standing about on their territories or simply sitting on the ground dozing. A favourite resting site was a small hollow or tunnel in the volcanic rock. A number of these were found, with the bird standing or sitting just in the entrance and with a little conical heap of droppings nearby to indicate long and regular usage.

## The Wrybilled Plover

*Photo 113*

*Anarhynchus frontalis* 20 cm.

The Wrybilled Plover is a unique New Zealand endemic. No other bird has a bill deflected to one side. The Wrybilled Plover is blue-grey above and white below and in breeding plumage has a black band across the chest. The bill is longer than the Banded Dotterel's and turns to the right. These plovers breed only in the South Island east of the Southern Alps and for practical purposes only on the extensive riverbeds of the large, many-braided rivers from the Wairau in the north to the Ahuriri in the south. They return to their breeding grounds in August and eggs may be found from September to November.

Wrybilled Plovers hold large territories and for breeding purposes demand large expanses of water-worn stones free of growth and debris. They will not nest near trees and the encroachment of willows has destroyed much of their habitat. They will tolerate lupins and gorse, but prefer to avoid them, and their ideal site is a bare shingle bank, 100 metres or so long, surrounded by water.

The nest is a scrape lined with small stones and the clutch is 2. The eggs are laid 48 hours apart and resemble exactly the stones among which they are laid. So good is their camouflage that, having located them, it is quite possible to turn, move back 5 or 6 paces and then not to be able to find them again without a stone-by-stone scrutiny.

Wrybilled Plovers can be extremely tame at the nest and will allow the quiet observer to sit closely beside them. Both sexes incubate and the incubation period is about 30 days. Wrybilled Plovers not only distract with broken wing but will run towards you with raised wings and harsh cries in an attempt to drive you away.

In winter, Wrybilled Plovers migrate to the extensive estuaries of the North Island where they feed on the mudflats and form dense, compact, resting flocks that attract to them many of the rare migrants from the Northern Hemisphere. Counts of these flocks give an estimated total Wrybilled Plover population of at least 5000 birds.

## Curlews, Godwits, Sandpipers, Snipe Scolopacidae

Wading birds with bills as long as the head or longer. Plumage mostly cryptic and without bold markings. Sexes similar. With the exception of snipe, all have a non-breeding plumage different to breeding plumage and all breed in the Northern Hemisphere and migrate south. Most breed in the Arctic, and, as a general rule, the Arctic breeders migrate further south than those of middle latitudes. Many cover prodigious distances. In the Southern Hemisphere most are coastal and in New Zealand the principal wader grounds are the tidal mudflats of Parengarenga, Kaipara, Manukau, Firth of Thames, Tauranga, Farewell Spit, Nelson and Invercargill.

Curlews and whimbrels are medium to large birds with long legs and long, down-curved bills. Godwits have long legs and long, straight, or slightly upturned bills. Snipe have short legs and long, straight bills. Sandpipers are small or medium-sized with straight, tapered bills. Stints are tiny sandpipers. All arrive in New Zealand in September and depart in March. Immatures of some species overwinter. *C.* 82 species; New Zealand 33 migrants recorded, 1 snipe endemic.

## The Far-eastern Curlew

*Numenius madagascariensis* 60 cm. (bill 18 cm.)

The Far-eastern Curlew breeds in Siberia and migrates south as far as Australia, where it is common. New Zealand receives perhaps 50 a year. A giant among the waders, it is easily identified by its size and very long, down-curved bill. The head is not streaked as in the smaller whimbrels. Its voice, seldom heard in New Zealand, is a far-carrying, haunting, *curl-ee, curl-ee*. They are wary birds. Immatures may overwinter.

## The Asiatic Whimbrel

*Photo 115*

*Numenius phaeopus variegatus* 42 cm. (bill 9 cm.)

The Asiatic Whimbrel breeds in eastern Siberia and about 50, perhaps more, regularly reach New Zealand on migration. It resembles a small curlew with a streaky head and is about the size of a godwit. In flight it has a conspicuous white rump which serves to distinguish it from the American subspecies *hudsonicus*. It is a very wary bird, difficult to get close to, and has a shrill, rippling call of about 7 notes. On rocky shores, whimbrels, like tattlers, are difficult to see; often the first indication of one is the rippling call as it takes wing. Small numbers overwinter.

## The American Whimbrel

*Numenius phaeopus hudsonicus* 42 cm. (bill 9 cm.)

Also known as the Hudsonian Curlew, this race breeds in arctic North America and normally migrates to Central and South America. One or 2 stragglers reach New Zealand almost annually. It differs from the Asiatic race in having a brown rump.

## The Little Whimbrel

*Numenius minutus* 32 cm.

The Little Whimbrel breeds in north-east Siberia and winters in Indonesia and northern Australia, where it is one of the most abundant wintering waders. In New Zealand it is a rare vagrant with about a dozen records. In appearance it is a miniature whimbrel, about the size of a Golden Plover.

## The Bristle-thighed Curlew

*Numenius tahitiensis* 48 cm.

The Bristle-thighed Curlew breeds in the mountains of north-east Alaska and winters in the central Pacific. Not till 1948 was the nest of this species discovered, and even today few have been seen. In its winter quarters it has the unusual habit of predating the eggs of terns and other seabirds. There is 1 New Zealand record, at Macauley Island (Kermadecs) in 1966. In general appearance it resembles a whimbrel but has a conspicuously rusty-coloured tail. Its call note is a clear *kee-vee*, quite unlike the rippling trill of the whimbrel.

## The Eastern Bar-tailed Godwit

*Photo 111*

*Limosa lapponica baueri* 40 cm.

The Eastern Bar-tailed Godwit breeds in eastern Siberia and north-west Alaska and is the commonest of the migratory waders to reach New Zealand — about 100,000 annually. It is to be seen the length of the country and regularly reaches

**94** The Weka.

**95** The Banded Rail.

**96** The Australian Coot.

**97** The Dusky Moorhen.

**98** The Pukeko.

**99** The Variable Oystercatcher.

**100** The Black-tailed Native Hen. A nomadic Australian species last recorded in New Zealand in 1957–8.

**101** The Takahe. Photographed at the Mount Bruce Native Bird Reserve.

**102** A South Island Pied Oystercatcher showing food to a 2-day-old chick.

**103** The Chatham Island Oystercatcher.

**104** The Australian Spur-winged Plover.

**105** The Banded Dotterel.

**106** The Black-fronted Dotterel.

**107** The Auckland Island Banded Dotterel.

**108** The Black Stilt.

**109** The Shore Plover.

**110** Shore Plover habitat. The flat rock shelves, which are washed at high tide, are where the birds do most of their feeding.

**111** The Eastern Bar-tailed Godwit.

**112** The female New Zealand Dotterel.

**113** The Wrybilled Plover.

**114** New Zealand Dotterel inhabit the heights above Port Pegasus, Stewart island.

**115** The Asiatic Whimbrel.

**116** Turnstones.

**117** The Wandering Tattler.

**118** The Grey-tailed Tattler.

**119** Turnstones are characteristically found on rocky shores.

**120** The Subantarctic Snipe. This is the Chatham Island race.

**121** The Pied Stilt.

the Chatham Islands. Stragglers have been recorded at Auckland, Campbell and Macquarie Islands.

Godwits can hardly be confused with any other shorebird; no others look quite the same. Their general colour is a mottled grey and brown, and they are pale underneath. They have long legs and long, straight bills, slightly uptilted at the end, pink at the base and dark at the tip. Females are larger than males and have longer bills. In breeding plumage male godwits turn red underneath, females buff, and it is not unusual to see birds in this plumage shortly before their departure. Godwits may be found in groups of 6 to 12, but are usually found in substantial numbers and often in thousands. In New Zealand any large flock of long-legged, long-billed waders can only be godwits, for the other large waders just do not occur here in such numbers.

Godwits are frequently accompanied by other shorebirds, notably Knots. They feed mostly at the edge of the tide and, when feeding, keep up a continuous and conversational musical chatter. They feed with rapid stabs of the bill and will probe nostril-deep into mud and ooze. They fly in compact flocks, twisting and turning in unison, and they are a sight to see when they pour into the high tide roosts from the huge feeding grounds of the northern harbours.

The Bar-tailed Godwit is the commonest of the migrants to overwinter; some thousands do so each year, especially in the north.

## The Asiatic Black-tailed Godwit

*Limosa limosa melanuroides* 38 cm.

This is a rare straggler to New Zealand from breeding grounds in north-eastern Siberia, where it breeds at lower latitudes than the Bar-tailed Godwit. At rest, it is difficult to distinguish from a Bar-tailed Godwit. In flight, it shows 3 conspicuous features: a black tail contrasting with a white rump, a white wing bar and a pure white underwing. It is an irregular visitor, sometimes 4 or 6 birds together, and it has been seen at the Auckland Islands.

## The American Black-tailed (Hudsonian) Godwit

*Limosa haemastica* 38 cm.

A rare straggler from breeding grounds in Alaska and Canada, this species normally migrates to South America, but single birds are recorded in New Zealand most years. It is distinguishable from the Asiatic Black-tailed Godwit by its black axillaries.

## The Upland Sandpiper

*Bartramia longicauda* 30 cm.

The Upland Plover breeds inland over most of North America and migrates to South America, principally east of the Andes. There is 1 New Zealand record: 1967. It is an unusual-looking wader, with a small head, thin neck and long tail; it is brown above and mottled and streaked below. It holds its wings up on alighting, and perches on posts. It prefers grasslands.

## The Lesser Yellowlegs

*Tringa flavipes* 27 cm.

This very rare straggler to New Zealand (10 records) breeds in Alaska and Canada and normally migrates to South America. *Tringas*, as a group, are solitary, slim and noisy, and stand with the body at right angles to the legs. The yellowlegs

(2 species) are identified by their long, yellow legs that extend beyond the tail in flight. In the Lesser Yellowlegs, the bill is 1½ times as long as the head or less; in the Greater Yellowlegs, it is twice as long.

## The Greenshank

*Tringa nebularia* 33 cm.

The Greenshank is a rare straggler to New Zealand from breeding grounds in northern Europe and Asia. In winter plumage, it is a very pale, almost white bird about the size of a godwit, with a white rump, long, greenish legs, a long, thin, dark, slightly upturned bill and a horizontal stance. It frequents freshwater habitats short distances inland, rather than the saltings.

## The Marsh Sandpiper

*Tringa stagnatilis* 25 cm.

The Marsh Sandpiper breeds in the steppes from central Europe to Mongolia and winters south to Africa, India and Australia. It is a rare vagrant to New Zealand, with about a dozen records. It resembles a small Greenshank though it is not as pale. The legs are conspicuously long, and are greenish-grey.

## The Wandering Tattler

*Photo 117*

*Tringa incana* 28 cm.

In winter plumage the 2 Tattlers are difficult to tell apart. Neither is common in New Zealand which is beyond their normal wintering range. The Wandering Tattler breeds in the alpine zone of Alaska and winters on the Pacific Islands. It is grey above and white below and has a white rump. The nasal groove extends two-thirds the length of the bill (as against half for the Siberian Tattler) and in winter plumage this is the only absolutely diagnostic distinction between the 2 species. Its call note is a musical whistle of 6-10 notes, as against the double note of the Siberian Tattler, but this cannot always be relied on. Tattlers prefer rocky shores and may be seen perched on posts and logs. At times they can be very approachable but are usually wary. In breeding plumage the whole undersurface, including the undertail coverts, is barred grey and white.

## The Grey-tailed Tattler

*Photo 118*

*Tringa brevipes* 25 cm.

The Grey-tailed Tattler is slightly smaller than the Wandering Tattler and more uniformly pale grey above. In breeding plumage the undersurface is barred grey and white. The nasal groove is only half the length of the bill, not two-thirds. It breeds in the remote mountain regions of eastern Siberia and its nest and eggs were not discovered till 1959. After breeding, it winters from Malaysia to Australia. It is a rare but regular straggler to New Zealand and may overwinter. It frequents rocky shores and perches on posts. Its voice is a clear double whistle. Warier than the Wandering Tattler, it is usually solitary, not associating with other species.

## The Common Sandpiper

*Tringa hypoleuca* 20 cm.

The Common Sandpiper breeds across northern Eurasia and Japan and winters south to Africa, India and Australia. It is a rare straggler to New Zealand, with 6 records. It is a slender bird, brown above and white below, with a slender bill and greenish legs. It constantly bobs its head and dips its tail, and perches on posts and snags. Its flight is distinctive — a series of short, clipped wing-beats alternating with short glides on down-curved wings. A solitary bird, it has a cheery *kitty-needy* whistling call.

## The Terek Sandpiper

*Tringa terek* 23 cm.

The Terek Sandpiper breeds from Finland to north-east Siberia and prefers tropical and subtropical wintering grounds. One or 2 reach New Zealand each year. It is one of the easiest waders to identify, with the diagnostic combination of a long, thin, up-curved bill and orange legs. In flight it shows a broad white trailing edge to the wings. It is an active bird with a characteristic, fast, crouching run.

## The Turnstone

*Photos 116, 119*

*Arenaria interpres* 23 cm.

Turnstones are prodigious travellers. They breed in the Arctic to the limit of the unfrozen shoreline and after breeding travel the globe. About 2000 reach New Zealand each year and they regularly reach the Chatham and Auckland Islands. Turnstones are unmistakable. Even in winter plumage Turnstones retain a distinct tortoiseshell pattern of black, white, chestnut and brown. In breeding plumage they are more colourful, with the patterning more distinct, but the assumption and loss of breeding plumage varies in timing from one bird to another, so a whole range of plumages may be seen in a flock. Turnstones have short, orange legs and a low-slung, dumpy look. The bill is short and slightly up-turned. Typically, they are birds of rocky shores but they also feed inland in company with Golden Plovers.

On the shore they feed busily and energetically, actively tossing tide wrack apart, turning over stones and arguing in chittering remonstrance with other members of the flock. On reefs they feed close to the breaking waves, where they are often forced into flight to avoid being drenched. Small flocks of immatures overwinter in northern harbours.

## The Subantarctic Snipe

*Photo 120*

*Coenocorypha aucklandica* 20–23 cm.

The Subantarctic Snipe is an endemic species now confined to islands that introduced predators have not reached. Five subspecies are described, one of which, the Stewart Island Snipe, is now extinct as a result of the disastrous invasion of Big South Cape Island by rats in the 1960s. This not only exterminated the Snipe and Bush Wren but would also have exterminated the South Island Saddleback, had it not been for the Wildlife Service rescue expedition which transferred the few survivors to a rat-free island nearby. Subantarctic Snipe are richly plumaged birds, streaked and variegated with russet, black and brown. The legs are short and the bill long and tapering. Females are larger than males and have longer bills.

Subantarctic Snipe are today found at the Chatham, Snares, Antipodes and Auckland Islands. At the Chatham Islands they occur on South East Island and the Star Keys and in 1970 were released on Mangere Island with great success. They are now firmly established. On South East Island they tend to be more nocturnal than diurnal and they keep to dense cover. The Chatham Island birds differ from the other races in being smaller and in having a plain and unbarred lower breast and abdomen. They feed among the leaf litter and probe deeply into soft soil and mud. Nests have been seldom found. Those reported were where they had overhead cover — under logs and the roots of trees.

At the Snares, Subantarctic Snipe are easily seen in the daytime and nests have been found in clumps of tussock, under dense vegetation and in the hollow ends of tree trunks. The clutch is 2 and both parents incubate. Snares Island birds have the undersurface barred throughout.

At the Antipodes Islands (a darker race) they are widely distributed over the uplands. They nest on the ground with a clutch of 2 and a nest I saw was at the base of a tussock that was grown through with fern.

At the Auckland Islands they have been exterminated on the main island by introduced cats but are present on Ewing, Enderby, Adams and Disappointment Islands. On none are they easy to find or observe. This race has the flanks but not the abdomen barred.

Subantarctic Snipe are considered a primitive and relict species whose survival from the past is attributed to the accident of isolation on remote islands with consequent protection from ground predators.

## The Japanese Snipe

*Gallinago hardwicki* 33 cm.

This species, which breeds in Japan and migrates to Australia, is a rare straggler to New Zealand. Skulking and shy, it has the typical, disruptive, streaked, snipe plumage in blacks and red-browns with the head streaked dark-brown and cream. The eye is large, the bill very long and the legs are short. It has a fast zig-zagging flight and is typically seen only as it explodes upward from near your feet.

## The Knot

*Calidris canutus* 25 cm.

In New Zealand Knots are second in frequency only to godwits; about 75,000 reach here each year. They breed far north of the Arctic circle and after breeding migrate to Australia, New Zealand, West Africa, South America and Europe. They are among the world's most numerous waders. In New Zealand they winter mostly in the North Island and are uncommon south of Farewell Spit. Knots are grey above and pale grey below. They have a pale eye-stripe, an indistinct wing bar and the legs and bill are neither long nor short. In breeding plumage they turn red underneath.

Knots form dense, compact flocks and often associate with godwits. Like them, they indulge in massed flights, swirling like clouds of grey smoke. They feed usually on the falling tide and, like other waders, have the habit when resting of standing on one leg and hopping reluctantly sideways when disturbed.

## The Great Knot

*Calidris tenuirostris* 29 cm.

The Great Knot breeds in the mountain regions of north-east Siberia and is a very rare straggler to New Zealand; about a dozen records. It is larger than the Knot. The crown is streaked dark and the undersurface is white with darkish spots on the breast and flanks. It does not turn red in breeding plumage; instead it becomes darker above and develops black spots on the breast that may coalesce to form a black band. The principal wintering grounds of this species are the coastal regions of southern Asia to northern Australia.

## The Sharp-tailed Sandpiper

*Calidris acuminata* 22 cm.

The Sharp-tailed Sandpiper breeds in north-east Siberia and migrates in enormous numbers to Malaysia and Australia where it is one of the commonest winter visitors. In New Zealand it is regular, but only in small numbers, and may be seen the length of the country. It is a richly marked species even in winter plumage. The crown is chestnut streaked with black and the upperparts are dark brown with pale-edged feathers. The underparts are pale with fawn streaks and spots on the neck and breast that fade gradually without sharp demarcation to a white abdomen. In breeding plumage the Sharp-tailed Sandpiper develops crescent-shaped spots on the flanks. This species prefers to feed in low-growing, salt marsh vegetation rather than out on the mudflats.

## The Pectoral Sandpiper

*Calidris melanotus* 22 cm.

The Pectoral Sandpiper breeds in arctic America and Siberia and migrates to Central and South America. It is a rare visitor to New Zealand, though probably regular. It closely resembles the Sharp-tailed Sandpiper but is differentiated by its more densely marked breast that is sharply cut off from the white underparts. As the Sharp-tailed Sandpiper, it prefers to feed in shallow, freshwater marshes with low herbage rather than on the open mudflats.

## Baird's Sandpiper

*Calidris bairdii* 18 cm.

Baird's Sandpiper breeds in subantarctic Siberia, North America and Greenland and normally winters at high elevations in the Andes of South America. It is a very rare vagrant to New Zealand, recorded in 1970, 1971 and 1976. It is a small wader with the upperparts dark and scaly, the breast buff, the abdomen white and the legs black. At rest, its dark wingtips project beyond the tail. The rump is black with white sides.

## The White-rumped Sandpiper

*Calidris fuscicollis* 19 cm.

This species breeds in Alaska and northern Canada and winters in South America east of the Andes. It was a vagrant to New Zealand in 1969 and 1971. It closely resembles Baird's but the rump is entirely white, not just the sides, and the neck and chest are finely streaked with grey.

## The Dunlin

*Calidris alpina* 20 cm.

The Dunlin breeds throughout the Arctic but rarely winters south of the equator. It was recorded in New Zealand in 1969, 1974 and 1977. In winter it resembles a winter-plumaged Curlew Sandpiper but for the rump which is black edged with white. In breeding plumage it develops a black patch on the belly.

## The Curlew Sandpiper

*Calidris ferruginea* 22 cm.

Curlew Sandpipers breed in arctic Asia with small numbers breeding in Alaska. It is one of the commonest migrants to Australia but, though regular, is rare in New Zealand and has mostly been reported from Manukau, Firth of Thames, Farewell

Spit and Lake Ellesmere. The Curlew Sandpiper has a slender, down-curved bill, a white rump, a white eyebrow and a white wingbar in flight. The bill is not as downcurved as one might expect from the name and in juveniles may be almost straight. In breeding plumage Curlew Sandpipers turn brick-red underneath, like Knots. They feed on the tidal mudflats; juveniles may overwinter.

## The Western Sandpiper

*Calidris mauri* 17 cm.

The Western Sandpiper breeds in Siberia and Alaska and winters in South America. It was recorded in New Zealand in 1964, 1970, 1971 and 1976. It is a small wader with a rather long, tapering and slightly decurved bill. The legs are black. In winter plumage it closely resembles Baird's Sandpiper.

## The Red-necked Stint

*Calidris ruficollis* 15 cm.

Red-necked Stints breed in Siberia and Alaska and winter south to Australia and New Zealand. They are tiny birds, about the size of a sparrow. In Australia they are abundant; in New Zealand they are regular but not common. They have short, straight, black bills and black legs. In winter plumage they are grey above and white below. In breeding plumage they turn red on the neck. Juveniles may overwinter. Stints are active little birds, twinkling briskly about on the wet sand, and are engagingly described in the New Zealand *Field Guide* as voracious feeders with a sewing machine action. With heads moving briskly up and down, they punch lines of stitches in the mud as they move busily along the water's edge. Stints are usually quite approachable, especially when resting with those most phlegmatic of waders, the Wrybills.

## The Sanderling

*Calidris alba* 20 cm.

The Sanderling breeds in the Arctic and migrates south with small numbers reaching New Zealand. In winter plumage it is a delicate pearly grey bird with white underparts and a black mark at the bend of the wing. In breeding plumage it turns chestnut red above and on the head and chest. It is typically seen on sandy beaches running rapidly on twinkling legs along the edge of the tide.

## The Broad-billed Sandpiper

*Limicola falcinellus sibirica* 18 cm.

This sandpiper breeds in the high Arctic and is a rare straggler to New Zealand, recorded here in 1960, 1963, 1965 and 1970. It is a small wader with a striped head and body plumage. The bill is longer than the head and slightly down-curved at the tip. The white stripes on the head above the eye form a V pointing towards the bill. The legs are short.

The following species have been recorded with a high but not absolute degree of certainty and in the 1979 *Amendments & Additions to the 1970 Annotated Checklist of the Birds of New Zealand* are retained on the Suspense List: the Semipalmated Sandpiper (*Calidris pusilla*), the Least Sandpiper (*Calidris minutilla*), and the Ruff (*Philomachus pugnax*). The first 2 are very small sandpipers closely resembling *mauri*. The Ruff resembles an Upland Plover.

## **Stilts and Avocets** Recurvirostridae

Medium-sized wading birds with long slender legs and bills. Bill either straight (stilts) or up-curved (avocets). Feet at least partly webbed. Sexes alike. Birds of shallow waters, marshes and braided rivers. Nest on ground, often colonially. Clutch 4. Incubation by both parents. Young fend for themselves, guarded by parents. Seven species; New Zealand 3, 1 endemic.

### The Pied Stilt — *Photo 121*

*Himantopus himantopus leucocephalus* 38 cm.

The Pied Stilt is the New Zealand representative of the cosmopolitan Black-winged Stilt and is widespread throughout lowland parts of the country wherever it can be near water. It is a black and white bird with very long, slender, red legs and a long, thin, straight black bill. The head and underparts are white; the wings, back and hindneck are black. In flight the long legs trail back behind the tail and the wings look triangular and pointed. Juvenile birds lack the black on the back of the neck.

Pied Stilts are nervous, excitable birds with a mincing gait and a high-pitched yapping cry. They are gregarious and usually nest in small colonies with the nests close to and often surrounded by water. The normal clutch is 4 and incubation, by both sexes, takes about 25 days.

Nesting Pied Stilts have most theatrical distraction displays. At one's approach, all the birds take to the air and fly round and round, yelping continuously. As one draws closer, a few birds dive past one's head with a crescendo of yapping cries but the majority land at a distance of some 30 or 40 metres, there to leap up and down on gangling legs, at first with excited vigour and much noise. Then gradually they quieten. They stagger. Their wings flap ever more feebly. Their legs give way. They sink to the ground. Finally they expire, only suddenly to leap to life and go through the whole extraordinary performance all over again.

After breeding, inland Pied Stilts move to the coast and many South Island birds migrate north. Return to South Island inland breeding sites occurs in August and these birds mostly nest from October to December. In the North Island nests have been found from July to February.

### The Black Stilt — *Photo 108*

*Himantopus novaezealandiae* 38 cm.

For practical purposes this rare, endemic stilt breeds today only in the watershed of the Waitaki river system. In the early days of settlement it was more widespread and in better numbers. Today it is down to about 50 birds, owing principally to predation of its eggs and small young by rats, cats and ferrets.

Black Stilts, when adult, are black all over and differ from Pied Stilts in a number of respects. They have shorter legs and are larger in the body. They are less excitable and much more confiding. They will, for example, accept a photographic hide within minutes of its being erected, something no Pied Stilt will ever do. Most of the Black Stilts remain in the Mackenzie Basin all year, again in contrast to the Pied Stilt, and those that do drift north in winter are mostly juveniles. Black Stilts are essentially solitary birds and even in winter family groups defend territories against other Black Stilts. They mostly nest on their own, though they may be attracted to colonies of Pied Stilts in areas of good food supply, and they tend to nest on dry ground rather than in swamps.

When juvenile, Black Stilts have a white head and white underparts and look like juvenile Pied Stilts. Shortly after fledging they develop black mottling on the flanks and belly and this plumage is retained over the winter. In the spring they moult into a mainly black plumage except for some white mottling on the head and underparts. The various stages of this moult for years caused much confusion because occasionally Black Stilts mate with Pied Stilts and many of these subadult birds were thought to be hybrids. When about 15 months old most Black Stilts lose all white mottling and become fully black.

Most Black Stilts spend the winter on the river deltas draining into Lakes Tekapo, Pukaki, Ohau and Benmore. In August they disperse over the Mackenzie Basin, some birds moving far up the rivers towards the Southern Alps. They nest mainly on the riverbeds and most have eggs by the end of September. The clutch is 4 and incubation, by both sexes, takes 25 days. The sexes change over with great frequency during incubation, often every 15 or 20 minutes, unlike Pied Stilts which change over every 2 hours. The young are slow to mature in comparison with Pied Stilts, taking about half as long again — some 45 days as against about 30. Black Stilts with eggs or young have none of the hysterical distraction displays of Pied Stilts. They may land nearby, yapping and waving their wings, but mostly they content themselves with flying round overhead, making occasional diving attacks.

All these differences indicate that the Black Stilt has been in New Zealand a very long time. By comparison, the Pied Stilt is a recent colonist, so recent that it is not yet any different from its Australian relatives.

In an endeavour to prevent extinction of the Black Stilt — which over the last 20 years has decreased from 150 to 50 birds — 3 projects are at present in operation. Selected nest sites are being surrounded by electric fences in an attempt to keep cats and other predators out. Other sites are being intensively trapped. The most effective interim measure, however, has been the collection of eggs for hatching artifically, for the chicks rear well. It is hoped eventually to achieve a captive breeding stock from which liberations can be made back to the wild.

## The Red-necked Avocet

*Recurvirostra novaehollandiae* 45 cm.

The Red-necked Avocet is an Australian endemic that visited and maintained small numbers in New Zealand between 1859 and 1878, chiefly in Canterbury and Otago. It then died out and the only subsequent records are for 1892, 1945 and 1 near Westport 1968-70. It is a long-legged, white bird with a chestnut head and neck, black wings crossed by a broad white band and a long, thin, upturned black bill. It is a bird of saline lagoons that breeds in compact colonies and its voice is a flute-like toot.

## **Phalaropes** Phalaropodidae

A family of 3 aberrant, small, sandpiper-like species with longish necks, small heads and thin, straight bills that breed in the Northern Hemisphere. Females are larger and more colourful than males and institute courtship. The males incubate. Two species spend their lives on the open sea between breeding seasons, where they form flocks and feed on plankton. They have lobed toes like grebes and coots and their plumage is dense like a duck's. They float high and typically spin on the water like tops when feeding. They are indifferent to man. Three species; New Zealand 2, both vagrants.

## The Red (Grey) Phalarope

*Phalaropus fulicarius* 20 cm.

This species breeds in the Arctic and, in the Pacific, winters off the west coast of South America along the Humboldt current. In breeding plumage it is red with a white face. In eclipse plumage it is grey above and white below. The bill and legs are yellow. Four New Zealand records on coastal lagoons.

## The Red-necked Phalarope

*Phalaropus lobatus* 19 cm.

This Phalarope breeds in the Arctic and winters as the Red Phalarope, though also on the seas north of New Guinea. In breeding plumage it has a white throat and the sides of the neck are rufous. In winter it is grey above and white below and the bill and legs are black. Two New Zealand records.

## **Pratincoles** Glareolidae

Aberrant Old World waders with long wings, long forked tails and short legs. The bill is short and slightly decurved. Flight swift and graceful, like that of swallows. Gregarious. Sexes alike. Feed on insects, taken mostly on the wing but also on the ground. The family also includes the Coursers. In all, 17 species; New Zealand 1 vagrant.

## The Oriental Pratincole

*Glareola maldivarum* 23 cm.

This Pratincole breeds in the arid regions of central and south Asia, wintering south to Australia. A rare straggler to New Zealand, there are 4 records, one of at least 5 birds. It has long wings, a long, deeply forked tail and a swallow-like flight. The upperparts are brown, the breast rufous, the abdomen white and the throat cream bordered by a black line. The bill is short and black and the gape is red.

## **Skuas** Stercorariidae

Aggressive, piratical, predatory birds, pelagic outside the breeding season. Resemble gulls but with mostly dark plumage. All show some white at the base of the primaries. Bill hooked. Feet webbed. Sexes similar. Females average larger. Breed in the Arctic and Subarctic and in the Antarctic and Subantarctic. Nest on the ground and defend territories vigorously. Clutch 2, incubated from the first by both sexes for about 28 days. Young clothed in brown down and fledge after 6-8 weeks. Five species; New Zealand 5.

## The Southern Skua

*Photo 122*

*Stercorarius skua lonnbergi* 63 cm.

In the New Zealand region Southern Skuas breed at Solander, Stewart and its outlyers, Chatham, Antipodes, Snares, Auckland, Campbell and Macquarie Islands. Elsewhere they breed all round the Southern Ocean and an isolated race, the Great Skua or Bonxie, breeds in the North Atlantic in a restricted area centred on Scotland, the Faroes and Iceland.

Southern Skuas are dark-brown, solidly built birds, somewhat resembling juvenile Black-backed Gulls, but evenly coloured and with a conspicuous white flash on the wings at the base of the primaries. They fly powerfully and when attacking pick up speed very quickly, hurling themselves at their victims and following with ease their twists and turns. Outside the breeding season they are pelagic, in general not close to land, and so are rarely seen in northern New Zealand waters. On what they feed at this time is uncertain, but piracy is unlikely to be a principal method, for victims are too few and the specialisation too risky. Prions are suggested as the most likely prey.

Most adults return to their breeding islands in September. There they establish themselves near penguin rookeries, on headlands near petrel colonies and near colonies of seals. They defend their territories with vigour, boldly challenging intruders with raised wings and loud, harsh calls. Man is dive-bombed furiously and on islands with high densities of skuas is subjected to constant bombardment for no sooner does he move out of the territory of one pair than he enters the territory of the next.

At their breeding islands, Southern Skuas prey on the eggs and small young of penguins and on incoming petrels, prions and shearwaters. They also scavenge offal, such as the placentas and dead young of sea lions and fur seals. They nest on the ground, making a well-formed nest of tussock, and have a liking for headlands with a commanding view. The clutch is 2 and incubation, by both parents, takes about 30 days. Normally only 1 chick is reared.

Where skua populations are high — such as at the Chatham Islands — it is common to have 3 birds (occasionally more) in attendance on the one nest. The complexities of these situations have yet to be worked out but it does appear that 3-bird groups rear more chicks than do conventional pairs and it is presumed that the odd bird of the group is the pair's last year's young, though this has yet to be proved.

Skuas usually dismember their prey at set feeding places and, like many birds, form pellets of indigestible material which they then regurgitate. These skua middens and pellets are often a most useful guide to the petrel species on small islands, especially if one's visit to the islands is of necessity brief and in daylight.

## The Antarctic Skua

*Stercorarius maccormicki* 53 cm.

The Antarctic Skua closely resembles the Southern Skua but is smaller and has a golden tinge to the feathers of the neck. It breeds only on the Antarctic continent and adjacent islands such as Balleny. After breeding it disperses widely and is regularly recorded off the coast of Japan. It is rarely reported in New Zealand waters.

## The Arctic Skua

*Stercorarius parasiticus* 43 cm. plus tail feathers 7 cm.

The Arctic Skua breeds in the Arctic and migrates to southern seas. Despite the fact that New Zealand has a resident breeding skua, this is the commonest skua seen over New Zealand inshore waters. It is a graceful bird with an effortless flight. Like all skuas it harries other seabirds, forcing them to disgorge, and it is piratical especially on gannets, gulls and terns.

This species has 2 plumage phases, a light and a dark. The light phase is white below and has straw-yellow cheeks and neck; the dark phase is dark brown all over. Both phases have dark wings with a small white patch at the base of the primaries and both have wedge-shaped tails with or without the central feathers elongated and pointed.

This skua is essentially a summer visitor but juveniles do stay on over our winter.

## The Pomarine Skua

*Stercorarius pomarinus* 48 cm.

This species breeds mostly north of the Arctic circle and migrates to the tropics. It is not common in New Zealand seas. It is larger than the Arctic Skua and shows more white in the wings. The central tail feathers, if present, are twisted and blunt ended. Once again there are 2 plumage phases: a dark phase, which is uncommon, and a pale phase which has the face and underparts white, the rump and upperparts dark brown and the crown black.

## The Long-tailed Skua

*Stercorarius longicaudus* 35 cm. plus 20 cm. tail streamers

The Long-tailed Skua is another Arctic breeder that migrates south, though few reach the south-west Pacific, which is outside their normal dispersal range. There is one New Zealand record: 1964. In breeding plumage, the central tail feathers are greatly elongated, but otherwise, this is a small skua, brown above and white below, with a black cap and a yellowish nape.

### Gulls, Terns and Noddies Laridae

Familiar birds of coasts and inland. Sexes similar. Gulls are strong, aggressive, predatory and scavenging. They generally have square tails and strong bills, legs and feet. They fly, walk and swim well but seldom dive. They feed their young by regurgitation. Terns are slimmer and more graceful than gulls and mostly have slender, straight bills, short legs, small feet and forked tails. Many plunge dive for food. Most bring food to the young held in the bill. Both gulls and terns are mostly white with grey or black on the uppersurface and have colourful bills and feet. Noddies are tern-like tropical birds. Three of the 5 species are black; 4 of the 5 feed the young by regurgitation. All 3 groups are gregarious and breed in colonies. Gulls: 45 species; New Zealand 3, 1 endemic. Terns: 37 species; New Zealand 12, 1 endemic. Noddies: 5 species; New Zealand 4.

## The Southern Black-backed (Dominican) Gull

*Photo 124*

*Larus dominicanus* 60 cm.

In the New Zealand region the Southern Black-backed Gull occurs throughout and breeds on every outlying island group except the Kermadecs and Snares. Elsewhere it breeds in Antarctica, South America, South Africa, Australia (which it has but recently colonised) and on all but 2 or 3 of the subantarctic islands. It is a species that has benefited greatly from man's activities; with access to rubbish dumps and offal it has increased markedly in numbers.

When adult the Southern Black-backed Gull has the head, neck, underparts and tail white, the back and upper wings black. The wing has a white rear edge and the outer primary has a white subterminal spot. The bill is yellow with a red spot near the tip and the legs and feet are yellowish or olive-green depending on age and breeding condition. When juvenile they are mottled brown and white and they take 3 years to attain full adult plumage, becoming progressively whiter with each moult.

Black-backed Gulls mate for life and stay together all year round. They breed mostly in colonies, with the nests well spaced, but also as isolated pairs especially in the mountains and on offshore stacks. Nests are often close to the nesting colonies of other seabirds and these days also to garbage tips. Most eggs are laid in early November and the usual clutch is 3. Incubation is by both sexes and takes 28 days. The chicks are downy and soon active and are fed on regurgitated matter, the parent first regurgitating onto the nest and then picking up bits to give to the chick. The young fledge when 7-8 weeks old.

Despite their very wide distribution over the Southern Ocean, Southern Black-backed Gulls are essentially coastal birds. They freely follow ships, but only in coastal waters. Once you start to lose sight of land, the gulls turn back and the mollymawks and Cape Pigeons take their place.

## The Red-billed Gull *Photo 123*

*Larus novaehollandiae scopulinus* 37 cm.

With its red eyelids, red bill, red legs and feet and pearl-grey and white plumage, the Red-billed Gull is a striking bird. It is essentially a coastal species, occurring the length of the country, and is also found at Chatham, Snares, Auckland and Campbell Islands. Elsewhere, other subspecies occur in New Caledonia and Australia (where it is known as the Silver Gull) and in South Africa (where it is known as Hartlaub's Gull).

Red-billed Gulls can be predatory, scavenging marauders and have benefited greatly from man's rubbish tips and offal outlets. They breed in densely packed colonies and the largest of all are on the Three Kings Islands and Mokohinau Island with numbers estimated in the region of 12,000 birds. Another large colony occurs on the Kaikoura Peninsula. All these particular colonies are placed next to plankton-rich waters with euphausid and small shoal fish being their principal food. Smaller colonies are often attracted to the colonies of other seabirds and some 80 colonies in all are known. Only 2 occur inland: at Lake Rotorua and at Kohukohu. Of the coastal colonies nearly all are on the east coast and those that do occur on the western coasts are mostly in sheltered waters. Much as Red-billed Gulls may maraud — and they can be quite devastating at tern colonies — when feeding young their supplies come principally from the sea.

Red-billed Gulls can breed at 2 years of age but most do not do so till 3 or 4. Like other gulls they mate for life and remain faithful to remembered breeding sites. Eggs are laid October-November with a normal clutch of 3 and an incubation period of 21 days. Both sexes incubate and both feed the young.

On the outer islands and especially at Chathams where there are high populations of skuas, Red-billed Gulls nest singly and in small, loose aggregations in crevices in rocks, under overhanging slabs, in caves and other such places that give protection from predation. It is quite strange to be walking over broken coastal ground and to have a Red-billed Gull suddenly take flight from some narrow crevice between 2 boulders at one's feet.

## The Black-billed Gull *Photo 126*

*Larus bulleri* 37 cm.

The Black-billed Gull is an endemic and is principally a bird of the South Island where it breeds inland on the riverbeds. Its largest colonies are in Southland. Like the other gulls it has benefited from man's activities, but in a different way. It gets much of its food from pastureland and is less interested in rubbish tips. It is less aggressive than the other species and is not often a predator. It does not, for example, like the Red-billed Gull, regularly descend with horrifying effect on the unprotected eggs of other species and it does not relate its colonies to the colonies of other birds.

The Black-billed Gull has a black bill, a red eye-ring and reddish-black legs and feet. The eye is white. When immature the bill and feet have a more reddish tinge which can cause confusion with immature Red-billed Gulls. If in doubt, the outer primaries of the Black-billed Gull are mostly white, those of the Red-billed Gull black with subterminal white spots.

The Black-billed Gull breeds mostly inland on the riverbeds of the South Island. The colonies are placed on shingle banks, often on an island between 2 streams, and most are full swing by October. The usual clutch is 3 and incubation (by both sexes) takes 21 days. After breeding most Black-billed Gulls move to the coast and a number move to the North Island where they form flocks in bays and estuaries up the east coast. Breeding in the North Island is uncommon. There is a long-standing colony associated with the Red-billed Gulls at Rotorua and small colonies have recently established near Gisborne and in the Firth of Thames.

## The Whiskered Tern

*Chlidonias hybrida* 33 cm.

A rare straggler to New Zealand with 3 records (1977 and 1978), the Whiskered Tern breeds in the warmer inland areas of Europe, Asia, Africa and Australia. In breeding plumage it is an overall grey bird, darker below. It has a jet black cap level with the top of the eye and a conspicuous white line across the face separating the black cap from the grey neck. The bill, legs and feet are bright red and the underwing is mostly white. In winter plumage it turns white underneath, mottled grey above and the bill, legs and feet turn blackish. The tail is only slightly forked. This species feeds by hawking over lagoons and fields, dipping down to pick items off the surface.

## The White-winged Black Tern

*Chlidonias leucopterus* 23 cm.

The White-winged Black Tern breeds in inland regions from eastern Europe to eastern Asia and then disperses north and south with a few reaching Australia and New Zealand. In breeding plumage the head and body are black and the tail white. The wings are pale grey above and grey below with black underwing linings. The bill and feet are red. In winter plumage it closely resembles a winter-plumaged Whiskered Tern — white below, mottled grey above and with blackish bill and feet. This is a rare but apparently regular visitor to New Zealand, mostly coastal but also inland in such places as the MacKenzie Basin. In 1973 a pair bred (unsuccessfully) at Milford Lagoon at the mouth of the Opihi River in South Canterbury, the only known breeding attempt in the Southern Hemisphere. These terns feed by hawking tirelessly over lagoons and estuaries. They do not dive.

## The Gull-billed Tern

*Gelochelidon nilotica macrotarsa* 42 cm.

This species breeds in Europe, Asia, North Africa, the Americas and Australia; chiefly inland. It is a straggler to New Zealand, with intermittent sightings since 1955. In breeding plumage it has a black cap, the upperparts grey, the underparts white, the bill black and gull-like (which diagnostic) and the tail only slightly forked. In winter plumage the head turns white with grey streaks and there is a dark patch behind the eye. It does not dive. It feeds by skimming hawk-like over lagoons and estuaries.

## The Caspian Tern *Photo 129*

*Hydroprogne caspia* 50 cm.

The Caspian Tern with its massive red bill and grating cries is an impressive bird. It is the largest of the terns and has a wingspan of 1.4 metres. It has a black cap and is grey above and white below. In New Zealand it occurs the length of the country, principally in coastal districts where it breeds in colonies on sandy beaches but also inland where it breeds as pairs on the Volcanic Plateau, at Rotorua and in association with the gull and tern colonies of the wide, braided riverbeds of the South Island. Elsewhere, Caspian Terns have a wide, if patchy, distribution over most of the world except South America.

Caspian Terns feed principally on fish, which they catch by diving from a height rather in the manner of a gannet, after first hovering overhead with bill pointed to the water. They nest in association with other gulls and terns, mostly on sand but also on shingle. The nest is a simple scrape and the usual clutch is 2. Incubation takes 21 days and is by both parents. The loss of eggs and chicks is high — partly from predation by gulls, partly from untimely high tides or flood. Human disturbance of colonies associated with Red-billed Gulls can be disastrous, for the gulls are less afraid of man than are the Caspians and descend like wolves on the Caspian's eggs. The result is ghastly. To the shocking uproar of squabbling gulls and barking Caspians, within minutes not a Caspian's egg remains whole.

For the first week after hatching the chicks remain in the nest-scrape guarded by one or other parent. They are then led away to the outskirts of the colony where they collect with other chicks on a nearby sandbank. Chicks that wander precociously or as a result of disturbance are pathetic sights, for they are pecked unmercifully by any Caspian or gull into whose territory they happen to stumble. Provided the chick remains in no-man's-land all is well, but as soon as it commits trespass it is promptly and severely pecked. The force of the blow is sufficient to send it staggering into the territory of the next Caspian where it is again pecked. And so on. Eventually it escapes but it can receive a fearful drubbing in the process.

The chicks are fed on fresh fish passed bill to bill. Should the fish be dropped the chick makes no attempt to pick it up off the ground. The size of the fish that can be swallowed is remarkable. Provided the chick can encompass the width, fish equal to its own length can be disposed of. Only flatfish give trouble: they are too wide.

After breeding, inland South Island Caspian Terns move to the coast and there is evidence that they then drift north.

## The Crested Tern *Photo 128*

*Sterna bergii* 47 cm.

The Crested Tern is a large, marine, plunge-diving, crested tern with a conspicuous yellow bill and a white forehead. The crest and top of the head are black; the uppersurface is grey and the underparts white. It breeds in the Indian Ocean, South-west Pacific and Australia. A rare straggler to New Zealand. Four records.

## The Black-fronted Tern

*Photo 125*

*Sterna albostriata* 30 cm.

The Black-fronted Tern is endemic to New Zealand and is principally a bird of the South Island where it breeds inland on the braided riverbeds that drain east from the Southern Alps. Except in winter it is uncommon in the North Island and it is rare at all times on the west coast of the South Island.

The Black-fronted Tern is a most attractive species. In breeding plumage it is grey above and grey below. The top of the head and the nape are black and the bill, legs and feet are orange. There is a white line below the eye and the rump is white. In winter plumage the top of the head turns grey.

Black-fronted Terns return inland at the end of August but take longer to settle to breeding than do the other riverbed birds. Display flights, during which they circle 2 or 3 together with trembling, upward-angled wings and chittering call-notes, occur from September onwards but it is often not till November that the birds finally make scrapes and lay eggs. Their nests are spaced well apart and consequently the colonies can straggle quite some distance along the river beaches. The clutch is usually 2 and incubation, by both sexes, takes about 21 days. Black-fronted Terns are fearless in defence of their nests and unmercifully harry intruding dogs, hawks, magpies and man with dive-bombing attacks pressed home with angry, grating cries. When man is the victim, the attack is often accompanied by a slap on the head from a foot as the bird swoops past, and by accurate discharge of messy regurgitated matter. Inspecting Black-fronted Tern colonies is a job that demands old clothes.

Black-fronted Terns feed mostly over fast flowing water, hovering with bill pointed downwards to suddenly dip down and pick items from the surface. They work always upstream, never down, and often swing back to their starting point to make their way back over the same stretch of water all over again. They evidently find most productive those stretches of river with rapid flow and are not often seen over quiet pools. They also obtain considerable insect life from cultivated fields, over which they hawk, and they will follow the plough.

After breeding, Black-fronted Terns move to the coast and from there a number go to the North Island. Others winter at Stewart Island. During the winter their main food seems to be coastal plankton which they sometimes obtain some kilometres out to sea.

## The Antarctic Tern

*Photos 127, 131*

*Sterna vittata* 40 cm.

In the New Zealand region Antarctic Terns breed on islands off the south-west coast of Stewart Island and at Snares, Bounty, Antipodes, Auckland, Campbell and Macquarie Islands. Elsewhere they breed on the Antarctic Peninsula and on most of the islands of the Southern Ocean.

Antarctic Terns resemble Black-fronted Terns in plumage pattern except that the bill, legs and feet are blood red, the tail more deeply forked and the overall plumage paler grey so that, for example, the white rump does not show so clearly against the tail which in the Antarctic Tern is almost entirely white.

At the Auckland Islands Antarctic Terns breed mostly in low-growing *cassinia* scrub and they may breed well inland. The colonies are not large and the nests are widely spaced. The usual clutch is 1 or 2 with incubation evidently from the first, for the eggs do not hatch together. In fact, the second egg often does not hatch at all. The chick is active by its second day and soon leaves the nest to hide under nearby scrub. When this happens the parents stay with the chick and abandon the second egg. The chicks are fed on small fish and the adults are to be seen fishing in small parties just offshore, plunge diving from a height. At Campbell Island they nest on rocks close to the sea but also in areas of low vegetation well inland. At the Snares they mostly nest on ledges overlooking the sea and have an incubation period of 24-25 days.

Antarctic Terns fledge at 27-32 days and as juveniles have a heavily barred dorsal plumage. In the New Zealand region Antarctic Terns apparently do not range far from their breeding grounds. In higher latitudes, of course, they are forced to do so by the onset of the winter night.

## The Arctic Tern

*Sterna paradisaea* 38 cm.

The Arctic Tern breeds in the Arctic and migrates south, some reaching the Antarctic. It is one of the most far-flying migrants. In breeding plumage it is virtually indistinguishable from the Antarctic Tern. However, in southern waters it is normally in eclipse plumage when the bill and legs are black and the forehead white. If seen perched the Arctic Tern has shorter legs than the Antarctic Tern. In New Zealand waters this is a passage migrant, seldom recorded.

## The Fairy Tern

*Sterna nereis* 25 cm.

In New Zealand the Fairy Tern is a very rare species confined as a breeding bird to isolated stretches of sandy beaches in the far north of the North Island. Elsewhere it occurs in New Caledonia, along the south and (especially) west coasts of Australia and in Tasmania. Everywhere it is essentially a solitary breeder, with nests sometimes many kilometres apart.

The Fairy Tern is white below and pale grey, almost white, above. It has a black cap, a white forehead and a black line running forwards through the eye that stops short of the bill (cf. the Little Tern). The bill, legs and feet are yellow.

In New Zealand Fairy Terns return to their breeding beaches in September. Eggs are recorded November to January and the normal clutch is 2. Incubation, by both parents, takes at least 18 days (20 in Australia) and the young fledge after about 24 days. After breeding Fairy Terns disappear from northern New Zealand, but where they go is yet unknown.

## The Little Tern

*Sterna albifrous* 25 cm.

In breeding plumage the Little Tern is separable from the Fairy Tern by the darker uppersurface, the black-tipped, yellow bill and the line through the eye reaching the base of the bill, not stopping short. It is an almost cosmopolitan species, breeding widely north of the equator and also in Australia. In New Zealand it occurs only as a rare visitor, albeit with some regularity.

## The White-fronted Tern

*Photo 132*

*Sterna striata* 42 cm.

The White-fronted Tern is a marine species breeding the length of the country and also at the Chatham and Auckland Islands. It has straggled to Snares, Campbell and Macquarie Islands. After breeding, large numbers, especially juveniles, migrate to Australia and recently (1979) a few pairs stayed to breed on an island off Tasmania.

**122** The Southern Skua.

**123** The Red-billed Gull.

**124** The Southern Black-backed Gull.

**125** The Black-fronted Tern.

**126** The Black-billed Gull.

**127** The Antarctic Tern. Photographed at the Auckland Islands.

**128** The Crested Tern.

**129** The Caspian Tern.

**130** Denham Bay, Raoul Island. Raoul is a lush, subtropical island of volcanic origin. Denham Bay is the site of a large Sooty Tern colony.

**131** The Antarctic Tern.

**132** The White-fronted Tern.

**133** The Common Noddy. Photographed at Lord Howe Island.

**134** The Sooty Tern.

**135** White Terns.

**136** The White-capped Noddy. Photographed on Meyer Island.

**137** The single egg of the White Tern is laid on the bare limb of a tree, usually at a great height.

**138** The Grey Ternlet.

139 The New Zealand Pigeon.

140 The New Zealand Pigeon.

141 The introduced Rock Pigeon.

**142** The Kakapo. Photographed in captivity.

**143** The Kea.

**144** The Antipodes Island Green Parakeet.

**145** The Yellow-crowned Parakeet.

**146** The Kaka. This is the South Island subspecies.

**147** The Antipodes Island Red-crowned Parakeet.

**148** A Red-crowned Parakeet photographed at the Kermadec Islands.

**149** The Crimson Rosella.

The White-fronted Tern has a black cap and a white forehead. The back and wings are grey and the underparts white. The tail is long and forked and in breeding plumage the outermost feathers extend as streamers. In eclipse plumage the crown becomes mottled.

White-fronted Terns breed in colonies numbering from a few to some hundreds. As a rule the small groups are on offshore rocks, the large ones at the mouths of rivers and on coastal sand dunes or shingle beaches. They are often associated with Red-billed Gulls and, like many terns, tend to change their breeding sites from one year to the next.

The display of the White-fronted Tern includes flying round with a small fish in the bill while uttering a grating cry. On the ground the 2 birds of a pair strut together side by side. Chittering remonstrance against trepass is common, with the birds face to face and rocking up and down.

The nest is simply a scrape in the sand or a depression in the rock and is usually unlined. Normally only 1 egg is laid but there may be 2. Incubation, by both sexes, takes 24 days and change-over at the nest is often accompanied by the ceremony of offering a fish. The chicks are fed bill to bill on small fish and fledge when about a month old.

## The Sooty Tern

*Photo 134*

*Sterna fuscata* 45 cm.

The Sooty Tern is one of the most widespread and numerous terns of tropical and subtropical seas. There are very large numbers at Norfolk and Lord Howe Islands. In the New Zealand region it breeds at the Kermadec Islands.

The Sooty Tern is black above and white below and has white cheeks and a white forehead. The black of the head extends forwards as a widow's peak and also as a triangle enclosing the eye and pointing out at the base of the bill. The tail is long and deeply forked and the legs, feet and bill are black.

Sooty Terns are also known as Wide-awake Terns, both from their harsh, twanging, *wide-awake* calls and from their noisy, incessant, nocturnal activity over their breeding grounds.

The Sooty Tern is a pelagic species that spends its life at sea between breeding seasons. Juveniles banded at Lord Howe Island have been recovered in the Central Pacific and banding results have shown that juveniles remain continuously at sea for at least their first 3 years. In view of this, it is surprising to learn that the Sooty Tern's plumage is poorly water-repellent and quickly becomes water-logged. Sooty Terns cannot rest on the sea, so if they sleep they must do so on the wing. Their food consists mostly of squid, which rise to the surface at night.

Unmolested, Sooty Tern colonies can reach enormous size. The colony at Denham Bay, Raoul Island, of the Kermadec Group, is predated by cats and rats to a horrifying degree and is today but a fraction of its original size; even so, it still contains some 25,000 pairs. At Lord Howe Island one colony alone contains at least 100,000 pairs.

Like all pelagic birds the Sooty Tern is a long-lived species — there are records of Sooty Terns still breeding when 30 years old — and it has a protracted breeding cycle. For 6 weeks or more the birds circle endlessly and noisily over the breeding grounds, at first only at night, later both by night and day. Then, as if on a signal, hundreds of birds descend, make scrapes and lay. Overnight, eggs by the hundreds will appear where before there were none. The clutch is invariably 1 and the incubation period is about 28 days. Both parents incubate, taking turns of 3 or 4 days at a time. When incubating they do not leave the nest except briefly to drink.

They drink seawater, excreting the excess salt through nasal glands. To walk through a Sooty Tern colony at this time is to receive a fine spray of moisture from hundreds of salt-excreting nostrils as the birds wheel in a screaming mass overhead.

The chicks are guarded for the first few days. Thereafter they are unattended while both parents hunt for food. The noise of a colony at this time is deafening. Indeed, without ear plugs, one wishes only for escape. Apparently the adults seek out their own offspring by sound, and with birds returning at all hours — for day or night makes no difference to a Sooty Tern — the noise is unrelenting. The Sooty Tern is one of the few true terns which feed their young by regurgitation; being pelagic, collecting their food from far out at sea, that is the only practical way. Carrying food in the bill is only for those species with fishing grounds close to the colony. Sooty Terns feed their young on squid, normally once a day. The young can survive long periods of starvation — an ability common to and necessary for the young of all oceanic species. The chicks fledge at 60-70 days.

In common with the colonies of all pelagic birds the colonies of Sooty Terns are ancestral; for obviously a pelagic species cannot aimlessly wander at the start of the breeding season on the off-chance of finding an island with some of its own kind present. Pelagic birds have an innate mechanism that directs them back to the same places year after year. It would be interesting to know not only how long colonies remain in existence but the mechanism by which new colonies are formed.

## The White-capped Noddy *Photo 136*

*Anous minutus* 34 cm.

In the New Zealand region the White-capped Noddy breeds at the Kermadec Islands. Elsewhere, it is widely distributed over the Pacific and also breeds in the Atlantic and Caribbean.

The White-capped Noddy is sooty-black all over except for a white forehead, a white crown and white eye-rings. It has a long, slender, black bill, short black legs and small black feet. The tail is long, wedge-shaped and slightly notched at the end. White-capped Noddies nest in trees and, for such long-winged birds, are remarkably dextrous in confined spaces: they float in and out of the trees on silent wings, and can hover and turn in their own length like a helicopter. In general, they are sedentary birds, remaining in the vicinity of their breeding grounds all year, and they return to their islands at night to roost.

The nest of the White-capped Noddy is a flat platform of twigs, leaves and litter, cemented together with guano placed on the fork of a horizontal limb, and takes about 3 weeks to construct. Only 1 egg is laid and incubation, by both sexes, takes 36 days. The chick is a delightful little ball of jet-black down and has the white cap clearly defined. It is brooded for the first 3 days and guarded, with one or other parent always present, for 3 weeks. Thereafter it is left much on its own and it flies at about 50-55 days. It is fed by regurgitation in the manner of a petrel chick; at first on an oily-looking fluid, later on plankton. On islands with no trees, White-capped Noddies nest on the ground, on rock ledges and on cliffs. Unlike the Common Noddy in such situations, they still build a substantial guano-cemented structure.

At sea, White-capped Noddies feed in flocks in the manner of Grey Ternlets — and often in company with them. Their food consists principally of fish, squid and plankton picked from the surface.

## The Common Noddy

*Photo 133*

*Anous stolidus* 39 cm.

For some reason this noddy, which breeds on virtually every major tropical and subtropical island group of the Pacific, Indian and Atlantic Oceans, does not breed at the Kermadec Islands, though it breeds at Norfolk and Lord Howe Islands. Its admission to the New Zealand list depends on 2 nineteenth-century reports.

In comparison with the White-capped Noddy the Common Noddy is larger, is brown rather than black, has less white on the crown and has a shorter bill. It nests usually on the ground, making a simple nest with little guano. After breeding it disperses widely and has been seen hundreds of kilometres from land.

## The White Tern

*Photos 135, 137*

*Gygis alba candida* 30 cm.

These ethereal birds breed in all tropical seas on almost every island group. In the New Zealand region they breed on Raoul Island of the Kermadec group, but are not common. The place to see them is Norfolk Island where they are in thousands.

White Terns are also known as Love Terns because when courting they perch close together side by side on a branch, preening each other's head feathers. The White Tern is pure white all over except for a narrow black ring round its beady black eye. The bill is black, slightly upturned, and blue at the base. The feet are black with a suggestion of yellow in the webs. When hovering against the light White Terns have a translucent, fairy-like quality to the wings and tail that is quite unmistakable.

White Terns return to Raoul Island in September. The breeding season is an extended one and details are yet to be fully documented.

During the early days of courtship and nest-site selection, the birds circle endlessly in and out and among trees, sometimes as pairs but often in threes. In these latter cases the third bird is presumed to be the pair's last year's young still accompanying its parents. The activity is most evident in the morning. By afternoon, most of the birds are settled on branches. In the evening they go back out to sea.

White Terns have a most unusual nesting arrangement. They lay their single egg on the bare branch of a tree, often 30 metres or more above ground, and often on a branch that appears impossibly narrow for the egg to remain in place. They make no nest but choose places that have a slight hollow or irregularity and these they may enlarge by scratching with their feet. Once laid, the egg is guarded with extreme care and is never willingly left. Change-over at the nest is accomplished by meticulous, sideways-shuffling steps.

White Terns have the most peculiar call-notes. Pairs displaying on a branch make noises like someone sawing wood and they have a habit of hovering overhead uttering strange wheezing and twanging sounds. Sometimes, especially if you have climbed a tree, the bird will hover in the air a few metres distant, staring you in the face with its beady eyes and uttering odd clicking noises.

When the chick hatches it is guarded for about 10 days. Thereafter it is left on its own. It is fed on small fish, which the parents bring held crosswise in the bill. The chicks have big feet and long claws which give them a tenacious grip of the branch. Nevertheless, high winds can cause devastation, and many chicks die through being dislodged and falling to the ground. Large chicks can climb back, which they do in the manner of a petrel climbing a tree for take-off — using the bill as a pick while heaving themselves up, a little at a time, with the wings and feet.

An unusual feature of White Tern chicks is that they can fly while still largely covered with down. When fully feathered they accompany their parents out to sea, but return to the nest to roost at night. At Norfolk Island the incubation period is 36 days and the chicks fly at 78 days.

## The Grey Ternlet

*Photo 138*

*Procelsterna cerulea albivitta* 28 cm.

Also known as the Grey Noddy, this small, dainty bird has a wide range across the South Pacific, breeding from Norfolk and Lord Howe Islands to Pitcairn and Easter Islands. In the New Zealand region it breeds at the Kermadec Islands and has occasionally bred at the Three Kings Islands and in the Bay of Plenty — on Volkner and Sugarloaf Rocks and at the Alderman Islands.

The Grey Ternlet has a pale grey plumage, darker on the wings and tail; a beady, black eye encircled by a narrow ring that is black in front and white behind; a small, slender, black bill; a bright orange gape; disproportionately large, gull-like, black feet with pinkish-yellow webs; a floating, unhurried flight and plaintive, rather querulous call-notes.

Grey Ternlets are present on all islands of the Kermadec group. On Meyer Islet large numbers nest along the coastal strip: in the cavities, crevices and ledges of cliff faces, in the shade of boulders on the beach and under clumps of vegetation along the cliff tops. The common denominator of all sites is all-day shade from the sun. No nest material is ever used and the single egg is laid on the bare rock.

The chick is hatched covered with grey down and is brooded for 3 days. Thereafter it is left for increasing periods of time. At 8 days it is on its own much of the day. At 3 weeks it is wandering freely but it does not fly till 5 weeks. It remains dependent on its parents for some time after it can fly. It is fed by regurgitation in the manner of a petrel chick, with the chick placing both its mandibles inside the mandibles of the parent. Food consists entirely of plankton. When the parent returns to the nest after fishing, the chick becomes very excited, uttering squeaking noises and pecking at the webs of the parent's feet — not at the parent's bill as one would expect. Only when the parent leans forward with wide open bill and with regurgitation on the way does the chick transfer its attention from the feet to the gape.

At sea, Grey Ternlets feed in flocks. They work into the wind, hovering and fluttering over the water like Storm Petrels, repeatedly dipping down to pick up plankton from the surface. As they run out of the feeding area they veer away to the side, circle round to rejoin the rear of the flock, and thence work their way forward again.

Grey Ternlets have very pretty display flights. Particularly attractive is an interweaving flight in which, hovering on the wind and following the pattern of an extended lazy-tongs, they float from side to side across each other's flight paths. The pattern is followed in unison and to watch them swinging apart, crossing over, swinging away to the other side, then crossing again, is quite delightful. In another display, the bird will position itself on the wind in front of its incubating mate and, with wings and tail elevated to an angle of about 45 degrees, will float up and down as if suspended by an invisible elastic string. Against dark, forbidding, volcanic cliffs these waif-like birds with their plaintive cries seem incongruous and out of place.

# COLUMBIFORMES

Two living families. One represented in New Zealand: Pigeons and Doves.

## **Pigeons and Doves** Columbidae

Land birds with short necks and small heads. Plumage soft and dense. Bill short and covered at the base with a fleshy, unfeathered cere. Gregarious. Nearly all species *coo*. All drink by sucking and without raising the head between sips. Nests are characteristically of flimsy appearance. Clutch 1 or 2. Incubation by both sexes, the male during the day, the female at night. The young hatch covered in a sparse, yellow down and with the eyes closed. When small, they are fed on a specialised crop secretion known as 'pigeon's milk'. Most species rear at least 2 broods a year. Two hundred and eighty-nine species; New Zealand 4, 1 endemic, 3 introduced.

## The New Zealand Pigeon

*Photos 139, 140*

*Hemiphaga novaeseelandiae* 50 cm.

The endemic New Zealand Pigeon is a forest species — one of a group known as fruit pigeons — that feeds on fruits, flowers and leaves. It occurs the length of the country and a subspecies now very rare (perhaps 50 birds) inhabits the Chatham Islands. It is a large pigeon, tame and easily approachable. The undersurface is white, the eyes, bill, legs and feet red. The head and uppersurface, especially in sunlight, are violet with bronze and green reflections and the tail is greyish. The sexes are alike.

Its flight is fast and noisy, with a characteristic swish to the wings, and is often interspersed with long glides. The bird also has a habit of swooping vertically upwards, stalling momentarily, and then diving away in another direction. Such display flighting may be seen most months of the year.

Pigeons occur in most areas of mixed forest. They cannot survive in pure beech forest, for that has insufficient year-round food. They eat a wide variety of vegetable matter and as their numbers have recovered from the excessive hunting of the early years of settlement they have become increasingly common visitors to the introduced trees of parks and gardens.

The nest of the New Zealand Pigeon is seldom seen. It is a typical pigeon's flat platform of sticks and is placed in both native and exotic trees at heights of up to 10 metres in situations where it is shaded all day from the sun. The clutch is 1 and incubation, by both sexes, takes 30 days. The chick is covered in a sparse, yellow down and is brooded continuously for its first 10 days. Thereafter it is left during the day for gradually increasing periods. It is fed only during the early morning. It is not fed during the day, nor does it make any demand to be fed. During the day it just sits phlegmatically in the nest, making little movement.

Feeding is by regurgitation, with the parent holding the chick's bill in its own and pumping a creamy-looking fluid down its throat. As the chick grows, vegetable pulp replaces the 'pigeon milk'. The chick remains in the nest about 45 days. Nests and eggs of the New Zealand Pigeon have been found from October to June, so it is possible that 2 broods are attempted each year.

Little is known about the Chatham Island race except that it survives in small numbers in the forest at the southern end of the main island.

## The Rock Pigeon

*Photo 141*

*Columba livia* 33 cm.

The Eurasian Rock Pigeon is the original stock from which the various breeds of domestic pigeon were derived, and the feral Rock Pigeons now seen throughout New Zealand are liberations or escapees of domestic birds. Principally birds of towns and cities, Rock Pigeons have reverted in many parts of the country to their ancestral life styles — breeding in the cavities of inaccessible cliffs and travelling to cleared and cultivated ground to feed.

Because the birds are descendants of domestic breeds, they show great variation in plumage. Basically they are blue-grey, with an iridescent sheen of green and violet on the neck. They have 2 black bars on the wings, a white underwing, red legs and feet, and a black bill.

Rock Pigeons breed throughout the year, with a clutch of 2, an incubation period of 18 days, and a fledging period of about 30 days. A number of broods may be reared in a season.

## The Spotted Dove

*Streptopelia chinensis tigrina* 30 cm.

The natural range of this species is India, China, Malaysia and Indonesia. In New Zealand, cage-bird escapees have established themselves in the Auckland region. It is a pinkish-brown dove with a white-spotted, black collar round the hind neck and a long tail conspicuously tipped white when fanned in flight. The sexes are similar.

The Spotted Dove is a rather wary bird. It may be seen waddling on short legs and with bobbing head along the paths of parks and large gardens but can be difficult to get close to. It nests in densely-foliaged trees where it is well hidden from view, and it lays 2 eggs on a typical flimsy-looking pigeon platform of sticks. The incubation period is about 14 days and the young fledge at about 21 days.

## The Barbary Dove

*Streptopelia risoria* 28 cm.

The Barbary Dove is a long-domesticated dove derived from the Collared Dove (*S. roseogrisea*) of the sub-desert areas of North Africa. Small numbers have established in the wild near Masterton since about 1970 and at Whakatane and near Rotorua since about 1978. It has an overall, sandy-coloured plumage, paler beneath, and a conspicuous, black collar on the hind neck.

# PSITTACIFORMES

## **Parrots** Psittacidae

Mostly brightly-coloured birds with the bill short, curved and rounded and the nostrils in a cere. Upper mandible hinged, giving a noticeable degree of movement. Feet with 2 toes forward and 2 back. Use the foot as a hand, and tend to be right- or left-'handed'. Powder down present. Nest in holes. Eggs smallish and white. Young hatch blind and naked and are slow to mature. Food mostly seeds, fruits and young shoots but also nectar, pollen, insects and insect larvae. Three hundred and thirty-two species; New Zealand 10, 6 endemic, 1 near endemic, 3 introduced.

### The Kakapo

*Photo 142*

*Strigops habroptilus* 63 cm.

The Kakapo is a large, nocturnal, flightless, ground parrot and one of the world's most endangered birds. The sexes are alike, though males average larger and have larger and broader bills. Above, the Kakapo is an almost iridescent moss-green barred with black and lemon-yellow; below it is yellow and pale yellow-green barred with brown. It has an owl-like facial disc which presumably serves, as it does in owls and Harriers, to increase hearing ability and it has a breeding behaviour that is unique among parrots and among flightless birds.

The Kakapo was once widespread over the wetter and forested areas of the 3 main islands. Today, because of the introduction of cats, rats, stoats and ferrets it is reduced to a total of 8 birds in Fiordland, all males, and perhaps 20 birds at the recently discovered colony at Stewart Island. The Kakapo is a gentle, tame, slow-moving, ground bird with a breeding behaviour that makes it totally vulnerable to introduced ground predators.

Kakapos are a forest species that inhabit the wetter forests of the main ranges from sea level to bushline and thence out into the high alpine basins. They have carefully tended tracks along the ridges and in past days some of these tracks extended for kilometres. When feeding at night Kakapos cover great distances. They are vegetarian, and one of their favourite plants above bushline is the snow tussock, which they chew in *situ*, extracting the juice and leaving a characteristic ball of macerated fibre still attached to the plant. Kakapos eat the leaves and fruit of many species, occupying the niche of a grazing and browsing animal.

Like kiwis, Kakapos have small eyes for a nocturnal bird and presumably like them rely greatly on hearing. They also have cat-like whiskers at the base of the bill, so presumably their sense of touch is also good. Kakapos stay mostly on the ground but they can clamber through trees and they are able to plane downhill on their rounded wings for distances of 40 or 50 metres.

It has recently been proved that the Kakapo is an *arena* or *lek* species. These terms denote a breeding behaviour in which males congregate at set display grounds to advertise themselves and mate with any females that appear. The males are promiscuous and take no part in nest building or rearing the young. The behaviour does not occur with any other parrot or with any other flightless bird. Kakapo chicks are hatched helpless and blind, as are all parrot chicks, but have to be reared by the female alone — who must leave them to forage — in a nest that is on the ground. The young of all other flightless species are active, not helpless, and leave the nest soon after hatching to fend for themselves. The Kakapo's unique behaviour can only succeed — can only have evolved — in the complete absence of ground predators. Once cats, rats, stoats and ferrets are introduced the species disappears for lack of females and young. There are now no female Kakapos in the South Island and no Kakapos at all in the North Island.

Male Kakapos display at 'booming-grounds' which are collections of shallow, saucer-like depressions often placed near a rock to throw the sound outwards. The boom is produced in much the same manner as the boom of a Bittern and sounds like a deep note of an oboe. Like the Bittern's boom, it can be heard a great distance. In full display the birds puff themselves up with feathers erected and wings spread. The birds boom for hour after hour, night after night, week after week. In all, booming may continue for 10 weeks. Lone birds will not boom. The stimulus of other males is required. Early observers remarked on the fact that Kakapos do not boom every year. It is now evident that when booming, Kakapos take very little time off to feed; as a result they become so reduced in condition by the end of the booming period that they may then take 2 or 3 years to recover. This is especially so since the introduction of deer which compete for the more succulent food plants and leave food supplies marginal for the Kakapos.

The survival of this species depends utterly on the provision of an environment totally free of introduced ground predators. This cannot be done in Fiordland — where it is now too late anyway — nor, it appears, at Stewart Island, where cats are reducing the population by 50 percent a year. Consequently, the only course is to transfer birds to offshore islands such as Little Barrier. This is in progress.

## The White (Sulphur-crested) Cockatoo

*Cacatua galerita* 50 cm.

A large, all-white cockatoo with a sulphur-yellow crest introduced to New Zealand from Australia, possibly by cage-bird escape. Now well established near Raglan and in the watersheds of the Rangitikei and Turakina rivers in the North Island. Occurs in some hundreds but little has been reported of its adaptation to New Zealand conditions.

## The Kaka

*Photo 146*

*Nestor meridionalis* 45 cm.

Kakas are large, gregarious, arboreal parrots dependent for existence on large areas of native forest containing big trees and dying forest giants. Like New Zealand Pigeons they cannot exist all year in pure beech forest which does not have sufficient all-round variety of food supply and they need decaying trees for the grubs of woodboring insects they contain. There are 2 subspecies: a rather dull-coloured bird, olive brown and dull green with a red rump and abdomen, a scarlet underwing and a grey crown, found in the North Island and on some of the neighbouring offshore islands, such as Little Barrier, Hen and Chickens and Kapiti; and a much brighter bird in the South Island and Stewart Island. This subspecies also occupies D'Urville and Inner Chetwode Islands in Cook Strait and Codfish and Big South Cape Islands off Stewart Island. It has a conspicuously grey crown, brighter and more extensive red on the undersurface and underwing, and a distinct reddish collar. The sexes are similar though males have larger and more powerful bills.

Kakas are noisy birds with a great variety of harsh cries and musical whistles. Kakas have an enormous repertoire of conversational, liquid, whistling notes and are in fact one of the most musical birds of the New Zealand forest. They keep constantly in touch with other members of the flock both when in flight and when feeding. They fly strongly and seem to delight in periodically breaking-off from steady flight to tumble about in the air, chuckling to themselves as they do so. They do not seem to sleep much and may be heard carrying-on and calling at all hours of the night.

Kakas feed on berries, shoots, nectar and insect larvae, especially those of wood-boring beetles — which they obtain by tearing into the rotten wood with their powerful bills.

Kakas nest in holes in trees. The usual clutch is 2 to 4, and incubation is by the female only. During this time the male gathers food and feeds his mate by regurgitation, calling her off the nest with a particular, diagnostic, 2-note, soft whistle. If you can imagine the well-known 'wolf-whistle' given quietly and rather coyly, then that is the sound. Incubation takes about 21 days. The chicks are fed by regurgitation by both parents at intervals of about 1½ hours, and fledge when about 9 weeks old.

## The Kea

*Photo 143*

*Nestor notabilis* 46 cm.

The Kea is confined to the South Island, where it is a bird of mountain regions and the upper reaches of the forest. It may be seen on the river flats, even at sea level, but it is as a bird of the high alpine basins that it is best known. Its call is a far-carrying *keee-aa*, a most evocative sound, especially when heard ringing through the swirling mists of rocky bluffs. Keas fly strongly and they delight in tumbling and playing on the gusty air currents of rough weather.

Keas are large, stocky, olive-green parrots with a scarlet underwing and a red rump. In the forest they may be confused with the Kaka — which is, however, a more colourful bird with a heavier bill and a conspicuous grey crown. The male Kea has a distinctly longer upper mandible than the female; juveniles have a yellow cere.

Like all parrots, Keas are predominantly vegetarian, feeding on berries and shoots, but they are extremely inquisitive birds, very tame, and have learnt to fossick through rubbish pits and to eat carrion. They are accused of killing sheep and for many years bounties were paid for their destruction. Just what the truth is about sheep killing is still not settled. Undoubtedly, Keas eat dead sheep and undoubtedly they will attack cast sheep that are in dying throes. To what extent they attack healthy sheep is the point at issue. The runholders say the Kea alights on the sheep's back and proceeds to dig into it with its beak and that as a result sheep are found either with large festering areas over the kidneys or with a virulent form of blood poisoning that kills them in a matter of hours. The scientist finds the whole subject most unsatisfactory, for he can never manage to witness the occurrences for himself — and so reserves judgement.

Keas are playful birds. They delight in sliding down the corrugated iron roofs of alpine huts and I have seen them rolling head-over-heels with obvious enjoyment. Around camp sites, however, they can be an absolute pest and the damage they can do should they find their way inside a tent can be unbelievable.

Keas are the only parrots known to be polygamous. They nest in holes in the ground, under logs and in the cavities between the jumbled boulders of old moraines now overgrown with scrub and trees. The usual clutch is 2 to 4 and eggs may be found most months of the year. Only the female incubates and incubation takes between 3 and 4 weeks. She is fed by her mate who calls her off 2 or 3 times a day. Feeding is by regurgitation and while she is being fed the female fluffs up all her feathers till she resembles a feather duster and makes peculiar, low, whining and grumbling noises. Males may be polygamous and have more than 1 female incubating within their territories. When the chicks hatch the male feeds the female, who then feeds the chicks. The chicks fledge at 13-14 weeks and are attended by the male till they become independent.

## The Eastern Rosella

*Platycercus eximius* 33 cm.

A brilliantly coloured Australian species introduced via cage bird escapes and now established in the wild in a number of places in the North Island and also near Dunedin. The sexes are alike. The head, neck and breast are red and the cheek-patch is white. The wings are black and yellow with blue edges, the undersurface is yellow and the tail green and blue. A rather wary bird in New Zealand, with little recorded of its life style.

## The Crimson Rosella

*Photo 149*

*Platycercus elegans* 35 cm.

This is another Australian species established as a result of cage-bird escape. It is brilliant red all over except for blue cheek patches, blue tail and blue-edged wings. The back is mottled black. Immatures are mostly green, which can be confusing. It has become established in the hills around Wellington since about 1963.

## The Red-crowned Parakeet

*Photos 147, 148*

*Cyanoramphus novaezelandiae* male 28 cm., female 25 cm.

In the New Zealand region the Red-crowned Parakeet occurs on the main islands (where it is now rare), on many of the offshore islands, and at the Auckland Islands. Separate subspecies occur at the Kermadec, Chatham and Antipodes Islands. Elsewhere, other subspecies are found at New Caledonia and at Norfolk Island. A subspecies once occurring at Lord Howe Island was exterminated as an agricultural pest; another subspecies occupying Macquarie Island was exterminated by introduced cats and Wekas.

Red-crowned Parakeets are now rare on the main islands of New Zealand. They are abundant, however, on many offshore islands and the same pattern prevails on those outlying islands where cats and rats have been introduced to the main islands of the group leaving only the offshore islets vermin free. At the Kermadec Islands there are no resident Red-crowned Parakeets on Raoul which is infested with cats and rats, though the species is abundant on the Herald islets and at Macauley. At the Chatham Islands they are restricted to South East and Mangere Islands. At the Auckland Islands, once again, on the main island, which has cats, they are rare but they are common on Enderby and other islands of the group. Undoubtedly, this is due, at least in part, to the Red-crowned Parakeet's penchant for feeding on the ground. This cannot be quite the full story, however, or the Yellow-crowned Parakeet, which also comes to the ground, though to much less extent, would tend to a similar distribution, and that is not the case. The Yellow-crowned Parakeet occupies the main islands of New Zealand and of the Auckland Island group; the Red-crowned Parakeet occupies the offshore islands.

The Red-crowned Parakeet is a long-tailed, green parakeet with a red forehead, a red crown, a red line through the eye — which is itself red — a red patch behind the eye and a red patch on each side of the rump. Its flight is swift and usually accompanied by a chattering call note. It feeds on young shoots, seeds and other vegetable matter, moving quietly in the trees, and it can be difficult to detect.

The Red-crowned Parakeet nests in holes in trees and in rock crevices. It is usually a late breeder with eggs not till November-December. The eggs number 5 to

9, laid 48 hours apart, and incubation is by the female only, fed by her mate who arrives nearby and calls her off with a specific call note. She is fed by regurgitation, the birds holding their bills crosswise; while being fed she makes a creaking noise rather like that of a squeaky gate. When the chicks hatch the female remains in the nest with them for the full fledging period. Food is supplied by the male who feeds the female who then feeds the young. The young fledge at about 40 days.

## The Yellow-crowned Parakeet *Photo 145*

*Cyanoramphus auriceps* male 25 cm., female 23 cm.

The Yellow-crowned Parakeet is the parakeet most often seen on the main islands of New Zealand where it is in places common, especially in beech forest. It occurs on a number of offshore islands, but with the exception of the Chetwode Islands in Cook Strait and some of the Muttonbird Islands off Stewart Island, it is usually well outnumbered in these places by Red-crowned Parakeets. A distinct subspecies, known as Forbes' Parakeet, larger and more brightly coloured, occurs at the Chatham Islands on Mangere and Little Mangere Islands. At the Auckland Islands it is the Yellow-crowned species that occupies the main island. On Enderby, Ewing, Rose and the others, where the Red-crowned Parakeet is now dominant, it is uncommon.

The Yellow-crowned Parakeet is an overall green parakeet, slightly smaller than the Red-crowned species, and has a red forehead, a yellow crown, a red line from the forehead to the eye but no red patch behind the eye. The eye is red and there is a red patch on each side of the rump. In behaviour it resembles the Red-crowned species except that it does not descend to the ground to the same extent. It nests in holes in trees, never in rock crevices, and eggs have been recorded from August to April.

## The Orange-fronted Parakeet

*Cyanoramphus malherbi* male 22 cm., female 20.5 cm.

The Orange-fronted Parakeet is a very rare, small parakeet known today only from the Lake Sumner region of the South Island. It resembles a small Yellow-crowned Parakeet but has an orange forehead, a yellow crown and an orange stripe from the forehead to the eye. It has no patch behind the eye and the patch on each side of the rump is orange. The eye is red. Virtually nothing has been recorded of the species' habits, for it has always been rare. Indeed, prior to its discovery near Lake Sumner in 1980, it had been recorded this century only 5 times.

## The Antipodes Island Green Parakeet *Photo 144*

*Cyanoramphus unicolor* male 31.5 cm., female 29 cm.

This species occurs only on Antipodes Island, which it shares with a subspecies of the Red-crowned Parakeet. It is the largest of the New Zealand parakeets and has a massive and powerful bill in comparison with the others. Like the other parakeets, it is predominantly green in colour. It has an emerald green face and a red eye but has no coloured markings on the head and rump.

The Antipodes Island Parakeet is a tame bird, easily approached with reasonable care. It tends to keep to the lower parts of the island where the vegetation (almost entirely tall, subantarctic tussock) is at its most dense and luxuriant. It feeds largely on the leaves of the tussock (*Poa litorosa*), passing them through its bill and extracting the juice rather in the manner of the Kakapo, except that the stems come out the other side like strips of corrugated cardboard! It fossicks around in the colonies of the Erect-crested Penguins for scraps of fat left on carcasses killed by skuas and for left-over contents of predated eggs. It also eats seeds and the leaves of low-growing *coprosma* shrubs. By contrast, the Antipodes Island Red-crowned Parakeet is seen mostly on the tableland; eats seeds, berries and insects rather than tussock, and is seldom seen fossicking the penguin colonies. Also, it breeds later in the year, which is in line with its behaviour elsewhere.

The Antipodes Island Parakeet nests in burrows in the peaty soil at the bases of the tussocks. Little has been recorded of the breeding cycle, owing to the infrequency with which this remote island is visited. However, it is evident that it nests earlier than the Red-crowned; for by February, when some Red-crowned birds still have downy chicks in the nest, the Antipodes Parakeets are all fully fledged, partly feeding themselves and nearing full independence.

# CUCULIFORMES

Two families; 1 in New Zealand: Cuckoos

## **Cuckoos** Cuculidae

Feet with 2 toes forward and 2 back. Bill without a cere. Most of the Old World species are parasitic, laying their eggs in other birds' nests. One hundred and twenty-five species; New Zealand 6, 1 endemic breeder.

### The Oriental Cuckoo

*Cuculus saturatus horsfieldi* 33 cm.

The Oriental Cuckoo is a rare straggler to New Zealand with about 10 records. It breeds from the Himalayas to Japan and migrates to southern Asia and Australia. In flight it looks like a hawk. The upperparts are blue grey and the abdomen is boldly barred dark-brown and white. The eyelids, legs and feet are yellow. It is a wary species, difficult to approach.

### The Pallid Cuckoo

*Cuculus pallidus* 30 cm.

A very rare straggler to New Zealand: 4 records. An Australian species parasitic mostly on honeyeaters. Very like the Oriental Cuckoo except that the abdomen is plain, not barred. In flight it resembles a hawk. It perches on posts and often raises its tail like a Blackbird on alighting.

### The Fan-tailed Cuckoo

*Cuculus pyrrhophanus prionurus* 25 cm.

The Fan-tailed Cuckoo is an Australian species recorded once (1960) as a straggler to New Zealand. The uppersurface is grey and the undersurface pale rufous. The tail is spotted and barred with white and is not particularly fan-like. This species often sits on posts — with its tail hanging down — and can be quite approachable. It raises its tail like a Blackbird when alighting. It is parasitic on Australian wrens and thornbills.

### The Shining Cuckoo

*Photos 150, 151*

*Chrysococcyx lucidus* 16 cm.

The Shining Cuckoo is a summer breeding migrant to New Zealand and the Chatham Islands and is parasitic principally on warblers (*Gerygone sp.*). Another race migrates to Australia where it is parasitic on their domed-nest species, of which they have a large number. The New Zealand birds winter in the Solomon Islands and the Bismarks. The Australian race winters in New Guinea and the Lesser Sundas.

Shining Cuckoos are small birds, difficult to see. They can be heard easily enough, for they are very vocal and have an unmistakable call, but the call is ventriloqual, and attempts to locate the birds can be quite exasperating. The Shining Cuckoo is bronzy green above and barred white and glossy green below. The call is a series of double, upward, whistled slurs, repeated 4 or 5 times, or more, and followed by a long, downward, whistled slur given once or twice; occasionally 3 times. Starlings often imitate it, for it fits their mimic repertoire beautifully.

The Shining Cuckoo arrives in late August but is not much noticed till well into September. It spreads the length of the country and is parasitic mainly on the Grey Warbler and the Chatham Island Warbler. Some evidently stop off at Norfolk Island where they parasitise the local warbler (*G. modesta*) and they used to parasitise the Lord Howe Island Warbler (*G. insularis*) in the days before that species was exterminated by rats. In New Caledonia it is parasitic on *G. flavolateralis.*

Shining Cuckoos are apparently promiscuous. Parties of a dozen or more are to be seen flying about the tops of tall trees, calling vociferously and apparently mating indiscriminately. Very little is known about the breeding behaviour of Shining Cuckoos other than that they are parasitic on Australasian warblers and their kin. Shining Cuckoos are difficult birds to come to grips with. For example, it is not known how many eggs a bird may lay in a season, nor in how many nests, nor how they are inserted. The incubation period, however, of a Shining Cuckoo's egg is 12 days, as against 19 days for a Grey Warbler, and consequently the Grey Warbler chicks have no chance of survival once the cuckoo's hatches.

Shining Cuckoos are insectivorous and, like many cuckoos, have a partiality for hairy caterpillars, something few other birds will touch.

## The Long-tailed Cuckoo

*Eudynamys taitensis* 40 cm.

The Long-tailed Cuckoo breeds only in New Zealand. It is a summer migrant wintering on the islands of the Pacific over a vast area from New Guinea to the Carolines and the Marquesas. It returns to New Zealand in October and spreads the length of the country where it is parasitic mostly on 3 related species: the Whitehead, the Yellowhead and the Brown Creeper.

The Long-tailed Cuckoo is an overall brown bird, liberally spotted with white, and rufous on the uppersurface. Underneath, it is white, streaked with brown. Its most conspicuous feature is the very long tail which is reddish brown and barred with black. The sexes are alike but with the females more rufous in colour.

In New Zealand the voice of the Long-tailed Cuckoo is a loud, long, drawn-out, rather intimidating screech: *shweesht*. (In its winter quarters it sounds quite different.) It also has a falcon-like *kik-kik-kik-kik*. On a number of occasions I have heard the screech of one bird being answered by *kik-kik-kik-kik* from another and I wonder if the sexes perhaps have different calls. As with the Shining Cuckoo, parties of a dozen or so birds may be seen in agitated commotion in the tops of tall trees, calling loudly.

Long-tailed Cuckoos are carnivorous and are predators on the eggs and young of many species but especially on those that make open nests such as the introduced Blackbird and Song Thrush. I have many times seen Long-tailed Cuckoos pursued through the forest by hysterical Blackbirds, the Blackbird's squab dangling from the cuckoo's beak. My wife once saw one of these cuckoos silently plane down out of a tree and lift a Blackbird chick out of a nest a few metres before her eyes. The whole sequence was done with smooth precision and with hardly a pause. She has also seen a Song Thrush egg taken in similar manner. Once a nest with chicks has been found the cuckoo returns again and again till all have been taken.

In the trees, Long-tailed Cuckoos often perch lengthways on a branch rather than across. They move in a sinuous, rather reptilian manner, holding the head low; with their baleful, yellow eyes, they are evil-looking birds.

The Long-tailed Cuckoo is parasitic principally on the Whitehead in the North Island, the Yellowhead and Brown Creeper in the South Island and the Brown

Creeper at Stewart Island. How the egg is transferred into the nest of the hole-nesting Yellowhead is not known, nor is the incubation period.

## The Channel Bill Cuckoo

*Scythrops novaehollandiae* 60 cm.

A very rare vagrant to New Zealand: 1 record, Invercargill 1924. A very large, grey bird with a massive pale, yellowish bill and a long tail. Voice a loud, raucous scream. Wary. Breeds north and east Australia, wintering to New Guinea and the Bismarks.

# STRIGIFORMES

Owls. Two families: Barn Owls, Typical Owls.

## **Barn Owls** Tytonidae

Barn Owls are large owls with a heart-shaped facial disc. The eyes are dark — not yellow or orange as in other owls — and are rather small compared to the large eyes of typical owls. Barn owls have a characteristic knock-kneed stance. Ten species; New Zealand 1 — a straggler.

### The Australian Barn Owl

*Tyto alba delicatula* 34 cm.

There are 3 records of this species as a wind-blown vagrant to the West Coast of the South Island. The undersurface and facial disc is white, the uppersurface is mottled yellowish-buff.

## **Typical Owls** Strigidae

Nocturnal birds of prey with soft plumage specialised for silent flight. Most are cryptically plumaged to make detection difficult when roosting during the daytime. The eyes are large, directed forwards for binocular judgement of distance, completely fill the eye-sockets, and are immovable. Movement is by the whole head which can rotate at least 180 degrees. The ears are large and hearing is aided by the disc-like arrangement of the facial feathers. Bill short and hooked but not especially strong: it is the feet that are powerful. Nostrils in a cere. Outer toe reversible but usually held to the side. Claws sharp and hooked. Sexes alike. Females larger. Swallow prey whole or in chunks and eject the indigestible bones, fur and feathers etc. in the form of pellets. Typically, are mobbed by small birds when discovered at day-time roosts. One hundred and twenty-three species; New Zealand 3, 1 introduced, 1 endemic probably extinct.

### The Morepork

*Photo 154*

*Ninox novaeseelandiae* 29 cm.

In New Zealand the Morepork occurs the length of the country and on most of the bushclad offshore islands from the Three Kings to Stewart Island. Elsewhere, it occurs in Australia (where it is known as the Boobook Owl), New Guinea, the Lesser Sundas and Norfolk Island. The race once inhabiting Lord Howe Island is now extinct.

Although essentially a bird of native forest, the Morepork is one of the species that has successfully colonised many man-made habitats and may now be heard and seen in many settled districts. It is a cryptically-coloured brown owl with a rounded head and the plumage spotted and streaked with white. It is larger and browner than the introduced Little Owl. Its voice is the well known double *more-pork* that can be imitated by blowing into cupped hands.

Moreporks are largely insectivorous but take lizards, small birds, rats and mice. They nest mostly in hollow trees, with eggs being laid in October or November. The normal clutch is 2, laid 48 hours apart, and incubation, by the female only, from the first egg, takes 30 days. The young are brooded and guarded by the female for

**150** The Shining Cuckoo.

**151** The Shining Cuckoo.

**152** The Little Owl.

**153** A Little Owl chick.

**154** The Morepork.

**155** A male Rifleman.

**156** A female Rifleman.

**157** A typical Rifleman nesting cranny.

**158** The Sacred Kingfisher.

**159** A female Rock Wren.

**160** A male Rock Wren photographed near the Homer Tunnel.

**161** A male South Island Tomtit.

**162** The introduced Skylark.

**163** The Welcome Swallow.

**164** A juvenile Black-faced Cuckoo Shrike.

**165** Black and Pied Fantails.

**166** A female South Island Tomtit.

**167** The Black Robin.

**168** A male South Island Robin at a typical nest site.

**169** The Mangere Islands. Little Mangere is in the distance. Big Mangere, to which the Black Robins were transferred when their habitat collapsed, is the foreground.

**170** Yellowheads.

**171** The Brown Creeper.

**172** The South Island Fernbird.

**173** The Yellowhead.

their whole time in the nest — about 5 weeks. When first hatched and for their first week or 10 days the female is most reluctant to leave the chicks, even at night, and during this time the male supplies all the food. As the chicks grow the female hunts too but stays in the nest during the day.

## The Laughing Owl

*Sceloglaux albifacies* 38 cm.

The Laughing Owl is a large endemic owl last reported in 1914 and now almost certainly extinct. It is larger than the Morepork, with long legs, a short tail and a yellowish-brown plumage streaked and spotted brown. The facial disc is mostly white (Morepork grey). In the early years of settlement it was reported from the North, South and Stewart Islands, and from both low and high rainfall areas. It may have fed much on the ground. Its voice was reported as loud and has been variously described as 'laughing', 'a series of dismal shrieks', 'like the yelping of a young dog'.

The species was apparently plentiful during the early years of settlement but by 1880 had become extremely rare. It nested among rocks with a clutch of 2 and incubation was by the female. If in fact it was predominantly a ground feeding species, as are so many of New Zealand's primitive endemics, then the introduction of cats, rats, stoats and ferrets can fairly be blamed for its demise.

## The Little Owl

*Photos 152, 153*

*Athene noctua* 23 cm.

The natural range of the Little Owl is Europe, North Africa and Asia east to Mongolia. It was introduced to the South Island of New Zealand between 1906 and 1910 in an endeavour to control the large numbers of other introduced birds that had become pests in Central Otago orchards. The effect, of course, was negligible — the Little Owl is not really a small-bird predator, though it does take some. Little Owls mostly eat invertebrates — earwigs, beetles, moths, spiders, earthworms and so on.

The Little Owl is a small, greyish-brown owl with a flat-topped head. Like the Morepork it is liberally speckled and spotted white above. Underneath, it is paler than the Morepork and has a white band across the throat. It now occurs throughout most of the South Island.

Little Owls may often be seen during the daytime perched on posts or the limbs of trees and in winter they have the habit of sunning themselves on warm afternoons. They fly in a characteristic, bouncy and undulating manner and they walk and run well.

Little Owls nest in ready-made holes in trees, buildings, hay stacks and clay banks. The clutch ranges from 2 to 5, usually 3, and most eggs are laid October-November. Incubation is by the female and takes 28 days. When the chicks are small the Little Owl, like the Morepork, is reluctant to leave them, and if you are gentle will allow you to lift her up to see how the chicks are progressing. Again like the Morepork, she stays in the nest during the daytime till the chicks are well grown but assists her mate to obtain food at night. Most chicks have left the nest by the end of December.

# APODIFORMES

## **Swifts** Apodidae

The fastest-flying and most aerial of birds. Wings long and scimitar-shaped. Legs short. Feet very small and weak. Bill tiny. Plumage plainly coloured. Sexes alike. Feed entirely on the wing. Perch by clinging to vertical surfaces. Use saliva in the construction of the nests. Seventy-one species; 2 reach New Zealand as stragglers.

### The Fork-tailed Swift

*Apus pacificus* 18 cm.

Breeds eastern Asia and Japan and migrates south. Regular in Australia, vagrant in New Zealand: about 10 records. Dark above and mottled below. Rump white. Tail long and forked. Throat whitish. Not as fast in flight as the Spine-tailed Swift.

### The Spine-tailed Swift

*Chaetura caudacuta* 20 cm.

Breeds Siberia to Japan and migrates south. Regular in Australia, vagrant in New Zealand but more frequent than the Fork-tailed Swift. A large, powerful swift and one of the world's fastest birds. Usually seen in small flocks. An overall, dark bird with long, scimitar wings, a square tail, white undertail coverts and a white forehead, chin and throat.

# CORACIFORMES

Hole-nesting birds with either 2 or all 3 front toes joined for parts of their length. Seven families; 2 represented in New Zealand: Kingfishers, Rollers.

## **Kingfishers** Alcedinidae

Thick-set, mostly very colourful birds with long strong bills, short legs and small feet. Sexes similar. Two main groups: the fishing kingfishers which plunge-dive for fish, and the forest kingfishers which live more on insects, lizards, crabs and the like and may be found far from water. The New Zealand species belong to the latter group. Eighty-four species; New Zealand 2, 1 introduced.

## The New Zealand (Sacred) Kingfisher

*Photo 158*

*Halcyon sancta vagans* 24 cm.

The New Zealand Kingfisher occurs the length of the country including many of the offshore islands and is also found at the Kermadec Islands. Elsewhere (where it is known as the Sacred Kingfisher) other subspecies occur in Australia, New Caledonia, the Loyalty Islands and at Norfolk and Lord Howe Islands.

The colour of the Kingfisher varies as the quality and direction of the light and also from bird to bird; usually, in full sunlight the uppersurface is brilliant blue with green reflections. Sometimes, however, the blue reflects as a more pastel, cobalt colour. In dull light it often just looks dark. The undersurface is white with a varying wash of ochre or rufous on the breast. A black band passes through the eye and encircles the neck and below that is a white or rufous collar. The bill is long, sturdy, tapered and black.

In New Zealand Sacred Kingfishers are most common in coastal districts and in the north. They may also be found far inland, in forest as well as open country, and though usually near water are not dependent on water for food.

Sacred Kingfishers feed on a wide variety of insects and small animals, from earthworms and grasshoppers to crabs, small fish, lizards, mice and even small birds. Prey is located by watching patiently from an elevated perch and captured by a sudden darting dive. They will perch for long periods, motionless except for an occasional bob of the head or nervous flick of the tail. If the area is unproductive they suddenly fly off to another perch 50 or so metres away and scan again. Telephone wires, fence lines, limbs of trees and isolated rocks on the shore-line are all favourite vantage points.

Except when breeding, Kingfishers are solitary, silent birds keeping to themselves. When paired for breeding, however, they become very vocal, uttering a 4-syllable *kik-kik-kik-kik,* endlessly and monotonously repeated. They nest in self-excavated holes in clay banks and rotten trees. In clay banks the tunnel is usually about 20 centimetres long, slopes slightly upwards, and is enlarged at the end to form a chamber. The entrance is characteristically squared-off rather than circular in outline and is typically situated just below the top lip of the bank. In trees, the holes may be at a considerable height. Most of the ones I have seen in the Eglinton Valley have been in the region of 5 to 10 metres. As a rule, Kingfishers like to make a new hole each year but old holes will be re-used.

Kingfishers commence their tunnels by flying at the bank or tree and hitting it hard with the point of the bill. They hit with considerable force and before launching themselves off, bob up and down and make churring noises as if egging themselves on. Once a dent has been made and a foothold achieved the rest of the tunnelling is done by clinging at the entrance and pick-axing with the bill.

The usual clutch is 4 or 5, and the incubation period is about 18 days. As breeding advances, food remnants and excreta accumulate in the tunnel, eventually to run down out of the entrance as a nauseating but tell-tale line of slime. Kingfishers are appalling housekeepers. The chicks in the nest keep up an incessant, wheezy, rasping note and fledge when about 20 days old. Most Kingfishers have eggs in October or November, and most have completed the cycle by January. Both birds excavate, both incubate and both feed the young.

## The Kookaburra

*Dacelo novaeguineae* 45 cm.

A very large Australian Kingfisher, well known for its laughing cry. Introduced to New Zealand between 1866 and 1880 and surviving in small pockets along the east coast north of Auckland. Mostly brownish-grey above and off-white below, it has a dark line through the eye and a streaky, brown crown. The tail is barred with russet and black and the shoulders are mottled blue. The bill is massive. In Australia this species breeds in cooperative groups of adults and last year's young but little is known about its habits in New Zealand.

## **Rollers** Coraciidae

Mostly tropical birds, so named for their spectacular flight displays during which they swoop and roll at speed. Robust, colourful birds mostly in blues. Sexes similar. Legs and feet weak. On the ground they hop clumsily; they do not walk. Nest in holes. Sixteen species; New Zealand 1 — vagrant.

## The Broad-billed Roller (Dollarbird)

*Eurystomus orientalis pacificus* 29 cm.

A breeding migrant to Australia from New Guinea, the Solomon Islands, and South-east Asia. A rare straggler to New Zealand, mostly juvenile birds wind-blown to the west coasts in late summer. A stocky, greenish-brown bird with a brown head and greenish-blue back and wings. In flight, the wings show a conspicuous white 'dollar' at the base of the primaries. Bill, eye-ring, legs and feet red. Usually seen sallying out from a perch after flying insects.

# PASSERIFORMES

Perching birds. Birds with 4 unwebbed toes joined at the same level with 3 toes forward and 1 back. All are land birds. A large and complex assemblage of over 5000 species in some 56 families. New Zealand 46 species of which 15 introduced and 3 extinct.

## New Zealand Wrens Acanthisittidae

An endemic family of 4 species of which one is extinct and another nearly so. Tiny birds of ancient and obscure origin whose ancestors probably became isolated in New Zealand during the early tertiary period.

### The Rifleman

*Photos 155, 156, 157*

*Acanthisitta chloris* 8 cm.

Except for the northern part of the North Island, the Rifleman occurs the length of the country, principally in native forest areas but also in exotic pine plantations and adjacent scrublands. It is also found on Great and Little Barrier Islands and on Codfish Island. It is most common in the South Island — in the beech forests east of the Southern Alps, where at times it may extend above bushline to occupy the habitats more usually associated with Rock Wrens.

Riflemen are New Zealand's smallest birds and have very short tails. Males are clear green above and white below and have a yellow rump, yellow flanks and a white eyebrow. Females are similar below but are streaked above with brown, white and yellow. Juveniles resemble the females but are streaky on the breast.

The Rifleman's most distinctive feature is the incessant flicking of the wings that accompanies its every move as it progresses in search of food. Riflemen are active little birds, forever on the go. They are insect feeders and from dawn to dusk may be seen exploring cracks and crannies, equally at ease whether hanging upside down or flicking their way through sprays of foliage. In the main, they are bark feeders and spend the greatest part of their time working with lilliputian jerks up the trunks of trees. They always work up the trunks, never down.

Riflemen nest in holes, mostly in rotting trees, but also in cliffs and old buildings, and they will use nest boxes. A favourite site is behind the peeling bark of a dead tree, with access gained through a narrow crack. In the cavity they build a globular nest of grass and moss lined with fine grass and feathers and the nest has a woven entrance in the side. Nests may be found at all heights from ground level to the tops of massive forest giants. Most, however, are between 3 and 6 metres. They nest, depending on latitude, from August to January, and early in the season any Rifleman seen on the ground is worth watching, for it is almost certainly looking for nest material and if quietly followed should reveal its nest in a few minutes. Both sexes build and sometimes more than one nest is started before one is finally taken to completion.

The usual clutch is 3 or 4 and the eggs may be laid at 48-hour intervals — a surprising discovery, for passerine birds normally lay their eggs daily. Incubation is by both sexes and takes 20-21 days, an unusually long time for a small bird. The young are fed by both parents, with visits to the nest every few minutes in bursts of about half an hour. The parents then break off for a while before the next session begins. Sometimes the young of a previous brood will help in feeding those of a later one and I have seen a number of nests that were attended by more than 2 adults. Six of these nests were attended by a male and 2 females, 2 by a female and 2 males (which was unexpected because Riflemen are territorial birds) and 1 by 4 birds: an adult male and female and a juvenile male and female.

The call note of the Rifleman is a high-pitched *zipt-zipt-zipt* beyond the range of some people's hearing.

## The Bush Wren

*Xenicus longipes* 9.5 cm.

The Bush Wren is now a very rare bird, bordering on extinction. Three subspecies are described, one for each main island, but the differences are slight. Bush Wrens resemble Rock Wrens more than Riflemen and the sexes are similar. The uppersurface is brown shading to green on the back and wings. The undersurface is grey. There is a white eyebrow, a yellow patch at the bend of the wing and a yellowish-green patch on the flanks. The Bush Wren bobs like a Rock Wren but inhabits forest areas rather than subalpine scrub. It is more likely to be confused with the Rock Wren than with the Rifleman and the best distinguishing feature is the grey undersurface.

In the North Island, the Bush Wren is feared extinct, the last sighting (unconfirmed) being Waikaremoana 1955. In the South Island it may just still survive; the last sighting was Nelson Lakes 1968. At Stewart Island it is definitely extinct, finally exterminated by the disastrous rat plague of Big South Cape Island and Solomon Island — its last refuges — during the mid 1960s. Prior to that it had already been exterminated on the Stewart Island mainland by cats. A hurried rescue attempt by the New Zealand Wildlife Service transferred the few remaining birds they could capture to Kaimohu Island but the birds failed to establish and when a party which my wife and I were privileged to join searched Kaimohu in 1976 no trace could be found. These birds bred on or near the ground, with a nest like a Rock Wren's, and were vulnerable in the extreme to introduced ground predators.

## The Rock Wren

*Photos 159, 160*

*Xenicus gilviventris* 9.5 cm.

The Rock Wren is confined to the alpine regions of the South Island where it inhabits screes, rockfalls and subalpine scrub. It extends the length of the island, from Nelson to Fiordland, but it is not found in every valley. In order to occupy its present habitat the Rock Wren has had to solve the recurring problems of alpine weather. Even in mid-summer high alpine basins can be blanketed in deep snow and if the birds are to breed above bushline, as they do, then their survival is dependent on their exploiting the possibilities of existence under the snow rather than retreat from it. Consequently, Rock Wrens occur only where there are extensive areas of jumbled fallen rocks and scree overgrown at least in part with subalpine scrub. In such places the birds find food and security in a mouse-like existence, hopping and running about the interconnected spaces while comfortably insulated by the blanket of snow above their heads. So well adapted are they to this life that even in winter Rock Wrens have yet to be reported descending lower than the subalpine scrub. In summer, and especially on cloudy days, more Rock Wrens will be heard underfoot than will be seen on the surface. Indeed, to find Rock Wrens good hearing is important. I am unable to hear them at all. Like the call of the Rifleman, their high-pitched *zipt* is beyond my range. At the Homer Tunnel my wife, whose hearing is much better than mine, consistently finds Rock Wrens where I keep walking over the top of them.

Rock Wrens are tiny birds with very weak flight, exceptionally large feet and a characteristic habit of bobbing up and down whenever they alight. In the northern part of their range both sexes are olive-brown above and white below, the males slightly greener above than the females. In the southern part, however, and especially south of the Hollyford River, male Rock Wrens are as green as male Riflemen. Male Fiordland Rock Wrens have bright green backs, bright yellow flanks and conspicuous white eyebrows. Female Rock Wrens, in Fiordland and elsewhere, have olive-brown backs, yellow flanks and buff eyebrows. Both sexes are white underneath.

Rock Wrens nest on or under the ground in the crevices between stones and among the ground-hugging branches of subalpine scrub. The nest is an igloo-shaped structure woven out of snow tussock and has a woven entrance tunnel. The cavity is lined with fine grass and feathers. The eggs are white and the clutch varies from 2 to 5. Neither the incubation nor fledging periods are yet reported but both sexes incubate and both feed the young. Food consists entirely of invertebrates: moths, caterpillars, beetles, grasshoppers, flies, grubs and the like. Beetles are often taken into the nest whole and are evidently broken up while inside, for after a while the parent reappears with all the prickly bits such as the legs and wing cases. Soft, downy feathers are regularly taken into the nest and worn feather-shafts are regularly cleared out. An interesting observation is that Rock Wrens often eat feathers, a behaviour once thought unique to grebes. In view of the number of hard-cased insects such as beetles and alpine grasshoppers in the Rock Wren's diet, no doubt the feathers have the same protective function for Rock Wrens as they have against fish bones for grebes. Whether Rock Wrens feed feathers to the young in the nest is of course impossible to say.

## The Stephen Island Wren

*Xenicus lyalli*

Extinct. This wren was confined to Stephen Island in Cook Strait where it was discovered in 1894 by the lighthouse keeper's cat which brought in about 20 specimens and then no more. It was seen twice by the lighthouse keeper, who said it did not fly but ran about like a mouse and was semi-nocturnal.

## **Larks** Alaudidae

Terrestrial birds of open country. The hind claw is usually long and the plumage cryptic. Nest on the ground. Seventy-five species; New Zealand 1, introduced.

## The Skylark

*Photo 162*

*Alauda arvensis* 18 cm.

The natural range of the Skylark is from Europe across Asia to Japan. Large numbers were introduced to New Zealand during the 1860s and later to the Chatham Islands. The species is now well established and has self-introduced to the Kermadec and Auckland Islands.

Skylarks are territorial birds whose song post is the sky. Their outpourings of continuous, liquid trills and runs seemingly without regard for the rules of taking breath are among the best known and most delightful of bird songs.

The Skylark is streaked brown and dark brown above and has a short crest. The underparts are buffy white and the breast is streaked brown. The outer tail feathers are conspicuously white. It has a very long hind claw. The Skylark does not bob its tail and it has a rather crouching stance — unlike the upright, tail-bobbing stance of the Pipit. It eats mostly small seeds whereas the Pipit eats mostly insects.

Skylarks nest on the ground in short herbage, building a neat, grass-lined cup and laying 3-5 eggs that are incubated, by the female only, for 11 days. The young are fed by both parents and when 9 or 10 days old leave the nest to hide in the surrounding vegetation. They fly well when about 20 days old.

## **Swallows and Martins** Hirundinidae

Small birds that feed by hawking for aerial insect life. Legs and feet small and weak. Bill small. Gape wide. Differ from Swifts in the presence of bristles round the gape and in having 12, not 10, tail feathers. Flight more erratic than Swifts' and not as fast. Perch readily and show little fear of man. Seventy-four species; New Zealand 2.

### The Welcome Swallow

*Photo 163*

*Hirundo tahitica neoxena* 15 cm.

The Welcome Swallow is a recent and welcome addition to the New Zealand fauna, self-introduced from Australia during late 1950s and the 1960s. The first New Zealand nests were discovered in 1958 and since then the spread of this species has been little short of explosive. Welcome Swallows now occur throughout the North Island and in much of the northern part of the South Island.

The Welcome Swallow is blue-black above and white below and has a rufous forehead, throat and breast. The tail is forked and the sexes are alike. In Australia the Welcome Swallow is a partial migrant and, like migrants generally, has the tendency periodically to move further afield. It is a bird of open countryside and has a distinct liking for nesting in man-made structures. Consequently, it is a species that benefits from man's clearance of land and erection of buildings. It is possible that in the past Welcome Swallows reached New Zealand only to find no foothold. Today they have evidently found conditions very much to their liking indeed.

Welcome Swallows so often use man-made structures for the placement of their nests that one wonders how they ever managed without them. The nest is a cup-shaped structure built by both sexes and made of small pellets of mud cemented together with saliva. It is lined with feathers and is always placed high up under an overhang or roof so that when completed there is just enough room for the bird to squeeze in between the roof and the lip of the nest. In New Zealand the most favoured site is under bridges though I have seen them far back in dark coastal caves and in old sheds. The clutch is 3 to 5 and incubation is by the female only. The male has no brood patch. The male roosts alongside the female at the nest at night. The incubation period is 16 days.

When the young are small the parents carefully carry away the faecal sacs and keep the nest clean. As the chicks grow, however, the droppings are simply ejected over the side of the nest, eventually to make a substantial pile on the ground beneath — a behaviour that gets rather messy when one has Welcome Swallows in residence on one's front verandah!

Welcome Swallows have no hesitation in dive bombing with a swish of wings and squeaks of protest should you approach too closely to the nest and they do the same in defence of chicks recently fledged. The chicks are dependent on the parents for about 3 weeks after leaving the nest and during this period return to the nest to roost at night. Later, the chicks of the first brood may help to feed the young of the second.

Welcome Swallows eat only insects caught on the wing. Their flight is fast, erratic, graceful and seemingly tireless. Between flights they perch on wires. Because they are dependent on flying insects, migration from colder districts in winter becomes necessary. The degree of movement within New Zealand, however, is as yet little known.

The range of this species in its widest sense takes in much of Polynesia, Australia, South-east Asia, southern India and Sri Lanka.

## The Australian Tree Martin

*Hylochelidon nigricans* 14 cm.

The Australian Tree Martin has a square tail and a white rump. It is black above and off-white below and has a reddish forehead. The sexes are alike. It breeds in Australia and migrates to New Guinea and the Solomon Islands for the winter. It occurs in New Zealand as a straggler, sometimes in small flocks, and a pair is reported to have nested in a mill at Oamaru in 1893. The species normally nests in colonies in holes in trees.

### **Pipits and Wagtails** Motacillidae

Small, slender, terrestrial birds of open country that walk and run, constantly tipping the tail up and down. They feed on insects and nest on the ground. Fifty-four species; New Zealand 1.

## The New Zealand Pipit

*Photos 180, 181, 182*

*Anthus novaeseelandiae* 19 cm.

In New Zealand the Pipit occurs the length of the country, from coastal beaches to mountain tops, wherever there is open ground. It occurs on most offshore islands and at the Chatham, Antipodes, Auckland and Campbell Islands. Elsewhere, the species (known as Richard's Pipit) has a very wide range over much of Australia, Asia, India and Africa.

The New Zealand Pipit is streaked brown and dark brown above. The underparts are white and the breast is streaked brown. The outer tail feathers are white and it has a long hind claw. It is a slimmer bird than the Skylark, stands more upright on longer legs and it constantly tips its tail. Its most common call note is *pee-pit*, but it also has a commonly heard rasping *screep*. In flight it has a rather undistinguished repetitive *cheet*. Its food is mostly insects, not seeds.

Pipits nest on the ground in rougher herbage than the Skylark, building a deep cup nest of grass. The clutch is 3 or 4 (occasionally 5) and incubation is by the female for 14 days. Both parents feed the young, which fledge at 14-16 days, and 2 or 3 broods may be reared.

At Antipodes Island the Pipits nest in the hearts of the big tussocks, a metre or more above ground and at the Auckland Islands I have seen one just inside the overgrown entrance of an abandoned rabbit burrow. At Campbell Island they are very rare and apparently surviving only on one or two offshore stacks.

### **Cuckoo-shrikes** Campephagidae

A tropical Old World family of birds somewhat resembling cuckoos in body shape and shrikes in their bill structure, but related to neither. Seventy species; New Zealand 2, both vagrant.

## The Black-faced Cuckoo-shrike *Photo 164*

*Coracina novaehollandiae* 33 cm.

A blue-grey bird with a black face and throat and a white undersurface and tail tip. It perches conspicuously and shuffles its wings on alighting. Flight undulating, with closed-wing 'glides'. About a dozen New Zealand records, widely dispersed, mostly of immature birds. The natural range is from Australia to India.

## The White-winged Triller

*Lalage suerii* 20 cm.

A small black-and-white Australian species. One New Zealand record: 1969, Otago Peninsula. Male black above and white below with white shoulders and a grey rump. Female brown above and grey below with buff coloured markings on the wings. Feeds on insects among the foliage and on the ground.

### **Bulbuls** Pycnonotidae

Adaptable, gregarious birds of Africa and Asia, some of which are popular as cage birds. The Red-Vented Bulbul *pycnonotus cafer* established itself during the early 1950s in Auckland but was successfully eradicated by 1955. None have been reported since.

### **Accentors** Prunellidae

Small, sparrow-like birds of Europe and Asia, mostly of alpine regions. Bill small and slender. Live on or close to the ground. Often flick wings and tail, especially in display. Eggs blue. Twelve species; New Zealand 1, introduced.

## The Hedge-sparrow (Dunnock) *Photo 175*

*Prunella modularis occidentalis* 14 cm.

Introduced during the late 1860s, the Hedge-sparrow is now one of the commonest small birds in New Zealand, occupying almost every habitat, both native and man-made, from coastal islands to subalpine scrub. It has spread to and is now resident and breeding on Antipodes, Auckland and Campbell Islands, and it has straggled to Snares Island. Its natural range is Europe and western Asia.

The Hedge-sparrow is streaky brown above and bluish-grey below. The head is grey with brown on the crown and ear coverts. The bill is slender. It is a skulking species, seldom seen far from cover, and it feeds mostly on the ground. Typically, it flicks its wings and tail, especially when courting.

Hedge-sparrows nest in dense cover, seldom above 2 metres, building a well-woven cup-nest of grass, leaves, moss and the like, lined with hair and wool, rarely feathers. The clutch is 4 or 5 and incubation, by the female only, takes 12 days. The young are fed by both parents and fledge at 12 or 13 days. Two broods may be reared.

## Warblers Sylviidae

A large and complex family of insectivorous birds variously classified. Five of the New Zealand species are contained in the subfamily Malurinae, the Australian warblers, and all 5 serve as hosts to the migrating, parasitic cuckoos. The Fernbird is contained in the subfamily Sylviinae, representatives of which are found over most of the Old World. *Bowdleria, Finschia* and *Mohoua* are endemic genera. *Gerygone* is Australian, with about 20 species, mostly in Australia and New Guinea. *C.* 400 species; New Zealand 6, all endemic.

## The Fernbird

*Photo 172*

*Bowdleria punctata* 18 cm.

Fernbirds occur the length of the country with separate subspecies described for the North Island — also on Great Barrier and the Alderman Islands, the South Island, Stewart Island — also on most outlyers that are free of Wekas and rats, Codfish Island and the Snares Islands. The Chatham Island subspecies became extinct about 1900, the victim of fire and introduced predators.

One's first brief glimpse of the Fernbird gives the impression of a rather nondescript, small, brown bird about the size of a lark with a long, bedraggled tail. Closer acquaintance, however, an easy matter, for the Fernbird is unafraid of man, reveals an attractive if quietly plumaged bird, rich brown in colour with dark, almost black, streaky markings, white eyebrows, a russet patch on the crown, a clean, white, speckled breast and abdomen and a characteristic, long, bedraggled-looking tail that droops downwards when the bird flies.

Fernbirds are birds of wet, peaty, scrubby, marginal country of the kind often drained and burnt for conversion to pasture-land. A favoured habitat is an association of rush, umbrella fern and low manuka scrub growing on damp, poor ground with the umbrella fern, as the name implies, forming an unbroken canopy over the surface. In this dense growth, which is roughly a metre tall, the Fernbirds spend their days, betraying their presence only by infrequent call notes and by brief appearances on the canopy, rather like a blowing porpoise — no sooner do they appear than they up-end and disappear back into the undergrowth. Fernbirds fly poorly and at most manage 30 or 40 metres, so are very vulnerable to fire.

Nest-finding in this habitat can be an absorbing pastime. Having decided on a 'possible' out of the various birds seen one has to follow its subsequent progress more by assessment of which vibrations and tremblings of the canopy of the fern are due to the bird and not to the wind, than by observation of the bird itself. Where the tremblings cease, there, if one has not been deceived, is the nest.

The nest is one of the most cleverly concealed I have seen. It is near the ground, woven of grass into the general mix of rush, fern, grass and stems, and has a characteristically deep cup lined with 2 or 3 feathers. The clutch is 3 or 4 and incubation, by both parents, takes 12 or 13 days. The young are fed by both parents and leave the nest at 12 or 13 days. They remain dependent for a long time after fledging, possibly as long as 6 weeks. Two broods may be reared, the eggs of the first being laid in September, of the second in January.

Fernbirds are duettists, as are so many birds that live in habitats where line-of-sight is limited. The call is *u-tick*. The *u* from one bird being answered immediately — the response is instantaneous — by *tick* from the other.

On the Muttonbird Islands of Stewart Island — those free of Wekas that is — Fernbirds are common and delightfully tame. Where on the mainland it is the Robin that comes for grubs when you chop wood, on the Muttonbird Islands it is the Fernbird. Few of these islands have much in the way of ground cover — the Muttonbirds see to that — so it is easy to see how the Fernbirds spend their days. They explore every habitat: running in and out of petrel burrows like mice, exploring the trunks of trees like Riflemen — always working up the trunk, never down — and carefully working through the accumulations of litter on the forest floor in a manner intriguing to watch because it is so unexpected. They methodically turn over the leaves with one foot, glance quickly underneath, then carefully replace the leaf before going to the next. They do not toss leaves aside like a Blackbird or scratch like a fowl.

## The Brown Creeper

*Photo 171*

*Finschia novaeseelandiae* 13 cm.

Brown Creepers occur only in the South Island, Stewart Island and some of the Stewart Island off-lyers such as Codfish Island. They are essentially birds of native forest and scrub but are one of the native species that has extended its range into exotic pine plantations. They are entirely insectivorous and obtain most of their food from the outer canopies of trees and shrubs. In tall timber they spend much of the day at a considerable height. They do not feed on the ground and they are never seen in open places.

Brown Creepers are attractive birds. The uppersurface is reddish brown and the undersurface pale cinnamon. The face and back of the neck are grey. The sexes are alike. They are tame and easily approached and are readily called down by squeaking noises made with pursed lips. Their song is an attractive warble in a minor key similar to one of the songs of the Yellowhead.

Brown Creepers mostly nest in tangled scrub adjacent to forest edges and have an especial liking for bushes densely overgrown with lawyer vine. The nests are difficult to locate and little has been reported on their breeding cycle. The nest is a neatly woven cup similar to that of a Tomtit and the usual clutch is 3 or 4. Only the female incubates and she is fed at or near the nest by her mate. The incubation and fledging periods are approximately 17 days each and nests may be found from October to January, so it is possible that 2 broods are reared.

After breeding Brown Creepers collect together in noisy flocks that move through the trees with a feeding behaviour very much like that of Yellowheads. Brown Creepers are one of the 3 main hosts of the parasitic Long-tailed Cuckoo.

## The Whitehead

*Mohoua albicilla* 15 cm.

The Whitehead is the North Island counterpart of the South Island Yellowhead, being white where the Yellowhead is yellow. It is today found only in the larger forest areas of the southern two-thirds of the island and on Great Barrier, Little Barrier, and Kapiti Islands. Unlike the Yellowhead it extends into exotic pine plantations and manuka scrub and it prefers to nest in manuka or other shrubs. In this respect it resembles the Brown Creeper. It is insectivorous, obtaining its food from the trunks of trees, from the leaf canopies and to a certain extent from the ground. It also eats seeds and small fruits. It is parasitised by the Long-tailed Cuckoo, which lays its eggs in the Whitehead's nest and predates the Whitehead's eggs and young.

The nest is a woven cup situated from 1 to 9 metres or more in height and the clutch is 2 to 4. Incubation is by both sexes and takes 17 days. Nests may be found from October to February and probably 2 broods are reared. As is the case with the

Yellowhead, nests may be attended by more than 2 birds, usually 4. Whether the additional birds are the young of a previous clutch or whether they are true polygamous groupings, however, has not yet been definitely determined.

## The Yellowhead

*Photos 170, 173*

*Mohoua ochrocephala* 15 cm.

The Yellowhead or Bush Canary is confined to the South Island and is strictly a native forest species, especially of beech forest. Unlike the related Whitehead and Brown Creeper it does not extend out to the scrublands or into exotic pine forests.

The Yellowhead is one of our most attractive species. Its overall plumage is yellow. The wings and tail are yellowish-brown, as are the back and rump. The sexes are alike except that the females have a brownish tinge to the back of the head. The eye is beady and black.

The Yellowhead feeds mostly in the high leaf canopy at the very tops of the trees, a habitat it shares with the parakeets. In really tall timber it spends its days so high that though its voice may be heard the bird itself is difficult indeed to see. It also has a fondness for rooting through the accumulations of debris that fall down and collect in the forks. To do this it grips the bark with one foot, digs its tail — the feathers of which are always abraded with the central shafts projecting as spines — into the trunk and scratches vigorously with the other foot, sending down a shower of debris. The action is very much that of a domestic fowl — a vigorous scratch, a look, another vigorous scratch and so on. In the foliage it hops through the leaves with quick, sprightly movements, investigating each twig in turn, and as it progresses, often stops to duck its head and dart perceptive, upward glances with its beady black eye at the undersurface of leaves, an action that locates many a lurking caterpillar. At the tips of the leaf sprays its sprightly movements cause it to swing up and down like a yellow ball on an elastic string.

The attractive, musical, canary-like trill of the Yellowhead is unlikely to be confused with any other bird song, though some of its briefer snatches resemble those of the Brown Creeper. Two calls worth mention are the alarm note — an unmistakable scolding — and the 'rattle' call, a series of rapid, staccato notes often added as a long trill at the end of its song.

Yellowheads nest in holes in rotting trees and usually at a considerable height. Of the 20 nests I have found most were over 10 metres and many were in the topmost reaches of ancient beeches. Rotting trees offer cavities of many sizes and shapes and Yellowheads use those with entrance holes about 8 centimetres in diameter. In the cavity they build a woven, cup-shaped nest of moss, rootlets and spider web, lined with fine grass. This is an unusual type of nest for a hole-nesting bird and it may be that hole nesting is a recently acquired trend. The nest site is selected by the male who demonstrates it to the female by repeatedly flying back and forth, alternately alighting at the hole and at her side. The nest itself is built by the female.

The eggs are laid in November or December and the normal clutch is 3 or 4. Incubation is by the female only and takes 21 days. Sometimes there are 2 females, in which case they take turn about. For the first 5 or 6 days after hatching the chicks are fed on a mush of caterpillars and such-like delivered from the parent's cheek pouches. Later, the food is brought held in the bill and consists of insects, moths, caterpillars and spiders of many kinds. Both parents feed the young, which fledge on their eighteenth day.

The nests of incubating Yellowheads are not easy to find. Apparently, the female comes off to feed only 3 or 4 times a day but when she does come off she stays off for at least an hour and often much longer. She is joined by her mate and the 2 birds feed together. This is where the 'rattle' call of the male becomes important, for a male Yellowhead joined by his incubating female gives this call with real timbre and quality, his tail visibly vibrating with the energy he puts into it. If you can keep the pair constantly in sight while they feed in the topmost canopy and mingle with other Yellowheads — so that your attention cannot be relaxed — you will eventually be rewarded by seeing the male escort his female back to the nest hole. That the hole will probably be 12 or 15 metres above ground in no way impairs your delight and relief at its discovery.

Yellowheads are predated and parasited by Long-tailed Cuckoos which both eat the eggs and nestlings and lay eggs in the Yellowhead's nest for the Yellowheads to rear.

At the end of the breeding season Yellowheads form flocks which travel noisily through the forest, constantly keeping in touch with call-notes resembling those of the Brown Creeper. These flocks are easily called down by making squeaks with pursed lips or by imitating the call of the Morepork.

## The Grey Warbler

*Photo 179*

*Gerygone igata* 11 cm.

The Grey Warbler is a small, greenish-grey bird with a red eye, a white abdomen and white spots on each side of the tail that show conspicuously in flight. It occurs the length of the country in both native and man-made habitats from sea level to subalpine scrub. It freely enters gardens and has adapted to pine plantations and other kinds of exotic vegetation. Its sweet, wandering melody in a minor key is one of our most appealing bird-songs.

Grey Warblers build penduline, pear-shaped nests suspended at the apex, with the entrance in the side near the top. They are constructed (by the female only) of moss, fibres, grass and wool and are cosily lined with feathers. The entrance is usually arched over with a small porch. They are usually suspended from the outer twigs of trees and bushes and at heights from 1.5 to 7 metres. The usual clutch is 4 to 6 and the incubation period is 17-19 days. The chicks leave the nest when about 18 days old and the parents continue to feed them for a further 2 or 3 weeks, during which time the female may also be constructing a nest for a second brood. The second nest may be built very quickly if, as sometimes occurs, the material comes mainly from the first nest.

The Grey Warbler is the principal host of the migratory Shining Cuckoo. Early clutches — those laid before October — escape, for the cuckoos are not then ready to lay. The cuckoos lay in the November-December clutches, though how the egg is inserted into the closed-in dome is unknown.

## The Chatham Island Warbler

*Gerygone albofrontata* 12 cm.

This species is confined to the Chatham Islands — Chatham, Pitt, South East, Mangere, Little Mangere and the Star Keys. It resembles the Grey Warbler but is slightly larger and has a heavier bill. It is mostly white underneath and has a white forehead. Some birds have a wash of lemon on the throat and flanks.

The nest and nesting behaviour are similar to those of the Grey Warbler and, like it, it is parasitised by the Shining Cuckoo.

Recently, Chatham Island Warblers have been part of a fostering experiment in which they have been used to rear, and perhaps save, the endangered Black Robin (see that species).

## **Flycatchers** Muscicapidae

A large assemblage of insectivorous birds that have the base of the bill broad and surrounded by bristles. Most catch prey by hawking from a perch but others glean from foliage in the manner of warblers. *Rhipidura* contains about 38 species, mostly New Guinea but extending to Asia and India. *Petroica* contains 12 species, mostly Australian with 2 in New Guinea and 1 extending to some Pacific Islands. *C.* 320 species; New Zealand 5, 3 endemic, 1 vagrant.

### **The Fantail**

*Photo 165*

*Rhipidura fuliginosa* 8 cm., 16 cm. with tail

In New Zealand the Fantail occurs the length of the country, including most of the bush-clad offshore islands, and it also occurs at the Chatham Islands. The sexes are alike. North Island birds have less white in the tail than the others. In this subspecies the 2 central feathers are dark, the remainder are about half white. South Island birds are dimorphic with black and pied phases, and the pied phase has about two-thirds of each tail feather white (except for the central 2). In the Chatham Island subspecies the outer tail feathers are almost entirely white and in flight this subspecies appears to have an all-white tail. Beyond New Zealand other subspecies of this Fantail occur in Australia, New Caledonia, the New Hebrides, the Solomon Islands and Norfolk Island. A race once inhabiting Lord Howe Island is now extinct.

In the South Island the black phase — which is sooty and brownish black all over except for a white spot behind the eye which may or may not be present — and the pied phase freely interbreed producing either black or pied young. Intermediates do not occur. The proportion of black to pied birds is about 1 to 8. Two Black Fantails paired together may have pied young but 2 Pied Fantails do not have black young. Pied Fantails are dark brown above and fawn below. They have a dark band across the breast and a conspicuous white eyebrow.

Fantails occur in all habitats where there are trees and bushes and they freely enter towns and gardens. They are among our most common and best-loved native birds, endearing themselves by their tameness and by their habit of entering buildings where they hawk from rafters and electric light cords, taking no apparent notice of the human activity below.

The Fantail is entirely insectivorous and obtains its food by hawking out from a perch with wildly erratic, jinking flight. Between forays it returns to the perch, or the next one along, where it twitters and restlessly twists from side to side. In the forest, it hunts at all levels from the topmost canopy to near the forest floor and in the sprays of foliage its restless movements and long tail help disturb insects that might otherwise remain hidden. It is when feeding in foliage that the fantail is best seen, for when the bird tips head downwards it nearly always fans the tail out to its fullest extent.

The nest of the Fantail is usually placed near water in the fork of a slender, outer branchlet and is shaped like a wine glass with a long, straggly tail hanging from below. It is neatly woven from plant fibre, moss and spider web and is built by both sexes. The usual clutch is 3 and incubation, by both sexes, takes 15 days. The chicks fledge when 15 days old, to be further cared for by the male while the female builds another nest and lays another clutch. Two or 3 clutches a year are normal, but 4 or even 5 have been recorded over a season extending from August to February.

## The New Zealand Tomtit

*Photos 161, 166*

*Petroica macrocephala* 13 cm.

The New Zealand Tomtit is a bird of forest and scrubland. Unlike the Robin it adapts to man-made habitats and exotic vegetation and freely enters pine plantations and the like. There are 5 subspecies. The North Island form (also on Hen and Chickens, Great and Little Barrier, and Kapiti Islands), known as the Pied Tit, has a black head, neck and uppersurface and a white undersurface. There is a white spot above the bill, a white wing bar and the outer tail feathers are white with black tips. Females are brownish where the males are black. The South Island form (also Stewart Island and outlyers) has the same overall pattern but is larger and has a yellow wash on the breast and abdomen sometimes separated from the black throat by a rich orange line. Females again are brown where the males are black. At the Chatham Islands is a subspecies resembling the South Island bird but with the female browner above and the legs longer. At the Snares Islands, the subspecies — the Black Tit — has both sexes entirely black. At the Auckland Islands is a subspecies where the female differs little from the male; both resemble a male South Island Tomtit. All races have a similar life style, though with variations on the outer islands according to local conditions.

Tomtits obtain much of their food from the foliage of trees and from the ground. Unlike the Robin, the Tomtit does not search while actually on the ground. Tomtits typically proceed by making short flights from one tree-trunk to the next, clinging sideways to the bark with a characteristic outward-leaning stance as they scan the ground beneath. When prey is sighted, the bird flies down and immediately returns to the perch with its catch. Only rarely do Tomtits chase flying insects in the conventional flycatcher manner.

South Island Tomtits nest from September to January, rearing 2 broods. The nest is a neatly woven cup placed where it has some overhead protection; a favourite site is in the hollows left by the falling of rotten side-limbs off the main trunks of trees. Most are placed 4-6 metres above ground, but I have found them at 1 metre and also at the very extremity of vision in the tops of forest giants. The clutch is 3 to 5, usually 4, and incubation, by the female only, takes 15 days. The young are fed by both parents and fledge when 16 or 17 days old.

Tomtits have a distraction display — not done by all birds — that may sometimes be triggered by one's too close approach to a nest. They raise and fan the wings and tail, twisting and turning on a nearby branch or on the ground, and the display is accompanied by harsh, hissing noises. It is surprising to see. Normally, one associates distraction displays with oystercatchers, plovers and their kin and not with small, passerine, forest birds.

At the Snares Islands the clutch is usually 3 and the nests are well hidden in hollow logs and under tussocks just over the edges of the cliffs. No details have been reported of the breeding of the Chatham and Auckland Island birds except that most have well-grown young out of the nest in December.

## The New Zealand Robin

*Photo 168*

*Petroica australis* 18 cm.

The New Zealand Robin is strictly a native forest species. It does not extend into exotic vegetation or into man-made habitats though it occurs on a number of offshore islands that have remained predator free. The sexes are similar though females are duller. The uppersurface is dark grey, the undersurface off-white and there is a white spot on the forehead prominent in threat display. The legs are long

**174** The introduced Blackbird.

**175** The introduced Hedge-sparrow.

**176** The Bellbird.

**177** The introduced Song Thrush.

**178** The Tui.

**179** The Grey Warbler.

**180** A young Pipit at the Chatham Islands.

**181** The New Zealand Pipit.

**182** A Pipit photographed at the Antipodes Islands.

**183** The introduced Greenfinch.

**184** The Red-wattle Bird. An Australian honeyeater recorded twice as a straggler to New Zealand.

**185** The Grey-backed Silvereye.

**186** The introduced Goldfinch.

**187** The introduced House Sparrow.

**188** The introduced Chaffinch. This is the female.

**189** The introduced Redpoll.

**190** The introduced Yellowhammer. This is the female.

**191** The introduced Indian Myna.

**192** The introduced Starling.

**193** The juvenile South Island Saddleback, once thought to be a separate species and known as the Jackbird.

**194** The North Island Saddleback.

**195** The introduced Australian Magpie. This is a male of the White-backed form.

**196** The North Island Kokako.

and the stance perky. Three subspecies are described. The North Island form (Central North Island, Little Barrier and Kapiti Islands) has a mottled throat and a rather streaky appearance to the uppersurface due to the shafts of the feathers showing whitish. The South Island form (Nelson to Fiordland and especially in the beech forests east of the Alps and also D'Urville, Chetwode and Pickersgill Islands in Cook Strait) has a smarter overall appearance and often a lemon wash on the breast in the male. The Stewart Island form (now rare on the main island and exterminated from Big South Cape Island by the rat invasion of the 1960s, but present on Poutama, Tamaitemioka, Pohowaitai, Jacky Lee, Motinui and Green Islands) resembles the South Island bird but is darker above and pure white below.

Robins are exceptionally tame and inquisitive birds and it is typical that they immediately arrive to investigate anything you may be doing in their territory. They will freely enter back-country huts and will hop around your feet for crumbs. They are strongly territorial and hold territory all year round.

Robins obtain much of their food from the ground and unlike Tomtits spend much of their time actually on the ground while seeking it. A certain way of attracting Robins is noisily to chop at old logs with an axe or simply to turn them over and kick them about. The Robin whose territory you have invaded will arrive immediately and, if your chopping is continued, neighbouring Robins may arrive as well. This immediately leads to territorial dispute. The first sign of anger is a raising of the feathers of the forehead to show a short line of white. This is visible from a considerable distance and if it fails then a determined chase follows. Robins will also direct the white spot display at man.

Chopping at rotten logs to supply grubs is a good way of finding Robins' nests. To follow the bird back when he has a beakful, however, is not always easy over tangled ground, for it is seldom possible to watch both the bird and your feet at the same time, and to take your eye off the bird even for a moment can be fatal. Robins can disappear as if by magic. If possible, you want to succeed with the first flight back because Robins have the habit of storing extra supplies of food in 'larders', which they then later visit in times of need. The larders are simply places, usually in the forks of trees, that both birds of the pair know about and both visit.

Robins nest from August to December, 2 broods being reared. The nest, a neatly woven cup of moss and fibre, is placed in the hollows of rotting trees and similar places with overhead protection. In general, they nest at lower levels than do Tomtits — around 3 metres — but I have seen them at the very tops of forest giants at heights I could only guess at. The normal clutch is 3 and incubation is by the female only, fed during this time by her mate and by visiting her mate's larders. The incubation period is 17-20 days and the fledging period 19-21 days. The young are fed in the nest by both parents and after fledging are fed for a further 3 weeks, each parent having charge of particular young.

Robins have a most attractive distraction display which is given by both sexes. It is provoked only by climbing up close to the nest. The birds fly up and land just above your head. Then with wings and tail raised and fanned they float silently down within 1 or 2 metres, turning and spiralling, till finally they land feather-like on the ground where, with wings and tail still widely fanned, they pirouette slowly from side to side.

The song of the Robin is a prolonged outpouring of staccato notes rising and falling in pitch and of surprising volume. Robins sing from high perches and can be heard from long distances.

## The Chatham Island Black Robin

*Photo 167*

*Petroica traversi* 15 cm.

At its low point of 5 birds the Black Robin was without doubt the world's rarest bird — every individual could be accounted for. It is a small Robin, black all over. It was originally found on Chatham, Pitt, Mangere and Little Mangere Islands but soon became reduced to a remnant population on Little Mangere Island following European settlement and the arrival of cats and rats. Unfortunately, Little Mangere Island is small (14 hectares) and is covered only with patchy degenerating forest. It is a sheer-sided stack, difficult to land on and climb. A visit in 1972 found 17 birds. By 1976 these had reduced to 7 by further degeneration of habitat and so that year all birds were transferred to Mangere Island by officers of the New Zealand Wildlife Service — a transfer not without difficulties and dangers.

For a small passerine, the Black Robin is a long-lived bird (one female is now 13 years old and still breeding) but it has the low reproduction rate that goes with evolution in a predator-free environment. The clutch is fixed at 2 but only 1 chick is reared and the chick is dependent on its parents for a long time after fledging. Two broods in a season are unknown, though the birds will re-lay should the first clutch be lost. Consequently, the Wildlife Service instituted a programme of fostering eggs on to other species thereby inducing 2 clutches a year from each of the 2 remaining pairs of Robins. The programme was not without its problems. The only foster species available on Mangere Island was the Chatham Island Warbler, which builds an enclosed nest and has chicks that excrete their droppings in faecal sacs. Black Robins build open cup nests and have chicks that excrete their droppings over the side. Consequently, the Black Robin chicks in the warblers' nests got into a wet and messy state. The problem was solved by supplying the fostering warblers with a freshly-built warbler's nest about every 5 days. Warblers are in considerable numbers on Mangere Island so this did not prove too difficult and the fostering warblers readily accepted the exchange of nests, provided the positioning remained reasonably as before. The next step was to foster eggs on to Chatham Island Tits on South East Island. This was most successful and at the time of writing the total population of Black Robins stands at 20: 8 on Mangere and 12 on South East. A major success story!

## The Satin Flycatcher

*Myiagra cyanoleuca* 16 cm.

A rare straggler from Australia. A broad-billed, restless, tail-quivering flycatcher with a rasping call-note. The sexes differ. The male has the head, neck, back, wings and tail black, and the breast and abdomen white. The female is brownish where the male is black and has the throat and breast chestnut-red. One record, of a female, Gisborne 1963.

## **Thrushes** Turdidae

A large, almost cosmopolitan family of song birds that obtain much of their food on the ground. They are related to the flycatchers and warblers. About 310 species; New Zealand 2, both introduced.

## The Song Thrush *Photo 177*

*Turdus philomelos* 23 cm.

Introduced from England in 1862 the Song Thrush is now widely distributed over New Zealand, including most offshore islands, and it has self-introduced to all outlying islands except Bounty, Antipodes and Macquarie — though in outlying areas it is not as numerous or as successful as the Blackbird. Its natural range is Europe and west central Asia. The sexes are similar. The upperparts are warm brown and the underparts buffy-white, spotted brown. The song is melodious and characteristically the phrases are repeated. In New Zealand, Song Thrushes breed from July to January and normally rear 2 broods. The clutch is 4 to 6. Incubation, by the female, takes 14 days, and the young fledge after a similar period.

## The Blackbird *Photo 174*

*Turdus merula* 25 cm.

Introduced from England in 1862 the Blackbird is now one of the commonest and most familiar birds in the country. It is a more aggressive coloniser of outlying areas than the Song Thrush and has self-introduced to all outlying islands except Bounty, Antipodes and Macquarie. Its natural range is from Europe across central Asia to China. The sexes differ. The male is black with an orange-yellow bill and a yellow eye-ring. The female is dark brown above and paler brown below with some indistinct mottling. The song is more mellow than the Song Thrush's and is not repetitive. Blackbirds typically lift the tail on alighting. In New Zealand, Blackbirds breed from July to January and normally rear 2 broods. The clutch is 4 to 5. Incubation, by the female, takes 14 days, and the young fledge after a similar period.

### **White-eyes** Zosteropidae

An Old World family of mostly tropical birds characterised by the presence of a ring of white feathers round the eye (absent in some) and by the habit of moving about in large flocks which makes them successful island colonists. They have brush tongues like the Honeyeaters for the extraction of nectar and pollen from flowers. They are small birds and the sexes are alike. They build delicately woven nests slung like a hammock from the forks of twigs and their eggs are blue. About 85 species; New Zealand 1, self-introduced.

## The Grey-backed White-eye (Silvereye) *Photo 185*

*Zosterops lateralis* 12 cm.

The Silvereye is an Australian species (occurring also in New Caledonia, the New Hebrides [Vanuatu], Fiji and Norfolk Island) that colonised New Zealand in 1856 when large flocks suddenly appeared near Wellington and Nelson. Since then, Silvereyes have become ubiquitous the length of the country from sea level to subalpine scrub. They have colonised Chatham, Snares, Auckland and Campbell Islands and have straggled to Kermadec, Antipodes and Macquarie Islands.

The Silvereye is green above with a grey back. The undersurface is whitish and the flanks are chestnut. The eye-ring (absent in juveniles) is white. Silvereyes are mostly seen in flocks, keeping in touch with plaintive *zee-zee* cries.

Despite their gregarious habit, Silvereyes mostly nest as isolated pairs, for they are territorial birds during the breeding season. They will, however, also breed in loosely-knit colonies, though the nests will not be all that close together. The nest is a woven hammock slung from the fork of a slender branch. It is made from grass, rootlets, hair and fibre and is sometimes so delicately constructed that the eggs can be seen through it. It may be placed at heights of from 1 to 10 metres. The usual clutch is 3 and both sexes incubate. The incubation period is one of the shortest known: 10-11 days. Both sexes feed the young, which fledge at 10-11 days, and 2 or 3 broods may be reared in a season.

Silvereyes eat a wide variety of invertebrate foods as well as pollen and nectar from flowers, soft fruits and small seeds. They come readily to household scraps and they are one of the common inhabitants of urban gardens.

## **Honeyeaters** Meliphagidae

A principally Australasian family of birds with flat foreheads, slightly downcurved bills and brush-tipped tongues for the extraction of nectar and pollen from flowers. They are active, restless birds, seldom still. One hundred and sixty species; New Zealand 4, 3 endemic, 1 straggler.

## The Stitchbird

*Notiomystis cincta* male 19 cm., female 18 cm.

Until the recent transfers to Hen and Chicken Islands as part of the programme of re-establishment of rare native species, the Stitchbird, originally an inhabitant of North Island forests, survived only on Little Barrier Island. It became extinct on the mainland about 1885.

The male Stitchbird has a black head, neck and upper breast, and a tuft of white feathers behind each eye. The uppersurface is brown and the undersurface pale brown. There is a band of golden yellow across the breast between the black breast and brown undersurface. The female is slightly smaller and is brown above and pale brown below. There is a white spot behind the eye but no tuft.

Stitchbirds are active, restless and quick moving. Characteristically, they cock the tail upwards when perched and when clinging sideways to the trunks of trees. They feed especially on nectar but also on insects and fruits. Their call note is an explosive *tzit* or *stitch* from which the name presumably is derived.

Stitchbirds are unique among honeyeaters in that they nest in holes in trees. The eggs are white, so presumably they have been hole nesters for a long time. Few nests have been discovered and most have been at a considerable height — to 18 metres. Like Yellowheads, Stitchbirds build a well-formed, cup-shaped nest within the hole. The clutch is 3 to 5 but details of incubation and fledging are little known. Both sexes feed the young, principally on nectar, at least during the early days, and fledging takes at least 2 weeks.

## The Bellbird

*Photo 176*

*Anthornis melanura* 19–20 cm.

Bellbirds occur the length of the country and on most forest-clad offshore islands. They are primarily birds of native forests but they extend into marginal lands and suburban gardens and they are establishing in exotic pine plantations. They are numerous at the Auckland Islands but do not occur at the Snares. A separate subspecies is described for the Three Kings Islands — slightly larger and less yellow — and another subspecies once inhabited the Chatham Islands but that became extinct in 1906.

The overall plumage of the Bellbird is green, with the flanks and undersurface yellow-green. Males have a purple gloss to the head and red eyes. Females, which are slightly smaller, are duller, have an olive-brown head with a white line running back below the eye from the angle of the gape. The eye is brown. Both sexes have dark, brownish-black wings and tail.

Bellbirds are renowned for their bell-like notes and when singing in chorus, as when collected at flowering trees, are indeed memorable. Their song varies at different times of the year and from one part of the country to another.

Bellbirds feed on nectar, pollen, insects and berries. I have seen them exploring tree trunks with the diligence of Riflemen and they will feed among leaf litter on the ground.

Bellbirds nest from September to January, 2 broods being reared. The nest is a woven, if rather untidy, cup, well concealed in dense tangles of vegetation. On the mainland it is usually placed fairly high: 10 metres. On islands it may be much lower, even at ground level. The clutch is 3 and incubation, by the female only, takes 14 days. The chicks hatch naked and blind and for the first few days are fed on nectar. Thereafter, insects, grubs, caterpillars, spiders and so on are supplied and the feeding process is extremely rapid. A few seconds suffice for the parent to arrive, feed the chick and depart. The chicks fledge at 14 days.

## The Tui

*Photo 178*

*Prosthemadera novaeseelandiae* male 31 cm., female 29 cm.

Tuis are native forest birds occurring the length of the country, including many well-forested offshore islands. They also occur at the Kermadec Islands and at the Auckland Islands. The birds at the Chatham Islands (slightly larger and with longer throat plumes) are described as a separate subspecies.

In dull light Tuis appear blue-black. In sunlight they reflect metallic greens and purples, the flanks bronze. There is a lacy collar of filamentous, white plumes round the hind neck and a double tuft of curled, white feathers from the throat. Females are slightly smaller than males, rather duller, and the throat plumes are smaller.

The song of the Tui is a mixture of bell-like notes interspersed with various clicks, rattles and wheezes that fall oddly on the ear. Tuis also have a whispering song of extremely high frequency, beyond the range of human hearing, delivered with the body hunched and all feathers fluffed.

The flight is strong, fast and noisy. Tuis hurtle through the forest with a whoosh of wings and out in the open have a habit of climbing fairly high, then closing the wings and plummeting earthwards to their destination.

Tuis are belligerent and aggressive and brook no trespass near their nests. The nest is a bulky, untidy structure with a broad flat lip and the cup lined with fine grass or similar material. On the mainland it is normally placed high — 10 metres or so — in dense tangles of lawyer vine or similar situations. On the offshore islands Tuis nest upward of 3 metres in the forks of leafy trees. Mostly they are late nesters — December-January. The clutch is 2 to 4 and incubation, by the female only, takes 14 days. The young are fed by both parents and fledge at about 21 days. As with the Bellbird, the feeding process is extremely rapid. The birds come and go in a matter of seconds.

## The Red-wattle Bird *Photo 184*

*Anthochaera carunculata* 34 cm.

A large, streaky, brown and grey Australian honeyeater with a red wattle behind and below the eye. Recorded twice in New Zealand as a wind-blown straggler: 1865 and 1882.

### **Buntings** Emberizidae

A large assemblage of small to medium-sized, seed-eating, terrestrial birds that build open cup nests mostly close to the ground. None are colonial. The sexes differ. About 320 species; New Zealand 2, both introduced.

## The Yellowhammer *Photo 190*

*Emberiza citrinella caliginosa* 16 cm.

Introduced during the 1860s the Yellowhammer is now widespread the length of the country on pastural and marginal lands with rough herbage. It does not enter forests, but it can be common in the subalpine scrub above bushline. It has self-introduced to the Chatham and Kermadec Islands and has straggled to Snares and Campbell Islands.

The male has a yellow head and a chestnut rump. The rest of the plumage is streaked yellow, chestnut and black. The female is duller and has a streaked head. Both sexes have conspicuous, white, outer tail feathers.

Yellowhammers nest on or very close to the ground, rearing 2 broods, October to February. The clutch is 3 to 5 and incubation, by the female only, takes 12-14 days. The fledging period is 12-14 days. The natural range of this species is Europe to Siberia and Mongolia.

## The Cirl Bunting

*Emberiza cirlus* 16 cm.

The Cirl Bunting was introduced during the 1860s, but it is not common and it has rarely been reported in the North Island. It is most common along the east coast of the South Island from Marlborough to Otago Peninsula, but the distribution is patchy, and it is uncommon inland.

The male has a yellow face, a dark crown, a black throat and an olive-brown rump. Otherwise it is rather similar to the Yellowhammer. The black throat and olive rump are the key differences. The female is duller and resembles the female Yellowhammer.

Cirl Buntings usually nest off the ground — to 2 metres. Few nests have been reported in New Zealand. The clutch is 3 or 4 and incubation, by the female only, takes 11-13 days. The fledging period is 11-13 days.

The natural range of this species is southern Europe, North Africa and western Turkey.

### **Finches** Fringillidae

Small to medium-small, seed-eating, arboreal birds that build cup-shaped nests in trees and bushes. None are colonial. The sexes differ in all but a few species. About 125 species; New Zealand 4, all introduced.

## The Chaffinch *Photo 188*

*Fringilla coelebs gengleri* 15 cm.

Introduced during the 1860s and now the commonest land bird in the country, occupying all habitats, both native and man-made, from sea-shore to subalpine scrub. It outnumbers all native birds in South Island beech forests. It has spread to all offshore islands other than the most barren and has self-introduced to Chatham, Snares, Auckland and Campbell Islands.

The male has a blue-grey crown and nape, a chestnut back, a green rump and warm brown underparts. It has a conspicuous white patch on the shoulder and conspicuous white outer tail feathers. The female is duller: olive-brown above and greyish below. Chaffinches have a squared-off look to the head that is unique among the small birds in New Zealand.

Chaffinches nest in trees and bushes, from 2 to 7 metres, building an exquisite cup nest. The clutch is 4 or 5 and incubation, by the female only, takes 12 or 13 days. The young are fed by both parents on food carried in the bill and fledge at 13 or 14 days. Only 1 brood is reared and nesting takes place between October and December. The natural range of this species is Europe, the Atlantic Islands, North Africa and western Asia.

## The Greenfinch *Photo 183*

*Carduelis chloris* 15 cm.

Introduced during the 1860s, the Greenfinch is now widespread, especially in man-made habitats. It has self-introduced to the Chatham Islands and has straggled to Kermadec, Snares and Campbell Islands. It enters beech forest but in general is not common at higher altitudes.

The male is olive-green with a yellow rump and conspicuous yellow patches on the wings. The female is browner and less yellow.

Greenfinches nest in hedgerows, bushes and trees, usually from just above eye level to about 5 metres, and sometimes in loosely knit groups, though without being colonial. The clutch is 4 to 6 and incubation, by the female only, takes 14 days. The young are fed by regurgitation at infrequent interval's by both sexes and fledge at 14 days. Two broods are reared. The natural range of this species is Europe and western Asia.

## The Goldfinch *Photo 186*

*Carduelis carduelis britannica* 12.5 cm.

Introduced during the 1860s the Goldfinch is now widespread in all man-made habitats, especially marginal lands with introduced weeds. It is not common above bushline and is only occasional in native forest edges. It has self-introduced to all outlying islands except Bounty but has not really established on any except Chatham: on the others is best described as a visitor and occasional resident.

In this species the sexes are similar. The face is red, the crown and nape black, and the cheeks and throat white. The wings are black with a conspicuous yellow band in the middle and the overall body plumage is sandy brown with the undersurface white. The Goldfinch is one of our most attractive aliens: a welcome addition to the avifauna.

Goldfinches built neat nests, typically lined either with wool or with the woolly fluff of black poplars, at heights of 1.5 to 4 metres in trees and bushes, often among the sprays of foliage that break away from the trunks of poplars and willows and in fruit trees. The clutch is 4 to 6 and incubation, by the female only, takes 12–13 days. The chicks are fed by both parents (who search for food together) at infrequent intervals by regurgitation, on the pulp of seeds and the like. Two broods may be reared.

The natural range of this species is Europe east to Iran and the Himalayas.

## The Redpoll *Photo 189*

*Carduelis flammea cabaret* 12 cm.

Introduced during the 1860s and now widespread over the country in a variety of habitats, the Redpoll is especially successful in the alpine zone of the South Island and on the Subantarctic Islands. It has self-introduced to Chatham, Snares, Auckland, Campbell (where abundant) and Macquarie Island.

The Redpoll is a small, streaky-brown bird with a red forehead, a forked tail and a diagnostic, plaintive *tsooeet* call note. In breeding plumage males have a red flush on the breast that in Central Otago birds exceeds in extent and brilliance of colour any written or illustrated description of Redpolls I have seen. Elsewhere, male Redpolls look as the descriptions say they should: reddish on the breast but not dramatically so. Females resemble males but develop no flush on the breast.

Redpolls nest from October to January, rearing 2 broods. The nest is a rather roughly woven cup lined with wool or feathers, placed in bushes and trees from 1 to 10 metres and nests may sometimes be grouped in loose associations. The clutch is 3 to 5 and incubation, by the female only, takes 11-12 days. Both parents feed the young, at infrequent intervals, on a regurgitated pulp of seeds, and the parents visit the nest together. The natural range of this species is throughout arctic and subarctic Eurasia and North America.

### Sparrows and Weavers Ploceidae

A family of small, principally ground-feeding, seed-eating birds, most of which are gregarious at all seasons, breeding in colonies and constructing enclosed nests. One hundred and thirty-three species; New Zealand 1, introduced.

## The House Sparrow *Photo 187*

*Passer domesticus* 14 cm.

House Sparrows have been introduced by man over much of the world and several liberations were made in New Zealand during the 1860s. House Sparrows are now ubiquitous in settled districts and have spread to Chatham, Snares, Auckland and Campbell Islands. House Sparrows, however, are dependent on man's activities and buildings, and in outlying regions maintain permanent populations only where man has regular business. Thus, at the Snares and Auckland Islands, which are uninhabited, House Sparrows retain no permanent foothold. At Campbell Island, which has a permanently occupied weather station, a few House Sparrows have at times resided near the station but not elsewhere on the island. At the Chatham Islands they occur on Chatham and Pitt Islands but not on the uninhabited offshore islands . . . and so the pattern repeats.

The male House Sparrow has a grey crown bordered with chestnut and has a black bib. The undersurface is dingy white and the uppersurface is streaked with black and brown. The female is duller and lacks the male's head pattern. Juveniles resemble females.

House Sparrows normally nest in holes in buildings, filling them with an untidy accumulation of grass and straw in the centre of which is a cosy, feather-lined cavity. They also nest in colonies in trees, building similar untidy, globular, feather-lined structures. The entrance is in the side. The clutch is 3 to 7 and incubation, by the female only, takes 12-13 days. Both parents feed the young on insects etc. brought in the bill; a number of broods — up to 5 — may be reared in a season.

## **Starlings** Sturnidae

An Old World family, widely introduced, of noisy, aggressive, mostly ground-feeding, open-country birds that walk and run but rarely hop. Many are good mimics and some can be taught to repeat human phrases. Most species nest in holes. One hundred and four species; New Zealand 2, both introduced.

### The Common Starling *Photo 192*

*Sturnus vulgaris* 21 cm.

Introduced during the 1860s Starlings are now ubiquitous the length of the country in both native and man-made habitats except for alpine regions and dense rain forest. They have self-introduced to Kermadec (abundant), Chatham, Antipodes, Snares, Auckland, Campbell and Macquarie Islands.

The sexes are similar and in dull light appear black. In sunlight they are glossed with green and purple. In winter, after the moult into fresh plumage, they are spotted with white and this spotting disappears as the plumage wears. In spring the bill is yellow with a bluish base in the male and a pinkish base in the female. In winter the bill is dark.

Starlings have a wide repertoire of bubbling and whistling songs and freely mimic other birds, especially oystercatchers, Spurwinged Plovers, Shining Cuckoos and California Quail. They nest in holes in buildings, trees and cliffs, collecting an untidy and sometimes massive accumulation of grass, straw, paper, feathers and such-like. The clutch is 5 to 7 and incubation, by both sexes, takes 12-14 days. The young are fed by both parents on food carried in the bill and fledge at 20-22 days. They remain dependent on the parents for some days after leaving the nest and as a rule only 1 brood is reared. After breeding, Starlings typically congregate in vast numbers to roost communally at night.

The natural range of this species is Europe and western Asia.

### The Indian Myna *Photo 191*

*Acridotheres tristis* 24 cm.

The Indian Myna was introduced to both islands during the 1870s but it has established only in the North Island, for the South Island is too cold for successful breeding of this tropical species. Like the House Sparrow the Myna has been an urban associate of man for a long time and in New Zealand is essentially an urban species though it has spread widely over farming districts.

The sexes are similar. It is an overall brown bird with a black head and neck, a black tail tipped white and has a conspicuous white patch on the wings in flight. The bill, legs and bare skin round the eye are yellow.

Mynas nest in holes in buildings, occasionally trees, in which they accumulate a heap of straw, leaves, grass, paper and so on without much real form or shape. The clutch is 3 to 6 and incubation is by the female. Males may sit on the eggs but have no brood patch. The incubation period is 14-17 days. Both parents feed the young on food carried in the bill and the young fledge after about 27 days. Mynas are late nesters in New Zealand and usually rear only 1 brood, though 2 do occur.

The natural range of this species is India to south-west China.

## New Zealand Wattle-birds Callaeidae

An endemic family of nearly flightless arboreal species of ancient and obscure affinity. All have wattles at the base of the billl. They progress by long, agile hops rather than by flying and consequently have strong legs and feet. Their reduced powers of flight are associated with a small keel on the breast bone for the attachment of the flight muscles, indicating reduced flight for a long time. Three species, 1 extinct.

## The Saddleback

*Photos 193, 194*

*Philesturnus carunculatus* 25 cm.

At the time of first European settlement Saddlebacks occupied native forests the length of New Zealand. By about 1890 they were extinct but for 2 island populations — on Hen Island in the north, and on Big South Cape Island and its satellites in the south.

Saddlebacks (the sexes are alike) are glossy black with a chestnut saddle across the back and wings, chestnut undertail coverts and reddish orange wattles at the base of the bill, larger in the male. North Island Saddlebacks have a yellow line separating the saddle from the back of the neck. South Island Saddlebacks have a distinct juvenile form — the 'Jackbird', once thought to be a distinct species — that is olive brown, paler below, with chestnut markings above the tail.

Saddlebacks leap and bound through the trees with great agility. They can fly, but not for any distance, and they are unable to sustain height. They feed much on the ground and one of the important aspects to be considered when transferring Saddlebacks to other islands is that the island's forest floor should have a good depth of leaf litter. Their food is varied: insects, berries, nectar, fruit and the larvae of wood-boring beetles which they extract by levering and tearing at rotting wood with their strong bills. Saddlebacks are always seen as pairs and presumably mate for life. They are territorial and have a loud, staccato *te-te-te-te* call that is unmistakable. Saddlebacks nest in holes in trees, in dense vegetation and other sites with overhead cover, often close to the ground, building a cup-shaped nest of twigs and fibre. The clutch is 2 and incubation, by the female only, takes 21 days.

The South Island Saddleback was very nearly exterminated during the early 1960s when rats got to Big South Cape Island and its satellites from fishing boats and underwent an appalling population explosion. Almost every living thing was killed and eaten. The local populations of Robin, Brown Creeper, Fernbird, Stewart Island Snipe and Stewart Island Bush Wren were wiped out and this has meant that those subspecies of Snipe and Bush Wren are now extinct, for Big South Cape and Solomon Islands held the last remaining populations. As to the Saddleback: 21 birds were trapped and hurriedly transferred by the Wildlife Service to Stage Island and 15 to Kaimohu Island. From these birds the present population of Saddlebacks derives. There are now no Saddlebacks on Big South Cape Island. Fortunately, Saddlebacks transfer well and they found Stage Island, in particular, very much to their liking. In no time, Stage Island had so many Saddlebacks that it was possible, indeed imperative, to make further transfers. South Island Saddlebacks are now on the following small islands off Stewart Island: Stage, Kaimohu, Betsy, Putahina, Kundy, Women's and North; also Maud Island in Cook Strait — with a total population of 180 birds.

With the lessons of the South Island disaster in mind, transfers have also been made of North Island Saddlebacks and these are now on Hen, 2 of the Chickens, Cuvier, Red Mercury, Fanal and Kapiti Islands with a total population of about 1000 birds.

Further transfers of both subspecies are planned as soon as islands can be made predator-free to receive them. For example, Little Barrier Island, after years of work, has finally been cleared of cats, a massive undertaking; it now looks likely to become one of the most important island refuges.

## The Huia

*Heteralocha acutirostris* male 45 cm., female 48 cm.

Presumed extinct since 1907, the Huia was known from the North Island only. It was a large, glossy, blue-black bird with orange wattles and a white-tipped tail. The male had a whitish, stout, slightly arched, short, chisel-like straight bill; the female had a whitish, long, thin, downcurved bill. The birds were always seen as pairs and obtained much of their food from the ground — over which they travelled in long leaps and bounds — and by chiselling into rotten wood for wood-boring grubs. They could fly but did so seldom.

Huias nested in hollow trees, building a substantial cup-shaped nest of sticks and fibre. One nest is recorded that contained 1 chick and another is reported to have contained 3.

## The Kokako

*Photo 196*

*Callaeas cinerea* 38 cm.

Kokakos are large, long-legged, blue-grey birds with a black mask on the face and wattles at the base of the bill. North Island Kokakos have blue wattles; South Island Kokakos have orange wattles.

Kokakos are specialised birds of dense native forests with a continuous canopy and a full range of understorey layers. They fly poorly and only downhill. Kokakos work their way up through a tree with long leaps and bounds and then glide down from the high canopy to the understorey of a neighbouring tree, thence to work their way up again. They are principally vegetarian and require a varied forest structure to ensure an all-year-round food supply.

The North Island Kokako occurs in isolated and scattered populations in the central North Island with outlying populations in North Auckland, the Coromandel ranges and Great Barrier Island.

The South Island Kokako is extremely rare if not extinct; the last acceptable report was in 1961.

The song of the Kokako is quite unlike that of any other New Zealand bird and consists of long, rich, musical, organ-like notes audible at a great distance. It is given, normally, at dawn and dusk. During the day various quiet notes are used by pairs keeping in touch but it is the organ-like notes that once heard one does not forget.

Kokakos are not easy birds to locate; their nests have been seldom found. They breed from November to March and the nest is a large, untidy structure situated fairly high in a tangle of branches or in a fork and the clutch is 2 or 3. Incubation is by the female and takes about 25 days; the chicks fledge in 27–28 days. Like Saddlebacks, Kokakos probably mate for life.

In 1982 4 Kokakos were transferred to Little Barrier Island — now cleared of cats — as part of the relocation programme for rare species.

## **Wood-swallows** Artamidae

An Australo-Papuan family, extending to India, of smallish birds that feed almost entirely on insects caught on the wing. Accomplished and graceful fliers but not related to the true swallows, they have a delta-winged flight silhouette akin to the Starling's and soar and glide in a diagnostic way. Unique among passerine birds in possessing powder down. All are highly social. Perch huddled close together in groups of up to 6 and should 1 bird take flight the remainder typically shuffle together to close the gap. At night they may roost in dense clusters of up to 50 birds like a swarm of bees. They are migratory and nomadic. Ten species; New Zealand 2, both vagrant, though 1 species bred.

### The Masked Wood-swallow

*Artamus personatus* 19 cm.

The male Masked Wood-swallow is grey above and pearly-grey below and has a large, black, facial mask bordered with white. The tail is grey, slightly forked and is tipped white. The female has a dull facial mask without the white border.

In Australia this and the following species regularly associate and even breed together in mixed colonies. During 1971-73 a pair of Masked Wood-swallows along with 4 male White-browed Wood-swallows temporarily resided in the exotic pine plantation of the Naseby forest and reared 2 young in the summer of 1972-73. They became tame and visited a local resident's bird table for household scraps. The New Zealand nest was not seen but Wood-swallows typically build flimsy nests of twigs and grass, placed in the fork of a tree, and the normal clutch is 2.

### The White-browed Wood-swallow

*Artamus superciliosus* 19 cm.

The male White-browed Wood-swallow is blue grey above and on the upper breast, has rich-chestnut underparts and a conspicuous white eyebrow. In 1971 4 males appeared at Naseby along with the above species. They became very tame, visiting a local resident's bird table, but disappeared after the 1973 winter. Neither species has been seen since.

## **Australian Bell-magpies** Cracticidae

An Australian family. Includes the Currawongs and Australian Butcherbirds. Plumage in all species black, white and grey. Predatory, scavenging and aggressive. Ten species; New Zealand 1, introduced.

### The Australian Magpie

*Photo 195*

*Gymnorhina tibicen* 40 cm.

There are 3 distinct geographical forms of this species, 2 of which have been introduced to New Zealand: the Black-backed Magpie (*G.t. tibicen*) and the White-backed Magpie (*G.t. hypoleuca*). The Black-backed form was introduced probably during the 1860s and is now established in Canterbury, Marlborough and Hawke's Bay but is nowhere as abundant as the White-backed form. The White-backed Magpie was introduced during the 1860s and is now widespread in both islands and still expanding its range.

Australian Magpies are conspicuous, black and white birds with strong, whitish, black-tipped bills. The male Black-backed Magpie is black with a white nape, white shoulders and wing band and a white rump. The female has the nape grey. The White-backed Magpie differs in that the back is white in the male, grey in the female and immature.

Magpies are superb songsters, alone or in chorus, uttering unmistakable, organ- or flute-like carollings from a high perch, especially in the mornings.

Magpies are birds of open country with scattered trees. They do not enter the forest. They feed mostly on the ground, taking a wide variety of invertebrate prey. They nest in trees, building a substantial structure of twigs lined with grass. In Australia the Black-backed form breeds in social groups of considerable complexity whereas the White-backed form nests more as conventional pairs. The clutch is 2 or 3 and the birds are uncompromisingly aggressive toward human interference. Much has yet to be discovered about their behaviour in New Zealand.

## **New Zealand Thrushes** Turnagridae

An endemic family of obscure affiliation. One species, probably extinct.

### The New Zealand Thrush (Piopio)

*Turnagra capensis* 26 cm.

Now considered extinct, the New Zealand Thrush — which has no relationship to the true thrushes, only a degree of resemblance of size and plumage — was last authentically recorded in the North Island in 1908 and in the South Island about 1930. Occasional reports since have periodically raised hopes, but none have been without doubt. The North Island subspecies is brown above and grey below with a white throat. The South Island subspecies is brown above and spotted white below. Both subspecies have a rust-red rump and short deep bills.

New Zealand Thrushes were plentiful in the early days of settlement. They were forest birds, exceptionally tame and confiding. Much of their food was obtained on the ground and they evidently hopped and bounded through the trees with the agility of Saddlebacks. They flew well, though usually only for short distances. South Island Thrushes built cup-shaped nests about 2 metres from the ground and laid 2 eggs in December. The nest of the North Island Thrush is not recorded.

## **Crows** Corvidae

An almost world-wide family of large, adaptable passerines, many with complex social structures. One hundred and two species; New Zealand 1, introduced.

### The Rook

*Corvus frugilegus* 45 cm.

A large, black crow with a white face bare of feathers, and shaggy thighs. Introduced during the 1860s, it is now established near Christchurch and in Hawke's Bay. Rooks are birds of open farmland with woods. They are gregarious and nest in colonies at the tops of tall trees, returning to the same place each year. In New Zealand most have eggs by September. The clutch is 2 to 5 and incubation, by the female, takes 18 days. The young fledge at 30 days.

The natural range of this species is from Europe to eastern China.

## Bibliography

*Annotated Checklist of the Birds of New Zealand,* The Checklist Committee (F. C. Kinsky, convenor) for the Ornithological Society of New Zealand Inc.; A. H. and A. W. Reed, 1970. Also *Amendments & Additions,* 1979.

*Birds of the Antarctic and Subantarctic,* G. E. Watson; American Geophysical Union, 1975.

*A Field Guide to the Birds of Australia,* G. Pizzey; Collins, 1980.

*A New Dictionary of Birds,* A. Landsborough Thomson, ed.; Nelson, 1964.

*The New Guide to the Birds of New Zealand,* R. A. Falla, R. B. Sibson & E. G. Turbott; Collins, 1979. (An essential companion — contains a wealth of information on all aspects of New Zealand birds.)

*New Zealand Birds,* M. F. Soper; Whitcoulls, 1976.

*Notornis,* The Journal of the Ornithological Society of New Zealand Inc., 1950-82.

# INDEX

Q



R

## V



## W



## Y



## Z